LOVING GOD

MIKE BICKLE

Charisma
HOUSE
A STRANG COMPANY

Most STRANG COMMUNICATIONS/CHARISMA HOUSE/SILOAM/FRONTLINE/REALMS products are available at special quantity discounts for bulk purchase for sales promotions, premiums, fund-raising, and educational needs. For details, write Strang Communications/Charisma House/Siloam/FrontLine/Realms, 600 Rinehart Road, Lake Mary, Florida 32746, or telephone (407) 333-0600.

LOVING GOD by Mike Bickle
Published by Charisma House
A Strang Company
600 Rinehart Road
Lake Mary, Florida 32746
www.charismahouse.com

Unless otherwise noted, all Scripture quotations are from the Holy Bible, New International Version. Copyright © 1973, 1978, 1984, International Bible Society. Used by permission.

Scripture quotations marked KJV are from the King James Version of the Bible.

Scripture quotations marked NAS are from the New American Standard Bible. Copyright © 1960, 1962, 1963, 1968, 1971, 1972, 1973, 1975, 1977 by the Lockman Foundation. Used by permission. (www.Lockman.org)

Scripture quotations marked NKJV are from the New King James Version of the Bible. Copyright © 1979, 1980, 1982 by Thomas Nelson, Inc., publishers. Used by permission.

Scripture quotations marked TLB are from The Living Bible. Copyright © 1971. Used by permission of Tyndale House Publishers, Inc., Wheaton, IL 60189. All rights reserved.

Cover Design by: John Hamilton Design, www.johnhamiltondesign.com
Executive Design Director: Bill Johnson

Library of Congress Cataloging-in-Publication Data:
Bickle, Mike.
 Loving God / Mike Bickle.
   p. cm.
 ISBN 978-1-59979-175-3 (casebound)
 I. God--Worship and love. I. Title.
 BV4817.B485 2007
 242'.2--dc22

                                                    2007015241

DAY 1

And so we know and rely on the love God has for us. God is love. Whoever lives in love lives in God, and God in him.
—1 John 4:16

No one can come face-to-face with what God is like and ever be the same. Seeing the truth about His personality touches the depths of our emotions, which leads us to spiritual wholeness and maturity.

PRAYER STARTER

Lord, there is nothing I want more than to experience a growing, ever more intimate relationship with You. Let me see You as You are so that I may be transformed in my own life and walk with You. Amen.

BEHOLDING THE GLORY OF WHO HE IS AND WHAT HE HAS DONE RENEWS OUR MINDS, STRENGTHENS US, AND TRANSFORMS US.

DAY 2

Then you will know the truth, and the truth will set you free.
—*John 8:32*

In our verse for today, Jesus tells us that we will know the truth, and the truth will set us free. What truths must we know to be free? First and most important, who is God? What is He like? What kind of personality does He have?

PRAYER STARTER

Lord, I want to be set free by Your truth. I want to become more like You. I want to exhibit the characteristics that I see in Your life. There are characteristics that I recognize in myself that are not like You. Help me to overcome these flaws as Your truth exposes each one and sets me free.

THE WAY TO OUR EMOTIONS IS THROUGH OUR MINDS.

DAY 3

I am the LORD, and there is no other;
apart from me there is no God.
I will strengthen you,
though you have not acknowledged me,
so that from the rising of the sun
to the place of its setting
men may know there is none besides me.
I am the LORD, and there is no other.
—*Isaiah 45:5–6*

Your ideas about God—who He is and what He is like—come naturally through your relationships with earthly authority figures. When these are distorted, so are your ideas about God.

PRAYER STARTER

Father God, I know that there are things about my earthly relationships that hinder me from understanding who You are. I don't want my ideas about You to be distorted. I commit to doing all I can to discover exactly what You are like by studying Your Word and by letting Your Spirit teach me more about You.

TO ACHIEVE LONG-TERM RENEWAL AND FREEDOM, WE MUST CHANGE OUR IDEAS ABOUT WHO GOD IS.

DAY 4

Great is our Lord and mighty in power;
his understanding has no limit.
The LORD sustains the humble
but casts the wicked to the ground.
—*Psalm 147:5–6*

In your most private thoughts, what do you believe God's personality is like? Your entire spiritual future is related to how you answer this question in the secret place of your heart, because inaccurate ideas of God will have a negative emotional impact on you.

PRAYER STARTER

God, help me to focus on Your awesome personality. Rid my mind of inaccurate ideas of what You are like. You are my Wonderful Counselor, my Mighty God, my Everlasting Father, and my Prince of Peace.

I BELIEVE THE GREATEST PROBLEM IN THE CHURCH IS THAT WE HAVE AN ENTIRELY INADEQUATE AND DISTORTED IDEA OF GOD'S HEART.

DAY 5

How great is the love the Father has lavished on us, that we should be called children of God! And that is what we are! The reason the world does not know us is that it did not know him. Dear friends, now we are children of God, and what we will be has not yet been made known. But we know that when he appears, we shall be like him, for we shall see him as he is.

—1 John 3:1–2

God will satisfy your hungry heart when He reveals Himself to you. As you encounter the awesome holiness and power of His personality, you will have the power to overcome temptation.

PRAYER STARTER

My heavenly Father, I am so hungry to have more and more revelations of Your wonderful love for me. Your love overwhelms me and fills my heart with the hope of growing closer and closer to You each day. I hunger for more and more of You. Fill me to overflowing, Father.

> GOD IGNITES US TO HOLY, PASSIONATE AFFECTION FOR A DEEPER UNDERSTANDING OF THE DIVINE EXCELLENCIES, PERFECTIONS, AND PASSIONS OF OUR LORD JESUS CHRIST.

DAY 6

Your ways, O God, are holy.
What god is so great as our God?
You are the God who performs miracles;
you display your power among the peoples.
With your mighty arm you redeemed your people,
the descendants of Jacob and Joseph.
—Psalm 77:13–15

As you focus on His heart toward you and encounter His passionate affection for you, then you will become more equipped to overcome temptation. Focus on four key elements of the gospel in your journey to understanding the fullness of God:

1. Who God is
2. What He has done
3. What you can receive
4. What you should do

We often place most of the emphasis on the last three: what God has done for us in Christ, the forgiveness and inheritance we receive as adopted children, and what we should do in our walk with God. The foundational element—who God is—is often tragically absent in our messages.

PRAYER STARTER

Father, more than anything I want to know who You are—to me. Thank You for the things You have done for me and the blessings You have given to me. Now reveal Yourself to me for exactly who You are in my life, right now. Amen.

THE GREAT NEED OF THIS HOUR IS TO MAKE KNOWN THE PERSONALITY OF GOD.

DAY 7

No one has ever seen God; but if we love one another, God lives in us and his love is made complete in us.... And so we know and rely on the love God has for us.
—1 John 4:12, 16

There is a powerful, concrete connection between *knowing* the truth about who God is as the way of *experiencing* passion for Him. It is the revelation of God's passionate affection for us that awakens ever-deepening feelings of love and passion for Him.

PRAYER STARTER

God, I know what Your Word has taught me about You. But I want to experience You, not just know about You. Help me to feel the passionate love You have for me.

SIMPLY PUT, WE LOVE HIM BECAUSE HE FIRST LOVED US (1 JOHN 4:19).

DAY 8

Yet the LORD longs to be gracious to you;
    he rises to show you compassion.
For the LORD is a God of justice.
    Blessed are all who wait for him!
—*Isaiah 30:18*

The precious insights into God's heart are near to every child of God. They are *within our reach!* They are there for the taking. God is accessible. He has made Himself available. Just how passionate for Jesus do we want to be? You and I are the ones who set those limits, not God.

PRAYER STARTER

God, You have been so gracious to me. I long to grow in my passion for You. Forgive me for the limits I have placed on my love for You. Remove the barriers and walls I've erected, and overwhelm me with a passionate love for You.

THE QUESTION IS, HOW MUCH INTIMACY DO YOU WANT?

DAY 9

Now the Lord is the Spirit, and where the Spirit of the Lord is, there is freedom. And we, who with unveiled faces all reflect the Lord's glory, are being transformed into his likeness with ever-increasing glory, which comes from the Lord, who is the Spirit.
—*2 Corinthians 3:17–18*

The promise of being transformed and ignited to holy passion by understanding and beholding God's glorious personality is for everyone. No matter how weak or strong you feel, regardless of your previous failures, irrespective of your natural temperament or personality, you can be ablaze with passion for Jesus.

PRAYER STARTER

Father, the hopeful thought that You can transform me to become more like You is almost too much to comprehend. Do a work in me that goes beyond my human understanding, that I may reflect Your personality in my own life.

> IF THE FIRST TWENTY YEARS OF MY LIFE TAUGHT ME ANYTHING, IT WAS THAT PASSION FOR JESUS DOES NOT COME FROM NATURAL HUMAN ZEAL OR ENTHUSIASM.

DAY 10

You search the Scriptures, because you think that in them you
have eternal life; and it is these that bear witness of Me; and *you are
unwilling to come to Me*, that you may have life.
—*John 5:39–40, NAS, emphasis added*

For the first time in my life, zeal was not enough. If anything, it
had turned on me and become my enemy—condemning me for my
spiritual failures. My human zeal was not able to deliver my heart. My
increasing anger toward God and people added to my burden of guilt
feelings. I was almost twenty years old by this time—and was a ball of
frustration on the inside because I viewed myself as a spiritual failure.

PRAYER STARTER

*Lord, I too, like Mike Bickle, have felt like a spiritual failure at times.
Help me to blaze with passion for You.*

> I SUDDENLY REALIZED I WAS LIKE THE PIOUS PHARISEES
> WHO STUDIED THE SCRIPTURES YET DID NOT ENJOY
> A RELATIONSHIP WITH THE PERSON THOSE VERY
> SCRIPTURES WERE ABOUT.

DAY 11

And he got up and came to his father. But while he was still a long way off, his father *saw* him, and *felt compassion* for him, and *ran* and *embraced* him, and kissed him.
—*Luke 15:20, NAS, emphasis added*

One day as I was reading the story of the prodigal son, the verbs in the verse above, regarding the prodigal's father, suddenly came alive. I had wondered so many times how God felt about me. Suddenly I knew, for through the prodigal's father I glimpsed the face and heart of God. My heavenly Father was a watching, running, weeping, laughing, embracing, kissing God! He was an encouraging, affirming, praising, affectionate kind of God.

PRAYER STARTER

Lord, like the prodigal son, I long for You to see me, feel compassion for me, run and embrace me, and kiss me. Lord, I will never stop expressing my love for You.

HE WAS A GOD WHO LOVED ME SO MUCH HE COULDN'T KEEP FROM EMBRACING ME.

DAY 12

The father said to his servants, "Quick! Bring the best robe and put it on him. Put a ring on his finger and sandals on his feet. Bring the fattened calf and kill it. Let's have a feast and celebrate. For this son of mine was dead and is alive again; he was lost and is found."
—*Luke 15:22–24*

Just as the prodigal's father was overwhelmed with joy at the return of his son, my Father God feels even more inexplicable joy when I come into His presence. He is a God who enjoys me even in my failure and immaturity, a God I don't have to strive to make happy, because He's already happy with me. He is a Father who cheers me on and enthusiastically calls me His son.

PRAYER STARTER

Father, Your love has changed my life and transformed my spirit. My heart is overflowing with the joy of knowing You have called me Your child.

I BEGAN MY JOURNEY OF UNDERSTANDING GOD'S AFFECTION FOR ME, WHICH POWERFULLY CHANGED MY LIFE, REPLACING MY GUILT WITH HOLY BOLDNESS AND AFFECTION FOR HIM.

DAY 13

Remember, O Lord, your great mercy and love,
for they are from of old.
Remember not the sins of my youth
and my rebellious ways;
according to your love remember me,
for you are good, O Lord.
—*Psalm 25:6–7*

When God saw me trudging toward His throne with my head bowed in shame, I suddenly realized that He, like the prodigal's father, was moved with affection and tenderness for me. The awesome truth came streaking across my soul, bursting in to light up my heart with this truth! I had been struggling to please God so that He would like me, when all along my heavenly Father had loved me as my dad loved me—*only far more!*

PRAYER STARTER

Father, no one, not even my earthly father, has ever loved me the way You love me. Like a child I want to crawl up into Your arms and feel You lifting me away from the bondages of my sinful life. You're my Abba, my Dad, my heavenly Father.

HIS ARMS WERE OUTSTRETCHED, REACHING FOR ME,
LONGING TO CATCH ME UP IN HIS LOVING EMBRACE.

DAY 14

I consider everything a loss compared to the surpassing greatness of knowing Christ Jesus my Lord, for whose sake I have lost all things. I consider them rubbish, that I may gain Christ and be found in him, not having a righteousness of my own that comes from the law, but that which is through faith in Christ—the righteousness that comes from God and is by faith.
—*Philippians 3:8–9*

During those years, in my zeal to please God, I had thought only of His holiness and how out of reach it was. Like the apostle Paul, I had come face-to-face with my sinfulness and weakness. Paul was filled with passion for Jesus as a result of seeing the glory of His personality. For the surpassing value of knowing a glorious *person*, Paul counted all things as rubbish that he might gain a deeper relationship with Jesus.

PRAYER STARTER

God, I don't like having to face my own human weakness, but unless I do, and recognize Your glory, You cannot cause me to be more like You. Show me the things that cause me to be so weak.

WHEN I SAW MY SIN, I WAS CONFRONTED WITH MY INABILITY TO CHANGE MY HEART.

DAY 15

The LORD your God is with you,
he is mighty to save.
He will take great delight in you,
he will quiet you with his love,
he will rejoice over you with singing.
—*Zephaniah 3:17*

I lived under crushing condemnation as I struggled under the misconception that God had judged me as a failure. Yet God was not focused on my failures; He saw the value of my sincere, yet failed, desire to please Him. He was delighting in me.

PRAYER STARTER

Thank You, Father, for looking beyond my failure to my heart. I really do long to do Your will. Teach me how to do it, and reveal Your plan for my life. I am Yours, Lord, all Yours. Use me any way You desire. Amen.

I WAS ONLY BEGINNING TO UNDERSTAND HIS AFFECTION FOR ME, EVEN IN THE MIDST OF MY SPIRITUAL FAILURE AND IMMATURITY.

DAY 16

I have loved you with an everlasting love;
I have drawn you with loving-kindness....
They will come with weeping;
they will pray as I bring them back.
I will lead them beside streams of water
on a level path where they will not stumble.
—Jeremiah 31:3, 9

The Father-heart of God was as thrilled with me—an immature, mess-making, spiritual infant—as with one of His spiritually mature sons who had just graduated with honors from the school of the Spirit. My heavenly Father enjoyed me while I was yet in the *process* of maturing, not sighing in disgust and waiting impatiently until I grew up. He loved and longed for me; He felt proud and was excited over me even while I was falling short.

PRAYER STARTER

Father, like Mike Bickle, I am an immature, mess-making, spiritual infant. Yet You love me so much that You enjoy me just as I am. It's so hard for me to comprehend that You could feel that way, Father, but my heart is overwhelmed with love because of it.

AS MY CONFIDENCE IN HIM GREW, MY HEART BECAME WARM AND TENDER TOWARD GOD.

DAY 17

"I will turn their mourning into gladness;
I will give them comfort and joy instead of sorrow.
I will satisfy the priests with abundance,
and my people will be filled with my bounty,"
declares the LORD.
—*Jeremiah 31:13–14*

Oh, the sense of anticipation that filled my heart as I realized that the Lord had real affirmation and affection for me. I began to feel confidence before Him. It was too good to be true! I wept for joy. And when the tears finally ceased, I could sense the anger, bitterness, guilt, and condemnation beginning to diminish in my heart. My little, flickering flame of human zeal was replaced by a blaze of passionate love for a glorious *person*. His intense devotion and ardent affection for me far exceeded that of my earthly father's…and I knew I would never, ever, be the same.

PRAYER STARTER

God, You—the Creator of all heaven and Earth—are really my friend! Your friendship causes a rush of excitement in me. I am filled with such great love for You, and I will spend my life loving You more and serving You with all that I am and have.

UNDERSTANDING GOD'S GREAT AFFECTION FOR ME WAS
BEGINNING TO REIGNITE MY LOVE FOR HIM.

DAY 18

Can you fathom the mysteries of God?
Can you probe the limits of the Almighty?
They are higher than the heavens—what can you do?
They are deeper than the depths of the grave—what can you
know?
Their measure is longer than the earth
and wider than the sea.
—*Job 11:7–9*

Our world is affected tragically every day by people who possess little or no sense of God's transcendence. Much of creation does not know—or care—that its Creator is unequaled, unrivaled, and supreme. Transcendence when in reference to God means that He exists not only in but also beyond our realm of reality. In other words, He's not like us—far from it. God is exalted far above His created universe, so far that even the brightest human minds cannot begin to fathom it.

PRAYER STARTER

Father, today I just want to stop to recite again everything that I know You are and everything that I know You are doing in my life. I'll never be able to fully understand who You are, Father, but I want to know more and more about You every day of my life.

MY INNER MAN IS CONTINUALLY IN THE PROCESS OF BEING RENEWED INTO A FULLER, MORE COMPLETE KNOWLEDGE OF GOD AND HIS GLORIOUS PERSONALITY.

DAY 19

God called to him from within the bush, "Moses! Moses!"
And Moses said, "Here I am." "Do not come any closer," God said.
"Take off your sandals, for the place where you are standing is holy
ground." Then he said, "I am the God of your father, the God of
Abraham, the God of Isaac and the God of Jacob." At this, Moses
hid his face, because he was afraid to look at God.

—*Exodus 3:4–6*

In Old Testament times, whenever God appeared to men, an overwhelming sense of terror and dread was the result. In contrast, many in our day are so blind to God's transcendence that they show shocking disregard for Him. If people are unaware of God's terrifying supremacy that transcends the universe and time itself, they will have little fear of Him. If we have no fear of God, nor the fear of consequences, then we will easily break His commands.

PRAYER STARTER

Father God, I stand in awe of Your power and might. Teach me to have a holy, reverential fear of Your glory so that my life will be lived in purity and holiness.

**THE DOWNWARD SPIRAL OF MORALITY IN OUR SOCIETY
IS DIRECTLY PROPORTIONAL TO THE LOSS OF OUR
UNDERSTANDING OF THE GREATNESS OF GOD.**

DAY 20

My son, if you accept my words
and store up my commands within you,
turning your ear to wisdom
and applying your heart to understanding,
and if you call out for insight
and cry aloud for understanding,
and if you look for it as for silver
and search for it as for hidden treasure,
then you will understand the fear of the LORD
and find the knowledge of God.
—*Proverbs 2:1–5*

Why does our society have such an irreverent and lowly view of God? The answer is simple. The church has not proclaimed it! The church's concept of God is much too small. The glory of God's personhood has not been clearly proclaimed to our generation. But when even the faintest light of God's surpassing greatness dawns upon our minds, we will walk carefully before Him as we work out our salvation with fear and trembling.

PRAYER STARTER

Father, help me to reverence Your name and never to trivialize Your power and might. Teach me to praise You as the Creator and God of the universe.

FOR MANY CHRISTIANS JESUS IS MORE LIKE SANTA CLAUS OR A POP PSYCHOLOGIST THAN THE HOLY OTHER WHO WILL JUDGE HEAVEN AND EARTH BY HIS WORD.

DAY 21

His body also was like beryl, his face had the appearance of lightning, his eyes were like flaming torches, his arms and feet like the gleam of polished bronze, and the sound of his words like the sound of a tumult. Now I, Daniel, alone saw the vision, while the men who were with me did not see the vision; nevertheless, a great dread fell on them, and they ran away to hide themselves. So I was left alone and saw this great vision; yet no strength was left in me, for my natural color turned to a deathly pallor, and I retained no strength.... Then behold, a hand touched me and set me trembling on my hands and knees.
—*Daniel 10:6–8, 10, NAS*

Daniel, a man greatly beloved by God, was granted an overpowering vision. He was left speechless and breathless, and all his strength was drained from him. The messenger in the vision Daniel saw was only a lower-ranked angel. What would it have been like to have beheld Michael or even the Lord Himself? Without doubt, such revelation would change our thinking about a lot of things. Our worship will be ignited with passion. Whether by insight and spiritual revelation or by visions in Technicolor, the effect is the same.

PRAYER STARTER

Lord, I long for a vision of You. Reveal Yourself to me, and show me the things that I must change in my life to become more like You.

A NEW REVELATION OF GOD'S HOLINESS ALWAYS SHINES THE SPOTLIGHT ON OUR OWN CONDITION.

DAY 22

Lift up your eyes to the heavens,
look at the earth beneath;
the heavens will vanish like smoke,
the earth will wear out like a garment
and its inhabitants die like flies.
But my salvation will last forever,
my righteousness will never fail.
—*Isaiah 51:6*

If only more believers understood that God is immutable—He never changes. God never suspends one attribute to exercise another. For example, He never diminishes in His holiness when He exercises His love and tender mercy. None of God's qualities ever diminish in even the slightest degree. In fact, when one immutable aspect of the nature of God is seemingly in conflict with another of His immutable attributes, it is at that place you will see glimpses of His greatness.

PRAYER STARTER

God, how wonderful it is to know that You never change. When everything around me—and in me—is full of change and confusion, Your love constantly surrounds me and keeps me secure.

WHAT GOD HAS ALWAYS BEEN, HE WILL EVER BE.

DAY 23

He has sent me…to bestow on them a crown of beauty.…
They will be called oaks of righteousness,
a planting of the LORD
for the display of his splendor.
—*Isaiah 61:1, 3*

Suppose there was a gardener who had planted and cared for a prize-winning bed of flowers. Which would he hate more: a weed in the common field or a weed in the bed of his prize-winning flowers? Obviously, he would hate the weed in his flower bed more because it chokes the life out of his prize-winning flowers and destroys the glory of his handiwork. In the same way God hates sin infinitely more in the lives of Christians because we are His vineyard, "the plantings of the Lord." The most wonderful thing of all is that He loves us with an everlasting love and reckons us as perfectly righteous because of our faith in Christ and His work on the cross.

PRAYER STARTER

Father, I don't want the weeds of sin in my life to choke out Your glorious presence and power. Show me those sins, and remove them from my life. I want only what is pure and holy and righteous from You.

NOTHING DESCRIBES GOD'S ABHORRENCE FOR SIN IN
THE WICKED BETTER THAN THE DEGREE OF ETERNAL
PUNISHMENT HE PRESCRIBES FOR IT.

DAY 24

Therefore do not let sin reign in your mortal body so that you obey its evil desires. Do not offer the parts of your body to sin, as instruments of wickedness, but rather offer yourselves to God, as those who have been brought from death to life; and offer the parts of your body to him as instruments of righteousness.

—*Romans 6:12–14*

When you begin to comprehend God's perfect and immutable holiness, and at the same time realize His unfathomable love for you, then you will begin to understand His hatred of sin in your life. The illumination of your heart with the knowledge of God transforms you into that same image. A casual attitude about sin comes from an incomplete understanding of God.

PRAYER STARTER

Make me holy, Father, and separate me from anything that hinders me from serving You with a pure heart. Transform me into the image of Your Son, who gave His life that I might live.

THE CROSS OF CALVARY WAS THE GREATEST DISPLAY OF THE CHARACTER AND ATTRIBUTES OF GOD.

DAY 25

God presented him as a sacrifice of atonement, through faith in his blood. He did this to demonstrate his justice, because in his forbearance he had left the sins committed beforehand unpunished—he did it to demonstrate his justice at the present time, so as to be just and the one who justifies those who have faith in Jesus.

—*Romans 3:25–26*

I have often been asked, "If God is a God of love, how could He send anyone to hell?" But the more appropriate question is this: If God is a God of perfect holiness, how could He send anyone to heaven? How can a holy and just God arbitrarily overlook sin? How could a loving God not forgive sin? Immutable holiness and unconditional love collide. The greatness of God was displayed, not in the fact that He forgave our sins, but in precisely *the way* He forgave them—He sent His Son as a perfect sacrifice for us. His love was displayed, and His justice was satisfied.

PRAYER STARTER

Jesus, I will comprehend Your willingness to give up Your life for mine! Thank You for Your sacrifice on the cross of shame for my sins. Forgive my sins, and prepare me to be worthy of eternity with You in heaven.

GOD WOULD NEVER VIOLATE HIS HOLINESS, NOR WOULD HE TURN AWAY FROM HIS LOVE.

DAY 26

Then he turned toward the woman and said to Simon, "Do you see this woman? I came into your house. You did not give me any water for my feet, but she wet my feet with her tears and wiped them with her hair. You did not give me a kiss, but this woman, from the time I entered, has not stopped kissing my feet. You did not put oil on my head, but she has poured perfume on my feet. Therefore, I tell you, her many sins have been forgiven—for she loved much. But he who has been forgiven little loves little."
—*Luke 7:44–47*

Some have such a dim view or low appreciation for both the holiness and love of God that the cross does not seem that significant. They understand neither the greatness of their need nor the glory of God's gift. Jesus taught that the one who has been forgiven much will love much. You will "love much" when you begin to comprehend the magnitude of what Christ has done on your behalf.

PRAYER STARTER

My heart overflows with love for You, dear Jesus. There is no one on Earth who loves me as You do. I have so much to thank You for, and I give my life to serving and loving You because of what You did for me.

PASSION IS BIRTHED IN YOU BY REVELATION OF THE KNOWLEDGE OF GOD.

DAY 27

I am still confident of this:
I will see the goodness of the Lord
in the land of the living.
Wait for the Lord;
be strong and take heart
and wait for the Lord.
—*Psalm 27:13–14*

In a *Dennis the Menace* cartoon, Dennis and his friend were walking out of Mrs. Wilson's house with cookies in both hands. Dennis's friend wondered what they had done to deserve the cookies. Dennis explained, "Mrs. Wilson doesn't give us cookies because we are nice. We get cookies because Mrs. Wilson is nice." It is God's goodness, not ours, that is the basis for blessing. Understanding this frees us to place our confidence and trust in God Himself instead of being forced to rely upon our own righteousness or upon whatever faith we can muster.

PRAYER STARTER

God, You are a good God! Out of Your goodness You have blessed my life abundantly. I place my trust and confidence in Your goodness, and I commit to living my life in faithfulness to You.

WE CANNOT TWIST GOD'S ARM OR THROW A TEMPER TANTRUM TO MAKE HIM GIVE US WHAT WE WANT.

DAY 28

The heavens declare the glory of God;
the skies proclaim the work of his hands.
Day after day they pour forth speech;
night after night they display knowledge.
There is no speech or language
where their voice is not heard.
Their voice goes out into all the earth,
their words to the ends of the world
—*Psalm 19:1–4*

Seeing the heart, mind, and character of God will cure our compromise and instability and motivate us to bright righteousness and holy passion. Personal, experiential knowledge of the person of Jesus will fuel obedience and zeal. It will put a stop to our restlessness and discontent. A new depth of intimacy with Him will extinguish our boredom and capture our hearts. Just a glimpse of Him…

PRAYER STARTER

God, I hate the compromise that creeps into my life at times. I long to be filled with holy passion and righteousness. Forgive my disobedient spirit and careless heart. Give me a fresh glimpse of Your love for me.

THE GREAT NEED OF THE CHURCH IS TO SEE, KNOW, AND
DISCOVER THE INDESCRIBABLE GLORY OF WHO GOD IS.

DAY 29

✑ I will sing of the LORD's great love forever;
with my mouth I will make your faithfulness known through all
generations.
I will declare that your love stands firm forever,
that you established your faithfulness in heaven itself.
—*Psalm 89:1–2*

John, whom Jesus nicknamed the "Son of Thunder" (Mark 3:17) because of his fiery temperament, became one of the most prominent of the apostles. As he walked with Jesus, John's fiery selfish ambition was replaced by fiery passion for Jesus. John's own Gospel makes it clear that he was greatly beloved by the Lord. He was one of the three apostles who were closest to Jesus.

PRAYER STARTER

✑ *Father, I want to be Your friend. I long to be worthy of being called "a friend of God." Take away my selfish ambitions, and give me a heart dominated by a desire to please You in everything I do.*

THINK OF IT. THE LIVING BIBLE SAYS JOHN WAS CHRIST'S CLOSEST FRIEND (JOHN 13:23).

DAY 30

I turned around to see the voice that was speaking to me. And
when I turned I saw...someone "like a son of man," dressed in a robe
reaching down to his feet and with a golden sash around his chest.
His head and hair were white like wool, as white as snow, and his eyes
were like blazing fire. His feet were like bronze glowing in a furnace,
and his voice was like the sound of rushing waters. In his right hand
he held seven stars, and out of his mouth came a sharp double-edged
sword. His face was like the sun shining in all its brilliance. When I
saw him, I fell at his feet as though dead.
—*Revelation 1:12–17*

When the Lord, whom John had served faithfully, appeared to him
in His awesome majesty and glory, John "fell at His feet as a dead
man" (Rev. 1:17, NAS). Imagine a man of John's spiritual stature and
experience being totally overcome by this brief glimpse of the beloved
Friend he had served faithfully for more than sixty years. When we are
exposed to even a portion of His consuming glory, as John was, we will
be motivated to live free from sin, die to selfishness, and give ourselves
passionately to the Lord.

PRAYER STARTER

*Take the world, Jesus, and give me only more and more of Yourself and
Your glory. Consume me with Your love, and stabilize me in Your will.*

> **WHEN WE GAZE UPON HIS LOVELINESS, WE WILL GLADLY
> DIE TO THOSE THINGS THAT ARE NOT LIKE HIM.**

DAY 31

> But we all, with unveiled face beholding as in a mirror the glory
> of the Lord, are being transformed into the same image from glory to
> glory, just as from the Lord, the Spirit.
> —*2 Corinthians 3:18, NAS*

While Jesus walked on Earth, His glory was veiled in human flesh. Veils were used in the Bible to hide the glory of God. A veil was put over Moses's face to hide the glory, a veil hid the holy of holies and glory of God in the tabernacle, and the writer of Hebrews spoke of the "veil, that is, His flesh" (Heb. 10:20, NAS). In his letter to the Corinthians, Paul discusses one other veil that hides the glory of God. It is the veil that covers the heart and prevents a person from beholding the glory of Christ.

PRAYER STARTER

Father, I do not want anything to hide the revelation of Your glory from my life. Remove the veil that covers my heart and prevents me from seeing You as You are.

THE REVELATION OF THE TRUE KNOWLEDGE OF THE
GLORIFIED CHRIST WILL TRANSFORM YOU.

DAY 32

This is what the Sovereign LORD says: I am about to set fire
to you, and it will consume all your trees, both green and dry. The
blazing flame will not be quenched, and every face from south to
north will be scorched by it. Everyone will see that I the LORD have
kindled it; it will not be quenched.
—*Ezekiel 20:47–48*

The enemy has assaulted the people of God. He has weakened and
destroyed our foundation of the knowledge of God. He has sought to
defeat us by diluting our passion for Jesus and diverting us from our
divine purpose. Satan has done his job well. But the blazing light and
majestic loveliness of the knowledge of God are about to shine into the
community of the redeemed, and all the dark forces of hell will not be
able to overpower it.

PRAYER STARTER

*Shine Your glory in my heart, Lord, and cast out all the darkness
Satan has tried to place within my life. Destroy his attempts to keep me from
following Your purposes for my life.*

IN HIS ARSENAL, GOD HAS RESERVED THE SECRET WEAPON
OF ALL THE AGES—THE AWESOME KNOWLEDGE OF THE
SPLENDOR OF THE PERSON OF JESUS.

DAY 33

His life is the light that shines through the darkness—
and the darkness can never extinguish it.
—John 1:5, TLB

John wrote his account many years after the other three Gospel writers. As he looked back, he commented on the irresistible nature of the knowledge of Jesus Christ. Compromise and passivity will be solved as the Lord allows us to gaze upon Him with deeper insight into His personal beauty and unveil His glory. The body of Christ will rediscover Christ's personhood and majesty. When we do, we will give ourselves to Him in unparalleled affection and obedience.

PRAYER STARTER

Your light is the light of my life, dear Father, and Your glory illuminates the deepest crevices of my being. Shine Your light ever more and more in my life so that I may behold Your majesty and glory.

THE SPLENDOR AND GLORY OF JESUS CHRIST WILL ONCE AGAIN CAPTURE THE AFFECTIONS OF THE CHURCH IN A NEW WAY.

DAY 34

Father, I want those you have given me to be with me where
I am, and to see my glory, the glory you have given me because you
loved me before the creation of the world. Righteous Father, though
the world does not know you, I know you, and they know that you
have sent me. I have made you known to them, and will continue to
make you known in order that the love you have for me may be in
them and that I myself may be in them.
—*John 17:24–26*

My love for Diane and my desire to be with her have helped me understand the love Christ felt for His bride. I remember when I noticed
this beautiful, young, blonde girl across the room. I flipped out! I had
never felt such intense emotions as I gazed across the room at Diane,
the girl who was to become my wife. Christ's prayer in John 17 especially moves me. Only hours before His agonizing death at Calvary,
my Lord was crying out to the Father with intense cravings for His
bride—for me!

PRAYER STARTER

*Father, I long to be where You are. I want to be Your Son's holy and
spotless bride, prepared to share eternity in the wonder of Your presence.*

**HE WAS CONSUMED WITH LOVE FOR HIS BRIDE AND LONGED
TO HAVE HIS BRIDE WITH HIM FOR ETERNITY.**

DAY 35

And I have declared to them Your name,
and will declare it, that the love with which You loved Me
may be in them, and I in them.
—*John 17:26, NKJV*

At the end of Christ's prophetic prayer in John 17, Jesus gave us a glimpse of the powerful and passionate church He would build. His focus changes from the first generation of Christians to the church throughout history. He intercedes for believers who will come to know Him after His death. We find prophetic promises for the church in this prayer.

PRAYER STARTER

Lord, I am Your church, Your sanctuary, and I want Your presence to overflow my life so that others may see Your great love for me—and for them.

HOW MAGNIFICENT IT IS TO SEE THE SON OF GOD PRAYING FOR THE CHURCH, HIS BELOVED BRIDE, ONE LAST TIME WHILE HE IS STILL CLOTHED IN HUMAN FLESH.

DAY 36

I pray also for those who will believe in me through their message, that all of them may be one, Father, just as you are in me and I am in you. May they also be in us so that the world may believe that you have sent me. I have given them the glory that you gave me, that they may be one as we are one: I in them and you in me. May they be brought to complete unity to let the world know that you sent me and have loved them even as you have loved me.

—*John 17:20–23*

These verses reveal that the answer to Christ's prayer lies not just in heaven. It will come to pass on this side of eternity so the unsaved can witness it. The beginnings of its fulfillment lie in this age. Jesus's prayer for such a church to love Him as the Father loves Him will undoubtedly be answered. It was directed by the Father, energized by the Holy Spirit, and prayed in accordance with the Father's will. Jesus never prayed amiss.

PRAYER STARTER

Lord, I despise the lukewarmness and lethargy in my spiritual life. Fill me to overflowing with Your Holy Spirit so that my life is energized to be a lighthouse to draw others to You.

> **JESUS PRAYED THAT THE WORLD WOULD BEHOLD A POWERFUL AND PASSIONATE CHURCH.**

DAY 37

I have brought you glory on earth by completing the work you gave me to do. And now, Father, glorify me in your presence with the glory I had with you before the world began. I have revealed you to those whom you gave me out of the world.
—*John 17:4–6*

I do not think Jesus Christ enjoys anything more than revealing to others the infinite splendor and awesome beauty of His Father. Every aspect of His ministry reflects the indescribable loveliness of the Father. We sometimes talk about the ministry of Jesus only in terms of physical and emotional healing or the preaching of forgiveness. But the ministry of Jesus was not confined just to miracles and forgiveness. The ministry of Jesus was most significantly defined by His making known the splendor of His Father.

PRAYER STARTER

Father, the wonder of Your splendor and beauty is too much for me to comprehend. Make my life a reflection of Your beauty, and show me how to reveal Your glory to those around me.

WHEN IT WAS ALL OVER, JESUS SUMMED UP HIS ENTIRE EARTHLY MINISTRY BY SAYING TO HIS FATHER, "I'VE MADE YOUR NAME KNOWN TO THEM."

DAY 38

But thanks be to God, who always leads us in His triumph
in Christ, and manifests through us the sweet aroma
of the knowledge of Him in every place.
—*2 Corinthians 2:14, NAS*

When people heard Jesus's words, observed His lifestyle, and beheld
His perfectly balanced personality and flawless character, they received
a glimpse of the beauty of what God the Father is like. It was Christ's
great joy to reveal His Father. You and I have the same privilege and
responsibility. The Spirit of God leads us into triumph and victory
so that we can manifest the sweet aroma of the knowledge of God
everywhere we go.

PRAYER STARTER

*Thanks be to God! Thank You, God, because You always lead me to vic-
tory when I place my hope and trust in You. Make me a sweet-smelling savor to
the world around me because of Your love, which permeates my being.*

**"I HAVE DECLARED TO THEM YOUR NAME" WAS
THE CONSUMING PURPOSE BEATING IN THE HEART OF JESUS
DURING HIS THREE AND A HALF YEARS
OF EARTHLY MINISTRY.**

DAY 39

And we eagerly await a Savior from there, the Lord Jesus Christ,
who, by the power that enables him to bring everything under
his control, will transform our lowly bodies so that
they will be like his glorious body.
—*Philippians 3:20–21*

God desires that we experience fellowship with the Holy Spirit so
that we will be transformed—led into victory from the inside out—a
victory touching our hearts, minds, and emotions. Then we will
manifest a measure of the sweet fragrance of the knowledge of God in
private, in public, and in all our casual interactions. That's what Jesus
did in fullness.

PRAYER STARTER

*Holy Spirit, allow me to fellowship with You each day. I long for You
to transform me by Your power so that everyone can see the transforming
power of Your presence in my life.*

**A SWEET AROMA IS OFTEN THE MANIFESTATION OF
THE PRESENCE OF GOD.**

DAY 40

But thanks be to God, who always leads us in triumphal
procession in Christ and through us spreads everywhere the fragrance
of the knowledge of him. For we are to God the aroma of Christ
among those who are being saved and those who are perishing.
—*2 Corinthians 2:14–15*

When we see God in another person, whether in their actions, words,
or quiet spirits, a pure freshness touches our hearts. Every time the
Spirit of God enables us to break a bondage or to triumph over an
addiction or weakness and come into victory, that conquest releases in
us more of the fragrance of our glorious Father.

PRAYER STARTER

*Lord, I see Your presence in some of the beautiful Christians that enter
my life. That's what I want to be evident in my life, too, dear Lord. I want
Your love to radiate from my life to the lives of those who pass through—or
stay in—my life.*

> **MINISTRY AT ITS MOST BASIC DEFINITION IS THE
> MANIFESTATION OF THE KNOWLEDGE OF GOD
> THROUGH OUR LIVES.**

DAY 41

And we pray this in order that you may live a life worthy of
the Lord and may please him in every way: bearing fruit in every
good work, growing in the knowledge of God, being strengthened
with all power according to his glorious might so that you may have
great endurance and patience, and joyfully giving thanks to the
Father, who has qualified you to share in the inheritance of
the saints in the kingdom of light.
—*Colossians 1:10–12*

The invisible aroma of the knowledge of God that the apostle Paul
talked about has power. It lifts us from one degree of life to another.
Our hearts become softer and more tender. We grow more caring,
compassionate, patient, and forgiving. We become more sensitive to the
Spirit of God. We are more like Jesus. In order to grow into maturity,
we must know God the Father more intimately.

PRAYER STARTER

*Father, help me to be aware of the things in my life that are not pleasing
to You. I want to grow and mature into Your likeness. Show me where I need
to be more caring, compassionate, patient, and forgiving.*

**OUR MOST VITAL MINISTRY IS REVEALING THE BEAUTY
OF GOD'S PERSONALITY TO OTHERS.**

DAY 42

Now it is God who makes both us and you stand firm in
Christ. He anointed us, set his seal of ownership on us, and put his
Spirit in our hearts as a deposit, guaranteeing what is to come.
—*2 Corinthians 1:21–22*

In the early days of my journey of becoming more intimate with God,
I struggled to feel His presence. I recall the day that I was in my office
praying. I had been worshiping at His feet for about fifteen minutes
when my secretary suddenly rang into my office. Annoyed at being
distracted, I picked up the phone. My annoyance left as I listened to the
caller's words: "God says that you are to set Him as a seal upon your
heart. He wanted you to know that right now."

PRAYER STARTER

*Sometimes, Lord, Your presence is so real to me that I feel as though
I could reach out and touch You. But at other times the cares of this world and
my own selfish desires keep me from being able to even sense Your presence.
Teach me to enter that secret place of intimacy with You.*

**IN THIS ENCOUNTER WITH THE LORD, THE HOLY SPIRIT
WAS REVEALING GOD'S HEART AND PASSION FOR ME.**

DAY 43

It was he who gave some to be apostles, some to be prophets, some to be evangelists, and some to be pastors and teachers, to prepare God's people for works of service, so that the body of Christ may be built up until we all reach unity in the faith and in the knowledge of the Son of God and become mature, attaining to the whole measure of the fullness of Christ.
—*Ephesians 4:11–13*

Jesus knew that after His resurrection, when He was seated at His Father's right hand, His priority would be to continue revealing the Father's name or His passions, desires, and pleasures to and through His church. Before Jesus comes *for* the church at the Second Coming, He will come *to* the church in revelation and power. His indescribable loveliness will be revealed to His people in a far greater measure in the great revival before His Second Coming.

PRAYER STARTER

Father, show me what I am to become in Your purpose and plan for my life. Mature me into the whole measure of the fullness of Christ.

THE CHURCH WILL BE FILLED WITH THE INTIMATE KNOWLEDGE OF GOD THE FATHER AND THE SON BY THE POWER AND REVELATION OF THE HOLY SPIRIT.

DAY 44

All things have been committed to me by my Father. No one knows the Son except the Father, and no one knows the Father except the Son and those to whom the Son chooses to reveal him.
—Matthew 11:27

Jesus's passion is to continue to reveal the Father. That's what He is doing now in His heavenly ministry at the right hand of the Father. That is what He will do through all eternity. Those who deeply encounter the ministry of the resurrected Christ will be captured by the beauty and splendor of the Father's name and personality.

PRAYER STARTER

Father, there is nothing I want more than to be qualified to reveal Your personality through my life. Let me show You to others so they will be captured by Your love for them.

THE CHURCH TODAY MUST BE IN AGREEMENT WITH THIS PRESENT MINISTRY OF JESUS—REVEALING THE FATHER TO PEOPLE'S HEARTS.

DAY 45

I have declared to them Your name, and will declare it, that the love with which You loved Me may be in them, and I in them.
—*John 17:26, NKJV*

Jesus is praying that the body of Christ will love Him the way the Father loves Him. This is an awesome prayer. Jesus will reveal the Father, and in turn, the Father will capture our hearts for the Son. Here we can see some of the dynamic cooperation at work within the Godhead. God the Father desires a people who love Jesus as He does, a people who see and feel what God sees and feels when He looks at His beloved Son.

PRAYER STARTER

Count me in, God. I want to be a passionate believer who sees and feels what You see and feel. Reveal Your Son in all His glory to my life.

> GOD WILL HAVE A PASSIONATE CHURCH THAT LOVES JESUS
> AS GOD LOVES HIM.

DAY 46

I have given them the glory that you gave me, that they may be one as we are one: I in them and you in me. May they be brought to complete unity to let the world know that you sent me and have loved them even as you have loved me.

—*John 17:22–23*

As the riches of the knowledge of God are revealed, the quality of love the Father has for the Son will be in the church. Jesus will dwell in His people; that is, He will manifest His supernatural life in and through them. The cycle goes all the way around. When Jesus manifests His life's ministry through us, we declare God's name and make Him known to others. Then we are, in turn, awakened with passion for Jesus, leading to lifestyles characterized by His presence.

PRAYER STARTER

Dear Jesus, manifest Your supernatural life in and through me. I want to reveal You to others. Awaken me with a passion to make You known to others so that we can live lifestyles characterized by Your presence.

THE SAME LOVE THE FATHER HAS FOR JESUS WILL FILL OUR HEARTS.

DAY 47

Father, I want those you have given me to be with me where I am, and to see my glory, the glory you have given me because you loved me before the creation of the world.

—*John 17:24*

It takes the power of God to make God known to the human spirit. This knowledge enables us to love God. It takes God to love God, and it takes God to know God. A revival of the knowledge of God is coming, and as a result the church will be filled with holy passion for Jesus. The heart of the Lord will be known by His people, and the church will love Jesus as God the Father loves His Son, Jesus.

PRAYER STARTER

It's only as I learn more and more about Your glory that my life will radiate Your love to others. I don't want anything to hinder me from the knowledge of God; revive my heart and fill me with passion for You.

DIVINELY IMPARTED PASSION IS ON THE HOLY SPIRIT'S AGENDA, AS SEEN IN JESUS'S PRAYER.

DAY 48

Righteous Father, though the world does not know you, I know you, and they know that you have sent me. I have made you known to them, and will continue to make you known in order that the love you have for me may be in them and that I myself may be in them.
—*John 17:25–26*

Passion for Jesus always comes from seeing God's name or personality because of Jesus's work on the cross. There is nothing Jesus wants more than a bride who loves what He loves and does what He does. He longs for a bride who will participate in the passions and purposes of His heart. We long to be a part of a glorious, spotless church in our generation—a church filled with the knowledge of God, reflecting His glory and consumed with passion for Jesus.

PRAYER STARTER

Father, I long to be able to tell others the wonder of all that You have done in my life. I want others to know You as I know You—as Savior, comforter, teacher, friend, and lover of my soul.

JESUS WILL HAVE AN ETERNAL COMPANION FILLED WITH HOLY AFFECTION FOR HIM.

DAY 49

Do not be afraid of those who kill the body but cannot kill the soul. Rather, be afraid of the One who can destroy both soul and body in hell. Are not two sparrows sold for a penny? Yet not one of them will fall to the ground apart from the will of your Father. And even the very hairs of your head are all numbered. So don't be afraid; you are worth more than many sparrows.

—*Matthew 10:28–31*

The soul of a human being is the seat of affection, where love and true worship flow. Who ultimately possesses the people's affections is of highest concern to the Father. We were made in His own image, uniquely designed for His holy purposes. God would only send His beloved Son to die for priceless, eternal human souls.

PRAYER STARTER

Father, every day I see people who are lost and hopeless without Your love in their life. Cause me to care deeply about their souls. Set me afire with a blazing desire to show them Your love.

NOTHING IN ALL CREATION IS MORE SIGNIFICANT TO GOD THAN THE SOUL OF A HUMAN BEING.

DAY 50

Jesus replied: "Love the Lord your God with all your heart
and with all your soul and with all your mind." This is the first and
greatest commandment.
—*Matthew 22:37–39*

God designed the human soul to be passionate and committed. This
is the only way that we can function to our fullest. Without abandonment to God, our hearts sink into restlessness, boredom, and
frustration. We must have something in our lives that is worth giving
everything up for. God intended our souls to be fascinated with Jesus.
Our highest development and greatest fulfillment lie in worshiping and
serving Jesus with all our heart.

PRAYER STARTER

*That's what I want to be, Lord—passionate and committed to You.
Let me find my highest development and greatest fulfillment in worshiping and
serving You with all my heart.*

**IF WE HAVE NOTHING TO DIE FOR, THEN WE HAVE
NOTHING TO LIVE FOR.**

DAY 51

For this reason I remind you to fan into flame the gift of God,
which is in you through the laying on of my hands.
For God did not give us a spirit of timidity,
but a spirit of power, of love and of self-discipline.
—*2 Timothy 1:6–7*

The Father will not insult His beloved Son by giving Him a bride that is bored, passive, and compromising. Passionless Christianity is no threat to the devil. It is focused on activities to the neglect of heartfelt affection and obedience to God. True Christianity sparks a flame in the human spirit. It ignites the heart with fervency.

PRAYER STARTER

Move me out of complacency and passivity to Your plan and purpose, Father. Wake me up and ignite my heart with fervency for my Savior.

AS AN INHERITANCE, GOD THE FATHER HAS PROMISED HIS SON A CHURCH FILLED WITH PEOPLE ABLAZE WITH AFFECTION.

DAY 52

Why do the nations rage, and the people plot a vain thing?
The kings of the earth set themselves, and the rulers take counsel
together, against the LORD and against His Anointed, saying, "Let us
break Their bonds in pieces and cast away Their cords from us."
—*Psalm 2:1–3, NKJV*

Satan, aware of the Father's agenda to fill the church with passion for
His Son, has devised an agenda of his own. To carry out his plans,
Satan is raising up wicked leaders who are committed to sin. They
are passionate in their resistance against the holy things of God. This
passion will become a hellish rage against Jesus just before He returns.
This raging conflict will be fought on many battlegrounds: religious,
social, and political ideologies; the economy; science and medicine;
morals and ethics; and education, music, and art.

PRAYER STARTER

*Father, I resist Satan's wicked agenda to keep people from turning to
You. I stand against his plans, and in Your Spirit I challenge him to release his
captive hold and set the prisoners free to place their trust and hope in You.*

> THESE WICKED LEADERS WILL VIOLENTLY OPPOSE
> THE IDEA OF A PASSIONATE PEOPLE FILLED WITH
> AFFECTION FOR JESUS.

DAY 53

Be self-controlled and alert. Your enemy the devil prowls around like a roaring lion looking for someone to devour. Resist him, standing firm in the faith, because you know that your brothers throughout the world are undergoing the same kind of sufferings.
—1 Peter 5:8–9

Satan always seeks to twist and pervert the issue to serve his interests. At his appointed time, rebellious, red-hot passion will develop around that issue. At the moment he may be promoting homosexuality, abortion, and sex education, which fosters an ungodly lifestyle, pornography, or other sin issues. But Satan's real, underlying motive goes far beyond that issue. His desire is to capture the passions of the human race, because that is the highest priority on God's agenda.

PRAYER STARTER

Lord, make me cautious, watchful, and diligent to recognize and thwart the attempts of Satan and his demons to ensnare Your people. Guard my passions, and set me as a watchman on the walls to keep the enemy away.

MARK IT: IF AN ISSUE IS IMPORTANT TO MAN, YOU'LL FIND SATAN'S FINGERPRINTS ALL OVER IT.

DAY 54

We know that anyone born of God does not continue to sin;
the one who was born of God keeps him safe, and the evil one cannot
harm him. We know that we are children of God, and that the whole
world is under the control of the evil one. We know also that the Son
of God has come and has given us understanding, so that we may
know him who is true. And we are in him who is true—even in his
Son Jesus Christ. He is the true God and eternal life.
—1 John 5:18–20

Satan's underlying motive goes far beyond a particular issue in society.
His goal is for the nations to erupt in rage against God. He is after a
militant, unified, passionate revolt against God's laws and Jesus's right
to reign over the planet. If you keep an eye on the spiritual tempera-
ture of national and international events, you will see the thermometer
climbing higher and higher. Satan and his cohorts are fanning and
feeding flames to explode in rage and reckless revolt against God's
ways.

PRAYER STARTER

*Father, I cry to You to have mercy on this nation. Cause a movement
of holiness and righteousness to sweep our nation, and forgive our sinful
disobedience and immorality.*

**POCKETS OF ANGER AND REBELLION ARE SMOLDERING
AMONG THOSE WHO INFLUENCE AND SET THE
COURSE OF MORALITY.**

DAY 55

Therefore the people wander like sheep
oppressed for lack of a shepherd.
My anger burns against the shepherds,
and I will punish the leaders;
for the LORD Almighty will care
for his flock, the house of Judah,
and make them like a proud horse in battle.
—*Zechariah 10:2–3*

First, Satan deceives the leaders. Then he unites them around his diabolical purposes. He motivates them to devise clever ploys to capture public opinion and undermine righteousness. They plot to erase the wise boundaries of right and wrong, good and evil that God has marked out in His Word for benefit of the human soul. The momentum of unholy passion is building. Dark-minded rulers from every level of society—lawmakers, educators, corporate heads, entertainers, advertisers, religious leaders, media moguls, and others—plot to attack the holy commandments of God. They seek first to dilute, then to demolish them from society, one by one.

PRAYER STARTER

Place in my heart the names of the leaders of this nation that You desire to capture for Your purposes. Keep me faithful in praying for them, and show me how I can partner with You to bring Your will to pass in this great nation.

HE PROVOKES LEADERS TO CAST OFF THE RESTRAINTS OF GOD'S WRITTEN WORD.

DAY 56

> I will declare the decree: The LORD has said to Me, "You are My Son, today I have begotten You. Ask of Me, and I will give You the nations for Your inheritance, and the ends of the earth for Your possession. You shall break them with a rod of iron; you shall dash them in pieces like a potter's vessel."
> —*Psalm 2:7–9, NKJV*

In this decree we see that the Bible is not just about God's plans and provision for mankind. It is also about God's plans and provision for His Son. We have an inheritance in which *our* delight and fulfillment are fundamental. God has an inheritance in which *His* delight is fundamental. We must be committed both to delight in and to give delight to God. The inheritance for us, the people of God, is the ability to experience both the blessings and the love of a passionate God. The inheritance for God is a passionate people.

PRAYER STARTER

> *Father, this is a nation that was founded on Your purposes and plans. Our inheritance is a covering of righteousness. Destroy the devil's attempt to snatch that inheritance away, and raise up an army of believers to restore this nation to purity.*

THE FATHER WILL EXPERIENCE HIS INHERITANCE ONLY AS WE BECOME RADICALLY COMMITTED TO HIM.

DAY 57

I pray that out of his glorious riches he may strengthen you with power through his Spirit in your inner being, so that Christ may dwell in your hearts through faith.
—*Ephesians 3:16–17*

What eternal riches God has offered mankind. What dignity and destiny He has bestowed upon the human race by designing us to live eternally for the praise of His glory. What a privilege to become the passion and pleasure of Christ Jesus. There are dimensions of pleasure and fulfillment that can never be experienced until we say a passionate, abandoned *yes* to the lordship of Jesus Christ. Yet so few believers have really said that *yes* to God.

PRAYER STARTER

Yes, Lord, yes! Whatever You want to do in my life—yes! However You want to transform my heart—yes! Wherever You want me to show forth Your glory—yes! Dwell in my life through faith and cause me to have an everlasting yes in my spirit to Your will.

IT IS LITTLE WONDER THAT THE UNBELIEVING WORLD LOOKS AT A BORED, COMPROMISING, BICKERING CHURCH AND SNEERS, "IF THAT'S WHAT A CHRISTIAN IS, FORGET IT."

DAY 58

Therefore, I urge you, brothers, in view of God's mercy, to offer your bodies as living sacrifices, holy and pleasing to God—this is your spiritual act of worship. Do not conform any longer to the pattern of this world, but be transformed by the renewing of your mind. Then you will be able to test and approve what God's will is—his good, pleasing and perfect will.

—*Romans 12:1–2*

The most powerful witness you and I can give sinners is a radiant life demonstrating that the will of God is good, acceptable, and perfect. Nonbelievers are looking for a contented, fulfilled people who aren't trying to cast off God's restraints—a people who are joyfully abandoned and totally committed to His cause. They need to see Christians who have taken up their crosses, turned their backs to the world, and given their all to the Christ who gave everything to them.

PRAYER STARTER

I want to be joyfully abandoned and totally committed to Your cause, God. Teach me Your ways so that I can prove Your good, acceptable, and perfect purpose in my life.

NONBELIEVERS LONG FOR SOMETHING OR SOMEONE THAT'S WORTH BEING PASSIONATE FOR—SOMETHING THAT COSTS THEM EVERYTHING.

DAY 59

Now therefore, be wise, O kings; be instructed, you judges of
the earth. Serve the LORD with fear, and rejoice with trembling.
—*Psalm 2:10–11, NKJV*

God is awesome in splendor and terrifying in His greatness. This royal
One has no superior—no equal. When we get a glimpse of His eternal
power and majestic beauty, we will be filled with reverential fear. We
tremble before His greatness. If we feel only trembling in God's presence, then we will not experience the fullness of His grace. David says
we are to rejoice before Him as well.

PRAYER STARTER

*Lord, You truly are awesome in splendor and terrifying in Your great-
ness. It is more than I can comprehend that You love me so much that You
bestow a righteous inheritance upon me. I rejoice in Your goodness to me and
bow in humble fear in Your mighty presence.*

WE ARE TO EXULT IN THE BENEFITS OF OUR INHERITANCE.

DAY 60

Kiss the Son, lest He be angry, and you perish in the way,
when His wrath is kindled but a little. Blessed are all those
who put their trust in Him.
—*Psalm 2:12, NKJV*

There is to be an intimate, affectionate, passionate dimension in our relationship with Jesus. Some churches emphasize awe and trembling, often leaving little room for rejoicing and affectionate worship. Others concentrate on rejoicing and blessing. Some of today's charismatic churches have focused on the authority of the believer and the privileges we have in Christ—to the exclusion of His awesome majesty and judgment. Still others are committed to affectionate intimacy with God with a passionate response of love toward Jesus. But God has fashioned the human spirit in such a way that we need all three dimensions—trembling, rejoicing, and kissing—in our relationship with Him.

PRAYER STARTER

Father, I have felt a trembling when I stand in Your presence, and I have abandoned my life to rejoicing in worship of such a great God. Now teach me to understand Your affectionate heart and to know the wonder of a loving, intimate relationship with You.

WE NEED TO ASK THE HOLY SPIRIT TO REVIVE IN OUR OWN HEARTS ALL THREE DIMENSIONS OF THE GRACE OF GOD.

DAY 61

*When Jesus entered Jerusalem, the whole city was stirred
and asked, "Who is this?" The crowds answered, "This is Jesus,
the prophet from Nazareth in Galilee."*
—*Matthew 21:10–11*

How about you? Maybe you have only seen a holy God who judges rebellion, and so you seek to walk in faithfulness as you fear God. You understand what it means to tremble. Do you rejoice in the benefits that are yours in Christ? Perhaps you do not experience much intimacy with God. The thought of kissing Christ makes you uncomfortable. It should, because David's call to kiss the Son is symbolic language that was not meant to be interpreted literal kissing. It refers to receiving God's love and then responding back to Him with wholehearted love.

PRAYER STARTER

Lord, I admit that the idea of "kissing Christ" is hard for me to comprehend. But show me the joy of crawling up into Your lap, throwing my arms around Your neck, and kissing Your holy face.

> **THE LORD WANTS TO INTERTWINE THESE THREE
> DIMENSIONS IN YOU. HE WANTS TO BRING THEM FORTH
> BY HIS HOLY SPIRIT.**

DAY 62

I will proclaim the decree of the LORD:
He said to me, "You are my Son;
today I have become your Father.
Ask of me,
and I will make the nations your inheritance,
the ends of the earth your possession.
You will rule them with an iron scepter;
you will dash them to pieces like pottery."
—Psalm 2:7–9

Remember that the shepherd boy who stood with holy confidence before Goliath while King Saul and the army of Israel cowered in the background is the author of this psalm. (See 1 Samuel 17.) Refusing to wear the cumbersome religious armor of his day, David charged out to face Goliath. He didn't see *big* Goliath and *little* David as he ran toward the battle line. He didn't see a huge sword and a little slingshot. All he saw were the powers of darkness mocking and defying the living God. David's stone and sling were irrelevant. He had the name of the Lord of hosts and the unshakeable confidence that His God would prevail!

PRAYER STARTER

Let me be a soldier in Your great end-time army, O Lord. Give me an unshakeable confidence in Your victory, and defeat the giants that try to intimidate me and cause me to forget Your awesome power and glory.

GOD WILL HAVE HIS END-TIME ARMY OF DAVIDS WHO ARE FILLED WITH THE KNOWLEDGE OF THEIR ALMIGHTY GOD. THEIR CAPTAIN IS THE LORD OF HOSTS, AND HE HAS NEVER LOST A BATTLE.

DAY 63

For he has rescued us from the dominion of darkness and brought us into the kingdom of the Son he loves, in whom we have redemption, the forgiveness of sins. He is the image of the invisible God, the firstborn over all creation.
—Colossians 1:13–15

We have taken God for granted. We have allowed materialism, secularism, and the love of things to smother the flame of God in our souls. We have created God in our own image, an image that is erroneous and tragically inadequate. Many in our generation have made for themselves a God they can use and control—a "heavenly butler" who waits on them hand and foot, catering to their every whim. To some believers, God is warm, approachable, and forgiving. To others, He is cold, aloof, and condemning. Regardless of how we see Him, what you and I think about God is the most important thing about us.

PRAYER STARTER

Forgive me, Father, when I have taken Your great love for granted. Forgive me for selfishly demanding my own will and way. Take the love of things out of my life, and cause me to love only You.

WE WILL EVENTUALLY BE SHAPED BY THE IMAGE OF GOD WE CARRY IN OUR MINDS.

DAY 64

Some people are like seed along the path, where the word is
sown. As soon as they hear it, Satan comes and takes away the word
that was sown in them.
—*Mark 4:15*

Satan goes to great lengths to distort our concepts of God. But because
such distortions can serve his "interests" in our lives, Satan is willing
to invest as much time and work as it takes to secure those vulnerable
areas of our minds for his own purposes. Those inaccurate, inadequate
concepts place us in great peril. To the degree that our ideas about
God are lower than the truth of God, to that degree we are surely
weakened and defeated. In those places and upon the foundation of
distorted truth Satan is able to gain ground and set up his strongholds
in our lives.

PRAYER STARTER

*If there are inaccurate, distorted images of You within my life, Father,
take them from me and reveal the truth of Your holiness. Satan will have no
stronghold in my life.*

WE DARE NOT DECIDE TO IGNORE AND JUST LEARN TO
LIVE WITH THE LIES AND MISCONCEPTIONS ABOUT GOD'S
PERSONALITY THAT HAVE BEEN PLANTED IN OUR MINDS.

DAY 65

Do not lie to each other, since you have taken off your old
self with its practices and have put on the new self, which is being
renewed in knowledge in the image of its Creator.
—*Colossians 3:9–10*

A spiritual fortress made of thoughts can be a fortified dwelling place
where demonic forces can hide. A stronghold in the mind is a collection
of thoughts in agreement with Satan—thoughts that are lies against
what God has revealed about Himself. Wrong concepts and ideas
about God are not automatically eliminated when we are born again.
We are continually in the process of being renewed by a true knowledge
according to the personality and likeness of God. Until we are walking
in that full, perfect knowledge of God, you and I must not make the
mistake of assuming that the process of change is over.

PRAYER STARTER

*Show me the strong places in my mind where Satan has kept me from
seeing the truth of Your revelation, Father. Tear these strongholds down, and
destroy anything that hinders me from being just like You.*

YOU AND I MUST NOT MAKE THE MISTAKE OF ASSUMING
THAT THE PROCESS OF CHANGE IS OVER.

DAY 66

> The god of this age has blinded the minds of unbelievers, so
> that they cannot see the light of the gospel of the glory of Christ,
> who is the image of God.
> —*2 Corinthians 4:4*

Jesus had no sin, wrong thinking, or impure motives that gave Satan
legal access to His life. Satan could find *nothing* in Jesus—not even
one square inch of territory—to which he could lay claim and thus
gain access to Jesus's heart. The enemy continually seeks occasions
where he can obtain a legal entry point in our lives. Sin and spiritual
ignorance open the door and invite his hold over us. This darkness is
like a veil that obscures the liberating light of the gospel in the minds
of unbelievers.

PRAYER STARTER

> *Shine Your glory in my life, and illuminate the dark recesses of my
> heart where Satan attempts to lay claim. In Your Spirit I resist his attack.
> I desire only to radiate the light of Your divine life.*

**AS A SHARK IS DRAWN TO BLOOD, SO THE DEVIL IS DRAWN
TO LIES AND DARKNESS.**

DAY 67

Rescue the weak and needy;
deliver them from the hand of the wicked.
They know nothing, they understand nothing.
They walk about in darkness;
all the foundations of the earth are shaken.
—*Psalm 82:4–5*

Satan's goal is to keep us in darkness. His strategy is to distort or restrict our knowledge of God so that it is erroneous and inadequate. Thus we are weakened and held in bondage. Satan seeks to lay claim to every area of spiritual darkness that he can find in us, including wrong ideas and thought systems, sympathetic thoughts toward sin, and self-excusing rationalizations. He utilizes these to erect spiritual *strongholds* in us to protect his investments and interests in our lives.

PRAYER STARTER

Father, when I am feeling weak, confused, and ineffective, help me to realize that a dark area in my spiritual life may be hiding some sinful habit or area of rebellion that needs to be exposed to God's light and then destroyed. Let Your light shine on all the dark areas of my life, O God, and bring me into spiritual maturity.

SATAN DOES NOT WANT THE LIGHT OF THE KNOWLEDGE OF GOD'S HEART TO INVADE OUR SPIRITUAL DARKNESS.

DAY 68

He will bring down your high fortified walls
and lay them low;
he will bring them down to the ground,
to the very dust.
—*Isaiah 25:12*

How does the enemy construct a spiritual stronghold in our lives? First, he starts with a foundation of lies and half-truths. Usually these are lies about the personality of God or about how God views us. Next, up go thick spiritual walls, brick by brick. They are built by inaccurate ideas about God and distorted perceptions of how God sees and feels about us, especially in our spiritual immaturity and when we sin. Held together by the mortar of mistaken reasoning, the walls rise higher and higher. Soon, lofty spiritual towers of vain imaginations loom inside us.

PRAYER STARTER

Father, I refuse to be held back from becoming more like You because of any spiritual strongholds Satan has erected in my life. Destroy all the walls of stubborn pride and vain imaginations in my life, and let me grow more and more into Your image.

SATAN ERECTS EVERY STRONGHOLD HE CAN TO KEEP US FROM THE TRUE KNOWLEDGE OF GOD.

DAY 69

It is because of him that you are in Christ Jesus, who has become for us wisdom from God—that is, our righteousness, holiness and redemption.
—1 Corinthians 1:30

We must adopt an offensive posture if we are to break free from a stronghold. We must hunger for God and long to know Him intimately as we look back over our shoulders at temptation and say no. Our strong-willed determination to overcome our weaknesses and addictions is not our sanctification. Our sanctification is found in a *person:* Jesus Christ! When we are given just a little glimpse of the truth about Christ's awesome beauty and splendor, we will bow before Him in awe, and with gladness and affection we will abandon ourselves to Him.

PRAYER STARTER

Lord, I do hunger and thirst after Your righteousness. My hope is found only in You, Lord Jesus, and I submit myself to Your will so that I may overcome all the weakness in my human heart.

IT'S BY KNOWING THE TRUTH, THEN PURSUING A PERSON (GOD), ALONG WITH RESISTING UNHOLY PASSIONS AND TEMPTATIONS, THAT WE CAN WALK IN VICTORY.

DAY 70

For he chose us in him before the creation of the world to
be holy and blameless in his sight. In love he predestined us to be
adopted as his sons through Jesus Christ, in accordance with his
pleasure and will—to the praise of his glorious grace, which he has
freely given us in the One he loves.

—*Ephesians 1:4–6*

I can remember when I began to think of God with a big smile on
His face. I imagined Him saying, "I enjoy you—knowing you brings
pleasure to my heart." I initially struggled with thoughts that are all too
common to many of us: "Who, me? Did You see my sin? How can You
enjoy me when I have such weaknesses?" However, the Father would
answer through the counsel of His Word, "I see the sincerity in your
heart. I see the cry in your heart to please Me even though you often
stumble. I delight in My relationship with you!"

PRAYER STARTER

*How awesome it is, precious Holy Spirit, to realize that Father God
truly takes delight and pleasure in me! How unbelievable that before He spoke
creation into being, He had already chosen to love me and to make me one of
His children.*

I SAW THAT GOD WANTED ME TO RUN TO HIM, NOT AWAY
FROM HIM, WHEN I FAILED.

DAY 71

I will sing of the LORD's great love forever;
with my mouth I will make your faithfulness
known through all generations.
I will declare that your love stands firm forever,
that you established your faithfulness in heaven itself.
—*Psalm 89:1–2*

I've been in the ministry for thirty years. Through those years I have grieved with many who have told me stories of their terrible hardships—stories of molestation, abuse, and perversion at the hands of cruel and hateful people. But I know that even if they had never experienced real love, God's Word offers each one bondage-breaking truth and joyful hope through the revelation of God's heart for them. The knowledge of God's pure, faithful, passionate affection for us is far more powerful and life transforming than anything we can receive from our earthly father.

PRAYER STARTER

The knowledge of Your love has transformed my life, O God. I long to pass that knowledge of love on to those I know who need the transformation of Your love to revolutionize their hearts and lives.

IT IS THE HOLY SPIRIT, NOT HUMAN WITNESSES, WHO REVEALS GOD'S LOVE FOR US AND MAKES HIM REAL TO OUR HEARTS, AND THAT REVELATION IS AVAILABLE TO EVERYONE.

DAY 72

May my cry come before you, O LORD;
give me understanding according to your word.
May my supplication come before you;
deliver me according to your promise.
—*Psalm 119:169–170*

People with wounded and broken spirits or perfectionists with performance-driven personalities often have difficulty receiving from God. Sometimes we become so caught up in our own pressures, pain, or anger that we don't even recognize His voice. As we persist in receiving the truth of God's Word about God's heart for us, then our hearts can progressively be healed of what earthly authority figures have done to us.

PRAYER STARTER

Father, I know so many people who have broken, wounded spirits or who are driven by a desire to perform. I want Your love, Your passionate affection for them, to be shown to them through my life.

THE HOLY SPIRIT WILL REVEAL THE WORD OF GOD TO US, GIVING US NEW AND FRESH UNDERSTANDING ABOUT THE PASSIONATE AFFECTION IN GOD'S HEART TO US.

DAY 73

Whoever lives in love lives in God, and God in him. In this way, love is made complete among us so that we will have confidence on the day of judgment, because in this world we are like him. There is no fear in love. But perfect love drives out fear, because fear has to do with punishment. The one who fears is not made perfect in love.
—1 John 4:16–18

Neither good experiences from our fathers nor even our zeal for God can produce abounding love for Jesus in us. I was an angry, frustrated Christian who constantly carried a heavy burden of guilt and failure for not measuring up. Only when I began to see the true knowledge of how God feels about me did the spiritual strongholds in my mind and heart begin to break down. The person who is afraid of God, who fears that He will judge all their failings, will live in torment. When I recognized that God's heart is filled with tenderness for me—even in my weakness—then it made me bold in my love for God.

PRAYER STARTER

Father, like Mike Bickle, I remember the spiritual issues that remained in my life even though I wanted to live a good Christian life. I thank You for the revelation of how much You loved me, because the knowledge of Your love for me is what allowed me to live in the peace and security of Your approval.

TORMENT IS THE OPPOSITE OF BOLDNESS.

DAY 74

Every valley shall be raised up,
every mountain and hill made low;
the rough ground shall become level,
the rugged places a plain.
And the glory of the LORD will be revealed,
and all mankind together will see it.
For the mouth of the LORD has spoken.
—*Isaiah 40:4–5*

God, who has never painted the same sunset twice, knows exactly how to reveal Himself to you. He will choose the perfect time and place to speak to you. He knows the precise way to illuminate your understanding, feed your hungry heart, or flow like healing oil over your wounded spirit. When you come to your heavenly Father for help, you will not be ignored or rebuked. You will not be ridiculed for your mistakes. He is extraordinarily kind and very patient toward you. He cares for you with affection and watchfulness. His love for you will never fail or end.

PRAYER STARTER

Father, I am overjoyed with the record of Your faithfulness to me. You have never ignored my pleas for help, and You have always poured the healing oil of Your spirit over my life.

GOD, HIS WORD, AND THE HOLY SPIRIT'S WORK IN YOUR LIFE ARE SUFFICIENT TO BRING YOU TO PERSONAL WHOLENESS AND SPIRITUAL MATURITY.

DAY 75

The king is enthralled by your beauty; honor him,
for he is your lord.
—*Psalm 45:11*

How do you think God sees you? Do you cringe at the thought? God is not the cold, aloof, rigidly legalistic being that religion has made Him out to be. He is not the demanding, impatient God so many of us have struggled to please. Oh, how the Lord longs for His church to receive a revelation of His ravished heart—filled with delight for us—even though we may not like or believe in ourselves. How His heart aches for us to become aware of His desire for us (Ps. 45:11).

PRAYER STARTER

God, may I never forget how You long to have an intimate, personal relationship with me. I want to spend time in Your presence. I want my life to be absorbed in Your love, Your will, and Your beauty.

> **OUR GOD IS NOT A THING OR AN IT. HE IS AN AFFECTIONATE, LOVING, DEEPLY PASSIONATE BEING.**

DAY 76

Let me understand the teaching of your precepts;
then I will meditate on your wonders.
My soul is weary with sorrow;
strengthen me according to your word.
—*Psalm 119:27–28*

Salvation is more than a legal exchange affecting our position before God. Salvation also includes the exchange of deep, loving affections and love. As God communicates His enjoyment and affections for us, we in turn respond in a similar way. An intellectual understanding of the legal aspects of salvation is essential, but it is not the full counsel of God. We will never have more passion for God than we understand that He has for us. We will never be more committed to God than our understanding of His commitment to us.

PRAYER STARTER

Lord, I want more than a head knowledge of the salvation You have so graciously given to me. May my heart be gripped by a revelation of your passion and love for me.

THE HOLY SPIRIT MUST QUICKEN OUR KNOWLEDGE OF GOD'S PASSIONATE LOVE AS THE WAY HE HAS CHOSEN TO IMPART IT TO OUR HEARTS.

DAY 77

Let him kiss me with the kisses of his mouth—
for your love is more delightful than wine.
Pleasing is the fragrance of your perfumes;
your name is like perfume poured out.
No wonder the maidens love you!
—*Song of Solomon 1:2–3*

Believers today are realizing that if our hunger for intimacy is ever to be satisfied, we must have Him whose affectionate love is far better than "churchianity" or the best wine of earthly experiences and possessions. Like the maiden who cried, "Your love is more delightful than wine," believers are coming to the point where they realize that money and material things are never going to supply the needs of our spirits. Prominence in the church or the world will never do it. No sensual or romantic relationship with another human being will ever satisfy the deep cravings of our spirits. We're becoming tired of powerless religion that can't deliver us from sin or from ourselves; tired of leaders filled with anger, striving, and immorality; tired of churches paralyzed in apathy.

PRAYER STARTER

Forgive me, God, for the "churchianity" that so often creeps into my life. I'm tired of powerless religion, of subtle sins that hide within my heart, and of the pew-sitting tendencies that keep me from serving You and loving You with passion.

WE'RE WEARY OF TRYING TO DRAW WATER FROM A DRY WELL IN THE NAME OF JESUS.

DAY 78

Because of the fragrance of your good ointments,
Your name is ointment poured forth.
—*Song of Solomon 1:3, NKJV*

A fresh abandonment, a holy recklessness for Jesus, is awakening in the spirits of God's people today. Before Jesus returns, God will raise up a church full of people who are hungering for God-centered Christianity and who refuse to return to man-centered Christianity. The denominational label will not matter. If the Son of God is being ministered in power, and His personal beauty is unveiled, people will flock to Him. Why do we want Him? We have discovered that the love and affection of God are better than anything the world has to offer, and we're beginning to see a little bit of the majesty and matchless beauty of the love of Christ Jesus.

PRAYER STARTER

Father, I sense the awakening of Your spirit within my heart anew. I want to live outside the box of man-centered Christianity. I want to arise out of my complacency and apathy to fulfill Your purposes in my life.

THE SPIRIT OF GOD IS CALLING US FORTH, TAKING THE
TRUTHS OF TIME AND ETERNITY AND USING THEM TO
AWAKEN US OUT OF COMPLACENCY.

DAY 79

Draw me after you and let us run together!
The king has brought me into his chambers.
We will rejoice in you and be glad;
We will extol your love more than wine.
Rightly do they love you.
—*Song of Solomon 1:4, NAS*

After the maiden in the Song of Solomon awakens to fervency, she then prays a twofold prayer: "Draw me after you and let us run together!" The order of that prayer is important. First we are drawn to Him in intimacy; then we run together with Him in ministry. It's easy for people to pray, "Let me run with You, Jesus," or "Increase my sphere of ministry and influence," without also fervently seeking to be drawn near to Him. God's order is that we be drawn to greater intimacy with Jesus as the way to greater effectiveness in ministry. That is what "running," or real ministry, is all about—bringing deliverance to the hearts of human beings so they can be drawn into knowing and worshiping God intimately.

PRAYER STARTER

Father, keep my steps running ever closer to You. Draw me close to You, and let me partner with You in bringing deliverance to others. Let me show them the path to intimacy with You.

IF WE ARE TO BECOME EFFECTIVE CO-LABORERS WITH
CHRIST, RUNNING WITH HIM, WE FIRST MUST FOCUS ON
BEING DRAWN AS WORSHIPERS TO ENCOUNTER
HIS AFFECTION FOR US.

DAY 80

Jesus replied: "'Love the Lord your God with all your heart
and with all your soul and with all your mind.' This is the first
and greatest commandment. And the second is like it: 'Love your
neighbor as yourself.' All the Law and the Prophets hang on these
two commandments."
—*Matthew 22:37–40*

A few believers say, "Draw me," but resist running with the Lord as
a partner with Him in His work in the earth. The Holy Spirit does
not draw us so we can hang up a "Do Not Disturb" sign and sit in
our little comfort zone, only singing love songs to Jesus the rest of our
lives. As fellow heirs with Christ, we are drawn into intimacy, and then
empowered in ministry to bring others into intimacy with the Lord.
The church will surely mature in the tension of drawing and running.
We will learn how to deliver broken people, prevail in spiritual warfare
and serve one another while maintaining our intimacy with Jesus.

PRAYER STARTER

*Father, draw me into an intimate relationship with You so that I may
be empowered to draw others unto You. I want to bring Your deliverance to
broken people. I want to prevail in spiritual warfare as others learn to turn
their hearts and lives over to You.*

BEING DRAWN INTO DEEP INTIMACY WITH JESUS AND
RUNNING IN SERVANTHOOD MINISTRY FULFILL THE TWO
GREAT COMMANDMENTS JESUS GAVE IN MATTHEW 22:37–40.

DAY 81

In him we were also chosen, having been predestined according to the plan of him who works out everything in conformity with the purpose of his will, in order that we, who were the first to hope in Christ, might be for the praise of his glory.
—*Ephesians 1:11–12*

Discovering that Jesus is the essential source of spiritual delight is an important part of our progression toward maturity, and the Lord does not want that process disturbed. He leaves us right where we are for a season: growing in the knowledge of His loveliness and faithfulness and feeling increasingly secure and satisfied. But while we are discovering His beauty and delighting ourselves in Him, the Lord is sealing our spirits. We will never again be content with a life of compromise that neglects spiritual intimacy. We have an inheritance in God, but God also has an inheritance in us. What an incredible thought: God, who possesses everything, has something He waits for—His inheritance in us.

PRAYER STARTER

Father, when I feel as though I am merely "marking time" instead of marching into victory, help me to understand that You are placing me in a season of spiritual growth and preparation for what lies ahead.

WE ARE EQUIPPED AND MATURED TO BE COHEIRS AND SHARE CHRIST'S HEART, HIS HOME, HIS THRONE FOREVER.

DAY 82

The voice of my beloved!
Behold, he comes
Leaping upon the mountains,
Skipping upon the hills.
—*Song of Solomon 2:8, NKJV*

Because the Lord loves us so affectionately and so deeply, He gives us a whole new revelation of Himself. At this stage of this beautiful song of love, the maiden sees her beloved in an entirely different dimension. She watches as he comes to her, leaping and skipping like a gazelle. The hills and mountains speak of obstacles that must be overcome. They include trials and tribulations of Christian growth. They also refer to our struggle against satanic principalities and powers. These obstacles may be the kingdoms of this world that oppose the gospel. It doesn't matter. No obstacle is insurmountable for our God.

PRAYER STARTER

Lord, I recognize the hills and mountains that bring the trials and tribulations of Christian growth. May I never lose sight of the fact that each step I take over these mountains brings me closer and closer to You.

LITTLE BY LITTLE IN THIS PROGRESSION OF HOLY PASSION, WE BEGIN TO FIGURE OUT THAT FERVENCY IS NOT THE SAME AS FULL MATURITY.

DAY 83

My beloved is like a gazelle or a young stag.
Behold, he is standing behind our wall,
He is looking through the windows,
He is peering through the lattice.
My beloved responded and said to me,
"Arise, my darling, my beautiful one,
And come along."
—*Song of Solomon 2:9–10, NAS*

In the early stages of our spiritual journey, we may have seen Jesus as the One whose presence satisfies our hearts, just as the maiden did. As we seek to go on to maturity in our walk with Him, we will surely encounter Him as the mighty King who skips on mountains. In these seasons, He is challenging the comfort zone in our life as He calls us to join Him in His war against all who oppose His kingdom in this world: "Arise, My beautiful one, and come with Me. You can't sit under the shade tree forever. Come and leap mountains with Me. Will you love Me enough to join Me in bringing My kingdom even to the places that oppose Me?"

PRAYER STARTER

Give me the courage, dear Father, to leave the comfort of my shady spot and to leap with You over the hills and mountains that threaten to inhibit my spiritual growth and that oppose Your kingdom.

CAN YOU RECALL A TIME WHEN THE LORD CHALLENGED YOU TO ARISE AND LEAVE YOUR COMFORT ZONE?

DAY 84

Until the day breaks
and the shadows flee,
turn, my lover,
and be like a gazelle
or like a young stag
on the rugged hills.
—*Song of Solomon 2:17*

Have you ever told the Lord no out of fear and weakness when He asked you to do something for Him? Just as He did with the maiden, the Lord calls us out of our comfort zone that we may become mature disciples who live for His pleasure and purpose.

PRAYER STARTER

Father, forgive me for the many times I've said no when You asked me to do something for You. I want to be mature, to have a constant yes in my spirit to the things You want me to do and be.

JUST LIKE THE MAIDEN IN THE SONG OF SOLOMON, I HAVE SOMETIMES REFUSED THE LORD'S FRESH CHALLENGES BY TELLING HIM TO GO LEAP ON THE MOUNTAINS OR GO AND CONQUER AREAS OF DARKNESS WITHOUT ME.

DAY 85

On my bed night after night I sought him
Whom my soul loves;
I sought him but did not find him.
I must arise now and go about the city;
In the streets and in the squares
I must seek him whom my soul loves.
I sought him but did not find him.
The watchmen who make the rounds in the city found me,
And I said, "Have you seen him whom my soul loves?"
—*Song of Solomon 3:1–3, NAS*

Sometimes the Lord gets our attention in discipling us by gently withdrawing His presence for a season. That is the way He caused the maiden to repent for refusing Him. When the Lord corrects His sincere, yet immature, disciples, He is not angry with us. He still loves and enjoys us in our immaturity; however, He loves us too much to let us stay there. Although we do not always understand it, He is bringing us forth to maturity. He knows what awaits us—the glory of being His bride and the spiritual treasures that come with being mature coheirs of the glorious Son of God.

PRAYER STARTER

In the seasons of the night, dear God, when Your presence seems far removed from my life, teach me to look forward to the morning when the light of Your love bursts into view and brings me into a new level of relationship with You.

OUR FEAR AND WEAKNESS DO NOT ANGER THE LORD.

DAY 86

My son, do not make light of the Lord's discipline, and do not lose heart when he rebukes you, because the Lord disciplines those he loves, and he punishes everyone he accepts as a son. Endure hardship as discipline; God is treating you as sons. For what son is not disciplined by his father? If you are not disciplined (and everyone undergoes discipline), then you are illegitimate children and not true sons.

—*Hebrews 12:5–8*

The Lord pries our fingers loose from the things to which we cling so tenaciously. Firmly, but tenderly, He woos us away from anything that would hold us back from that which is His best for our lives. He could say to us, "If you only knew the glory that you will inherit, you would never refuse Me. Have I ever led you into a place where I could not meet you and provide for you? I will never take anything from you that will not be restored tenfold. My disciplines are good. They seem sorrowful for the moment, but afterward they yield the fruit of righteousness."

PRAYER STARTER

I feel Your gentle tug on my fingers, Lord, prying them loose from those things You know must be dismissed out of my life. I release them to You, Lord. May they never hinder me from growing more like You each day I live.

> **WHEN THE LORD'S PRESENCE DEPARTS FROM US IN OUR PLACE OF COMPROMISE, WE MUST ARISE IN OBEDIENCE AND FAITH AND SEEK HIM.**

DAY 87

Until the day breaks
and the shadows flee,
I will go to the mountain of myrrh
and to the hill of incense.
All beautiful you are, my darling;
there is no flaw in you.
—*Song of Solomon 4:6–7*

We see our failures and shortcomings, and we may automatically think that God is accusing and condemning us. The devil has deceived us, leading us to attribute to God what is true of himself. Satan, not God, is the accuser of the brethren. God is our affirmer—our encourager. He believes in our sincere desires to obey Him more than we do and calls us forth in ways we would never dream. He says, "I love you! I have great affection for you! I will transform a fervent, immature maiden into My reigning, mature bride."

PRAYER STARTER

When my failures and shortcoming seem to overcome me, Lord, give me the courage to recognize the work of the accuser. You do not accuse me, Lord, but You affirm my desire to obey You, and You call me forth into my destiny in You.

CHRIST SEES OUR DESIRE FOR OBEDIENCE EVEN WHEN IT IS ONLY IN SEED FORM IN OUR HEARTS.

DAY 88

Therefore, I urge you, brothers, in view of God's mercy, to offer your bodies as living sacrifices, holy and pleasing to God—this is your spiritual act of worship. Do not conform any longer to the pattern of this world, but be transformed by the renewing of your mind. Then you will be able to test and approve what God's will is—his good, pleasing and perfect will.

—*Romans 12:1–2*

Some people think the will of God is always hard, but that's not true. The will of God is good, satisfying, and perfect. We find great fulfillment and joy in doing the will of God. On the other hand, there are times when we must say no to the desires of our flesh, times when our own carnal passions conflict with the will of God. At such times we must deny ourselves, and yes, that is difficult. That is what Jesus meant when He said, "If anyone wishes to come after Me, let him deny himself, and take up his cross daily, and follow Me" (Luke 9:23, NAS). If we want to be co-laborers with Jesus, fulfilling His purposes in the earth, we must step out of the comfort zone and move into the life of faith where our only source is the invisible God and the integrity of His Word.

PRAYER STARTER

I no longer want to dwell in comfort, Lord, if comfort means I have failed to deny Your cross daily and to follow You. Your purposes are what I crave to fulfill, and I commit to living the life of faith in utter trust in You.

CHRIST SAID WE CANNOT BE HIS DISCIPLES IF WE DO NOT PICK UP OUR CROSS AND FOLLOW HIM.

DAY 89

You have ravished my heart,
My sister, my spouse;
You have ravished my heart
With one look of your eyes.
—*Song of Solomon 4:9, NKJV*

What does it mean to "ravish" the heart? According to the dictionary, the word *ravish* means "to take away by violence; to overcome with emotions of joy or delight; unusually attractive, pleasing or striking." The bride had captured his heart, filling it with ecstasy and delight. As the maiden heard the Lord wooing and affirming her, her fears melted away, and she gained courage to follow Him. Remember: all that she has done at this point is say yes. Yet she has ravished the heart of God with her sincere desire to obey Him.

PRAYER STARTER

Is it possible, dear God, that my willingness to follow You could ravish Your heart with love for me? Your love is more than I can comprehend, but it is my sincere desire to follow You wherever You ask me to go.

DID YOU KNOW THAT YOUR YES TO CHRIST—YOUR IMMATURE BUT SINCERE COMMITMENT TO HIM—RAVISHES HIS HEART?

DAY 90

But since we belong to the day, let us be self-controlled, putting on faith and love as a breastplate, and the hope of salvation as a helmet. For God did not appoint us to suffer wrath but to receive salvation through our Lord Jesus Christ.

—*1 Thessalonians 5:8–9*

It is this revelation of Jesus's ravished heart for us that awakens our hearts to fervency for Him. It ignites holy passion in us. It is His love for us and our response of love and devotion back to Him that act as a breastplate of love, guarding our hearts with holy affections in times of temptation.

PRAYER STARTER

If Your love is so passionate for me, dear Father, then I am filled with such an intense longing to devote my heart and life to pleasing You. Guard my heart, dear Father, and draw me ever closer to You.

JESUS YEARNS FOR YOU WITH A LONGING FOR AN EVEN MORE INTIMATE RELATIONSHIP WITH HIM.

DAY 91

His pleasure is not in the strength of the horse,
nor his delight in the legs of a man;
the LORD delights in those who fear him,
who put their hope in his unfailing love.
—*Psalm 147:10–11*

Perhaps you have grown so accustomed to the constant, condemning barrage from the enemy, from your own accusing thoughts or the criticism of others, you hardly know what it is like to live without a sense of sin, failure, and rejection clouding your heart. You may have come to view yourself as failing, utterly unlovely and worthless, but that is not the way your beloved Lord sees you. As you look to Jesus and set your soul to follow Him at any cost, one loving glance seizes His heart and carries it away. "You have ravished My heart with one look from your eyes!" He exclaims. "I am overwhelmed by your devotion. You are so lovely, such a source of joy and delight to My heart!"

PRAYER STARTER

There are times, dear God, when I feel like such a spiritual failure. But when I place my eyes back on You instead of on myself, I am filled afresh with the wonder of Your love, which enables me to rise above my weakness and become all You desire me to become.

GOD CALLS US FORTH IN WAYS WE WOULD NEVER DREAM,
YET WE ACCUSE OURSELVES SO TERRIBLY.

DAY 92

> Let the beloved of the LORD rest secure in him,
> for he shields him all day long, and the one the LORD loves
> rests between his shoulders.
> —*Deuteronomy 33:12*

Every time Satan comes to weight down your heart with his lies, speak what the Word says back to him. The next time your own heart points a merciless, judgmental finger at your own failings, listen to the loving voice of Jesus as declared in His Word that says, "We are pleasing and beautiful to Him. Yes, we have ravished His heart!"

PRAYER STARTER

I hear Your loving voice, my Father, and it drowns out the depressing, lying voice of the enemy. I will not hear his voice; I will not believe his lies. You are my hope, my sustenance, and my joy.

WHEN YOU HEAR THE AFFIRMING WORDS OF YOUR BELOVED, DO NOT OPEN YOUR MOUTH TO PROTEST. ACCEPT THEM. BELIEVE THEM. THEY'RE REALLY TRUE.

DAY 93

How much better than wine is your love, and the scent of
your perfumes than all spices! Your lips, O my spouse, drip as the
honeycomb; honey and milk are under your tongue; and the fragrance
of your garments is like the fragrance of Lebanon. A garden enclosed
is my sister, my spouse, a spring shut up, a fountain sealed.
—*Song of Solomon 4:10–12, NKJV*

This verse reveals a very important spiritual principle that has application for you and me as believers. The knowledge of God's affection prepares us to experience His fullness and to remain strong and faithful to Him in times of persecution and testing. Jesus declares that our love for Him is better than wine—it is better than all the kingdoms of the world, better than all the glorious works of His hands. The beloved finds wonderful delight in his beautiful bride in three ways—her perfume, the sweetness of her lips, the fragrance of her garments.

PRAYER STARTER

*I know there will be times of persecution and testing in my life, dear
Lord, but Your love keeps me strong. No matter what comes into my life,
I will follow You with all my heart all the days of my life.*

TRULY, THE HEART OF JESUS IS UTTERLY RAVISHED BY THE
RESOLUTE HEART, THE LOVING ABANDONMENT OF HIS
CHURCH FOR HIM.

DAY 94

You number my wanderings;
Put my tears into Your bottle;
Are they not in Your book?
When I cry out to You…
In God I have put my trust;
I will not be afraid.
What can man do to me?
—*Psalm 56:8–9, 11, NKJV*

The scent of the bride's perfume can represent her inner thought life, which emanates as a lovely fragrance to the Lord. God hears the secret cry of our spirits that no one else hears, and it ascends as a beautiful perfume before Him. God sees the secret intentions of our hearts as we long to please Him, even when we come up short. The cry of the saints to the Lord is as fragrant incense to Him. In our verse today, David was weeping over his own failings. Our tears of repentance and sorrow are precious to the Lord.

PRAYER STARTER

May my life carry the aroma of purity and holiness before You. My heart breaks because of my inadequacies and failings, but Your love reminds me that my tears are precious to You.

> **INSTEAD OF CONDEMNING OURSELVES AND OTHER CHRISTIANS WHO FALL, WE MUST REALIZE THAT OUR TEARS ARE PRECIOUS TO GOD.**

DAY 95

Your lips, O my spouse,
Drip as the honeycomb;
Honey and milk are under your tongue;
And the fragrance of your garments
Is like the fragrance of Lebanon.
—*Song of Solomon 4:11, NKJV*

What are the milk, honey, and fragrant garments the beloved mentions? Just as milk and honey help nurture bodies, the lips dripping with milk and honey are the bride's edifying, life-giving words that nurture the faith of the young instead of accusing, slandering, criticizing, and finding fault. Her fragrant garments are her righteous deeds of service. Our intent to lay our lives down for the Lord, crucifying our own self-centeredness, ascends like a pleasing perfume to the Lord.

PRAYER STARTER

Lord, let my lips bring Your life and salvation to those I meet. May my acts of spiritual service bring others to You. I lay my life at Your feet and pray that it will be a pleasing perfume to Your heart.

WHEN THE INTENTION OF OUR HEARTS IS TO BE A SERVANT, OUR SERVICE EXUDES A BEAUTIFUL FRAGRANCE IN THE PRESENCE OF GOD (2 COR. 2:15–16).

DAY 96

Awake, O north wind,
And come, wind of the south;
Make my garden breathe out fragrance,
Let its spices be wafted abroad.
May my beloved come into his garden
And eat its choice fruits.
—*Song of Solomon 4:16, NAS*

As the Lord lavishes His love upon the maiden, she breaks out with one of the great prayers of the Song of Solomon. The north wind communicates the cold, bitter winds of winter, and the south wind is the warm, refreshing wind that comes during the sowing of the seed and the summer season of growth. The bride asks for both winds. She asks for the harsh north wind to blow on her in order to reveal what is in her heart, but she also asks for the blessing and refreshing of the south wind.

PRAYER STARTER

Father, give me courage to ask for the north winds of winter to come into my life as well as the warm, refreshing winds of harvest. Sow Your seeds of blessing during the winters of my life, and allow me to praise You for the harvest.

**WE NEVER OUTGROW OUR NEED FOR THE
SOUTH WINDS OF BLESSING.**

DAY 97

Submit yourselves, then, to God. Resist the devil, and he will flee from you. Come near to God and he will come near to you.
—James 4:7–8

When we can ask for both winds—His dealings and His blessings—we are saying, "If You love me so much, I know it's safe to be Yours. I deeply trust You. I'm not afraid of difficult circumstances. You do not give anything that takes away real life. You have guarded my every step." Don't confuse the north wind with the attack of the devil. We must always resist his onslaughts. We don't invite his attack. That's absolute foolishness, for we must always resist the devil and his dealings with us. We can trust our Beloved absolutely. Therefore, we are not afraid to pray this prayer: "I love You, Jesus. I want all my immaturity to be gone. I want my heart to be yoked with Your heart. Your inheritance in me is the most important thing in my life. Therefore, awake, O north wind!"

PRAYER STARTER

Lord, in the winter of discouragement and spiritual attack from Satan, I resist his plans to destroy my life, and I desire the inheritance of a blessed and faithful life.

GOD CAN USE THE ATTACKS OF SATAN TO STRENGTHEN OUR HEARTS.

DAY 98

I opened to my beloved, but my beloved had turned away and had gone! My heart went out to him as he spoke. I searched for him, but I did not find him; I called him, but he did not answer me. The watchmen who make the rounds in the city found me, they struck me and wounded me; the guardsmen of the walls took away my shawl from me. I adjure you, O daughters of Jerusalem, if you find my beloved, as to what you will tell him: for I am lovesick.

—*Song of Solomon 5:6–8, NAS*

Now comes the maiden's ultimate twofold test: the Lord withholds His presence, and even His people reject her. The first test is the loss of the conscious presence of God that so satisfies her soul. This is a temporary test. This withdrawing of His presence is not due to disobedience but rather because of her obedience and desire for full maturity. It is as if the Lord is saying, "Let Me ask you, My bride: Am I only the source of your satisfaction, or am I the consuming reason for your very life? Am I a means to your end, or am I the very end goal of your life? Will you serve Me if there are no spiritual feelings? When My discernible presence is gone, will you still say, 'I am Your loving bondservant'?"

PRAYER STARTER

Lord, in the seasons of my life when You seem far away, there have been times when I've also felt the rejection of people around me. Help me to remember in those times that I am Your inheritance and that You will keep me secure and safe in Your love.

SOONER OR LATER, YOU AND I WILL ALSO CONFRONT
THIS TWOFOLD TEST.

DAY 99

The watchmen found me
as they made their rounds in the city.
They beat me, they bruised me;
they took away my cloak,
those watchmen of the walls!
—*Song of Solomon 5:7*

The second test occurs when the watchmen or the leadership in the church strike and wound her and then take her covering away. Have fellow Christians—people to whom you have committed yourself—ever misunderstood you and risen up against you? Do you know what it is to stand bleeding and naked, feeling as if God Himself has left you? It appeared as if the maiden lost her entire inheritance in Him. She was stripped of the sense of His presence and of His favor in the church.

PRAYER STARTER

When misunderstandings and rejection from others enter my life, Jesus, teach me to remember Your sufferings and to abandon myself to You. Teach me to wait for the harvest times when the winter will be far gone.

WHEN WE STAND FOR TRUTH, SOMETIMES EVEN THE LORD'S SERVANTS WILL STRIKE US. WE MUST ENDURE THE MISUNDERSTANDING AND REJECTION OF OTHER BELIEVERS.

DAY 100

> O daughters of Jerusalem, I charge you—
> if you find my lover,
> what will you tell him?
> Tell him I am faint with love.
> —*Song of Solomon 5:8*

Like Job, this maiden did not know that the test she was experiencing would be only for a season. In the midst of pain, she was maturing in the Spirit. It is as if we can hear her proclaiming, "I'm not in it for myself anymore. I'm in it for You, my beloved King. You are my passion and portion." Next, we find her saying to the daughters of Jerusalem, the spiritually immature believers: "If you find my Beloved, tell Him I'm not angry. I'm not offended because He withdrew and let this happen to me. I love Him. I'm lovesick, not angry." When the Lord sees that response of love in us, even while we are walking in the midst of the fiery test, He exclaims, "Yes! That is the heart of My true bride!"

PRAYER STARTER

> *All I desire, dear Father, is to live in Your presence. No matter what comes into my life, help me to search for the way back into Your presence and to be willing to walk through the fiery test to stand before You as Your purified bride.*

IN THE MIDST OF PAIN, SHE WAS MATURING IN THE SPIRIT.

DAY 101

How is your beloved better than others,
most beautiful of women?
How is your beloved better than others,
that you charge us so?
My lover is radiant and ruddy,
outstanding among ten thousand.
—*Song of Solomon 5:9–10*

In my opinion, Song of Solomon 5:10–16 is the most outstanding statement of love in the Word of God. The maiden stands stripped and wounded before her accusers and proceeds to describe some of the precious attributes of her beloved king in symbolic language, mentioning his head, hair, eyes, cheeks, lips, hands, body, legs, countenance, and mouth. She praises the excellence of who he is, the infinite loveliness of everything he does. "He's dazzling!…This is my beloved and this is my friend," she cries. It is the knowledge of her beloved that stabilizes her. She is overflowing in worship as she declares the splendor of his personhood through these ten attributes. Her response is not one of offense with him for withdrawing his presence and allowing rejection from others. Rather, she magnifies his greatness as one who is lovesick.

PRAYER STARTER

Lord, the beauty of Your person and the glory that surrounds You are infinitely brighter than anything else. You bring the light of Your presence into my life and dispel the darkness that surrounded me.

**SHE FOCUSES ON THE REALITY OF HIS
MAJESTIC PERSONALITY.**

DAY 102

Where has your beloved gone,
O most beautiful among women?
Where has your beloved turned,
That we may seek him with you?
—*Song of Solomon 6:1*

What is the response of others when they see you standing utterly resolute in your commitment and unwavering in your affection for Jesus even in the midst of suffering, rejection, and persecution? What is their response when they see that price is no object to you and that you are totally committed to Jesus regardless of what comes your way? As the Holy Spirit reveals more and more of the personality of Jesus to our hearts, our commitment will deepen, and we will inspire even more to passionately follow Jesus. God is raising up a company of believers whose impassioned devotion to Him will inspire many.

PRAYER STARTER

I want to be a part of that great company of believers whose impassioned devotion to You will inspire many. Let my life be a witness to the lost. Let Your Spirit reside within so that anyone looking at me sees only You.

OTHERS CRY OUT, "WE WANT WHAT YOU HAVE IN HIM. WE WANT HIM, TOO!"

DAY 103

Place me like a seal over your heart,
like a seal on your arm;
for love is as strong as death,
its jealousy unyielding as the grave.
It burns like blazing fire,
like a mighty flame.
Many waters cannot quench love;
rivers cannot wash it away.
—*Song of Solomon 8:6–7*

Let me encourage you to take the Song of Solomon and turn its verses into devotional meditation. This beautiful song of divine love is breathtaking when we begin to understand the prophetic nature of its words. They are life changing when we realize our Beloved is also speaking them over us, affirming and drawing forth qualities not yet fully developed in our lives. Oh, that God would give us new eyes to see His affectionate, yearning heart for us while we're still growing, still failing, still weak in so many ways. Never allow the truths in God's beautiful love song to be forgotten and fade away in your heart.

PRAYER STARTER

Emblazon the words of Your love song upon my heart. Let the fire of Your love be the strength of my life. Wash over my life with the anointing waters of Your Spirit, that I may never forget the depths of Your love for me.

CHERISH THE MESSAGE OF GOD'S LOVE FOR YOU.

DAY 104

Woe is me, for I am ruined!
Because I am a man of unclean lips,
And I live among a people of unclean lips;
For my eyes have seen the King, the LORD of hosts.
—Isaiah 6:5

When Jesus is revealed in His glory, a new hunger for purity results. Isaiah saw the Lord lifted up and cried out for his own cleansing; then he offered himself for any service the Lord wanted, crying out, "Here am I. Send me!" (Isa. 6:8). Jesus is not coming for a church that's gritting her teeth, struggling to stay free from sin, secretly wishing she could indulge in a little immorality. No, Jesus is coming for a church utterly devoted to Him—one that is free on the inside.

PRAYER STARTER

Lord, the revelation of who You are—to me and to this world— motivates me to the highest level of obedience to Your Word. I want to be Your bride without spot or wrinkle and to stand before You in absolute purity.

THE GREATEST MOTIVATION FOR OBEDIENCE COMES AS WE ENCOUNTER MORE REVELATION OF WHO JESUS IS.

DAY 105

He told them, "The harvest is plentiful, but the workers are
few. Ask the Lord of the harvest, therefore, to send out workers into
his harvest field. Go! I am sending you out like lambs among wolves."
—*Luke 10:2–3*

So many Christians today are content to sit behind the church's
stained-glass windows in their own little comfort zones, unconcerned
with the disastrous plight of unbelievers outside the door of the church.
Too many today are focused primarily on seeking to find the good life
for themselves. They are seeking Jesus as the way to make life happier.
This is the extent of their focus. Why are we Christians lolling around
passively in our own little comfort zones, tuning out the Holy Spirit,
neglecting the place of prayer and the Word of God? Why are we
ignoring God's promptings to reach out to the lost and needy? Why do
we compromise and backslide? What are we doing? The Lord of indescribable splendor and glory is going to reveal Himself to the church.
That revelation will awaken a deep response of absolute obedience and
affection. We will never turn back to our compromise and passivity.

PRAYER STARTER

*Grip my heart with the brokenness of others who are lost in sin. Let me
see their hopelessness when they pass me on the street; let their cries for help fill
my ears and cause me to take the hope of Your great salvation to them.*

**MANY BELIEVERS ARE UNWILLING TO TAKE ANY NEW RISKS
OR TO STRETCH BEYOND THE KNOWN COMFORT OF THE
CHURCH TO TAKE THE LOVE OF GOD TO THOSE WHO
KNOW NOTHING OF IT.**

DAY 106

Do you not say, 'Four months more and then the harvest'? I tell you, open your eyes and look at the fields! They are ripe for harvest.
—*John 4:35*

I believe a great revival is coming, as well as a great harvest of souls. God's people must be ready, since we are the ones who will be caring for the multitudes that come. History reveals that we will reproduce converts after our own kind. I sometimes find myself praying, "God, don't fully release the harvest until You release something in Your church that is worthy of imparting to the multitudes of new converts. Don't allow another generation of easily offended Christians who lust for money, power, position, and pleasure to come forth. Please fill us with the knowledge of Your Son's splendor and loveliness before You bring hundreds of millions of new believers to us for training." Remember, Paul prophesied that the knowledge of Jesus would continue until we *all* attain to unity, intimacy, and maturity.

PRAYER STARTER

Lord, I'm no longer content to keep You all to myself while those around me live in sin and hopelessness. Train me in Your ways so that I can be a part of Your great army moving in unity, intimacy, and maturity to win the lost.

> WE WILL IMPART WHAT WE POSSESS INTO THOSE
> NEW BELIEVERS.

DAY 107

Although I am less than the least of all God's people,
this grace was given me: to preach to the Gentiles the unsearchable
riches of Christ, and to make plain to everyone the administration of
this mystery, which for ages past was kept hidden in God,
who created all things.
—*Ephesians 3:8–9*

God isn't interested in making men, ministries, or churches famous. He's committed to spreading the fame of His Son throughout the nations. He's looking for believers who are ablaze with passion and devotion to His Son and who will say, "I have only a moment on Earth. My citizenship is in heaven, and I want to spread Your fame. I want to capture the hearts of the people for You!" God ultimately desires to give His people greater grace and power. But I believe He will reserve the greater power—the mightier release of His Spirit—for the time when the church seeks to proclaim the riches of Christ's marvelous personality. He will anoint and empower believers who seek to capture the hearts of others for His Son—not for themselves.

PRAYER STARTER

I long to be a part of the generation that sees a mighty release of Your Spirit in our world. Anoint me and empower me to seek the lost and bring them into a transforming personal relationship with You.

THE DAY OF THE SPIRITUAL SUPERSTAR IS OVER.

DAY 108

Christ also loved the church, and gave himself for it;
that he might sanctify and cleanse it with the washing of water by the
word, that he might present it to himself a glorious church,
not having spot, or wrinkle, or any such thing; but that it
should be holy and without blemish.
—*Ephesians 5:25–27, KJV*

The Holy Spirit wants to impact people for Jesus, not for the latest exciting ministry in the nation or for the pastor with the biggest building. But strangely enough, the Holy Spirit does anoint men and women who do not glorify Jesus in their personal lives. He does it all the time. The church in the last days will have tenacious loyalty to the person of Jesus. If some of the ministries today have that loyalty, then imitate them. But if they don't, please don't be impressed just because some people fall down when the preacher prays for them. That's not enough. I believe some of that may continue happening, but something more, something far better is on the horizon. We are about to discover what it means to live and minister in an overflow of our personal experience of the satisfying knowledge of the person of Christ.

PRAYER STARTER

If all the world forsakes You, Lord, I will not. I want more than just a spiritual façade in my life; I want to be radically overflowing with the joys of Your great salvation in my life.

THERE'S SOMETHING GREATER THAN PEOPLE FALLING DOWN WHEN WE PRAY.

DAY 109

I keep asking that the God of our Lord Jesus Christ, the glorious Father, may give you the Spirit of wisdom and revelation, so that you may know him [Jesus] better.
—*Ephesians 1:17*

I have made you known to them, and will continue to make you known in order that the love you have for me may be in them and that I myself may be in them.
—*John 17:26*

Do you long to impact people for Jesus? Do you yearn to glorify Him in your personal life? Then I urge you to make our Scripture verses for today two of the paramount prayers of your life. Read those two verses over and over. Meditate on them. Write down what comes to your mind as you pray them. Begin asking God for a spirit of revelation in the knowledge of Jesus's beauty. Ask that you might love the Son as the Father loves the Son. We must persevere in these prayers until we are "strengthened with power through His Spirit in the inner man" (Eph. 3:16, NAS).

PRAYER STARTER

Father, give me the Spirit of wisdom and revelation so that I can know You better. Make Yourself known to me in new and fresh ways each day of my life. Give me a spirit revelation in the knowledge of Your splendor and beauty.

WE WILL BE RESTLESS UNTIL WE BECOME PRISONERS OF GOD. AS CAPTIVES OF HIS DIVINE PURPOSE, WE WILL LEAD OTHERS INTO PASSION FOR JESUS AND INTO CAPTIVITY TO HIM.

DAY 110

Whoever does not love does not know God, because God is love. This is how God showed his love among us: He sent his one and only Son into the world that we might live through him. This is love: not that we loved God, but that he loved us and sent his Son as an atoning sacrifice for our sins....How great is the love the Father has lavished on us, that we should be called children of God! And that is what we are!
—*1 John 4:8–10; 3:1*

Through a series of divine coincidences and interventions, some friends of mine who had remained childless through twenty-three years of marriage, and who hadn't even had their names on an adoption list because they were considered over the age limit to adopt, were blessed with a beautiful little boy just a few days old. They knew they would love their little son devotedly whether or not he ever returned their love, but they set out to win the child's love by demonstrating their love and affection for him. Then the day came when the couple's little son began to return their affection. The father's heart melted. What he felt was just a small expression of what our heavenly Father feels when His children start returning love back to Him.

PRAYER STARTER

Let me fill Your heart with joy and love as I return to You a portion of the great love You have given to me. Teach me how to praise You better, to love You more, and to express my heart to You in thankfulness for all that You have done for me.

WE WILL NEVER EXHAUST THE FULLNESS OF THE DEPTH OF LOVE GOD HAS DEMONSTRATED FOR US BY MAKING US HIS SONS AND DAUGHTERS IN HIS OWN HOUSE.

DAY 111

For you did not receive a spirit that makes you a slave again to fear, but you received the Spirit of sonship. And by him we cry, "Abba, Father." The Spirit himself testifies with our spirit that we are God's children. Now if we are children, then we are heirs—heirs of God and co-heirs with Christ, if indeed we share in his sufferings in order that we may also share in his glory.

—Romans 8:15–17

What best motivates a child to want to be like his parents? Is it affirmation and respect, or fear of rejection and guilt? The same principle is true in the spiritual realm. Using wrong motivations to encourage believers to pursue intimacy with Christ—manipulation, fear, or guilt—may seem to obtain quick results, but those results do not last. Even spiritual disciplines such as prayer, fasting, and Bible study, which are vital, can often result in legalism, pride, insecurity, or morbid introspection if pursued with the wrong motivation. Our spirits cry for more of Him when we begin to grasp the implications of being adopted as His children.

PRAYER STARTER

Father, all that You are cause me to want to be more and more like You. Show me how to become more like You each day of my life.

THE KNOWLEDGE OF GOD'S DEEP AFFECTION AND OF OUR FULL ACCEPTANCE AS HIS BELOVED CHILDREN IS THE BEST MOTIVATION FOR CONSISTENT SPIRITUAL GROWTH.

DAY 112

I pray that out of his glorious riches he may strengthen you with power through his Spirit in your inner being, so that Christ may dwell in your hearts through faith. And I pray that you, being rooted and established in love, may have power, together with all the saints, to grasp how wide and long and high and deep is the love of Christ, and to know this love that surpasses knowledge—that you may be filled to the measure of all the fullness of God.

—*Ephesians 3:16–19*

Being rooted and grounded in the strong, secure love of God motivates us to greater consistency, spiritual passion, and maturity. We long for a fuller, more intimate knowledge of God and for heart-to-heart fellowship with Him. As you and I pursue intimacy with Jesus, it will become apparent that we are God's royal children. *We will manifest our family's likeness* by conforming to Christ. *We will seek to further our family's welfare* by loving our brethren. *We will maintain our family's honor* by avoiding what our Father hates, pursuing what He loves, and seeking His glory.

PRAYER STARTER

There is nothing I want more, O God, than to be rooted and grounded in Your everlasting love. I want to manifest Your likeness. Let me live in purity and holiness as I show Your love to others.

WE DESIRE TO BECOME WISE CHILDREN WHO BRING JOY TO OUR FATHER.

DAY 113

Christ loved the church and gave himself up for her to make
her holy, cleansing her by the washing with water through the word,
and to present her to himself as a radiant church, without stain or
wrinkle or any other blemish, but holy and blameless.
—*Ephesians 5:25–27*

Just as you or I need a daily physical bath, we also need a daily spiritual bath to remove some of the "grime" and defilement. If the grime is allowed to accumulate, it will lead to spiritual dullness and insensitivity in our spirits. Inner corruption such as anger, slander, impatience, and sensuality grieves the Holy Spirit and makes our spirits insensitive and unable to respond fully to Him. The accumulation of information about the Scriptures and the mental discipline of hours of Bible study will never thoroughly cleanse the inner man in the way that devotional, worshipful meditation upon God's Word will. When our Bible study leads into personal dialogue with Jesus as we meditate upon His cleansing Word, we also experience growth in spiritual hunger, sensitivity, and nearness to Him.

PRAYER STARTER

Wash me in Your Word, dear Father. Cleanse me of my dull, insensitive spirit. Take the hidden, inner sins from my life as I meditate on Your Word and will for my life.

WHEN WE FIX OUR HEARTS ON THE PERSON OF JESUS AND
DIALOGUE WITH HIM, THE WORD OF GOD
WASHES OUR SPIRITS.

DAY 114

As the deer pants for streams of water,
so my soul pants for you, O God.
My soul thirsts for God, for the living God.
When can I go and meet with God?
—*Psalm 42:1–2*

We will never be empowered to walk in purity without the foundation of affection for Jesus. External disciplines and commitments to high standards of holiness without a living devotion for Jesus have little real power or life in them. A person named Jesus—not regulations and rules—guards our souls. As affection for Jesus is increased in our hearts, we find a new empowering to resist temptation. When passion for Jesus is built into your spiritual foundation, it repels the sensual communications that others may send your way. It returns the message, "No, I'm not available." That strong, clear message rises from within your spirit.

PRAYER STARTER

I thirst after You, dear God. Whatever it takes, whatever I must get rid of, whatever I must grow into, that is all I desire.

WE ARE FILLLED WITH SUCH LONGING FOR JESUS THAT WE HAVE GREATER RESOLVE TO REPEL SENSUALITY AND RESIST WRONG RELATIONSHIPS.

DAY 115

When I was a child, I talked like a child, I thought like a child,
I reasoned like a child. When I became a man, I put childish ways
behind me. Now we see but a poor reflection as in a mirror; then we
shall see face to face. Now I know in part; then I shall know fully,
even as I am fully known. And now these three remain: faith, hope
and love. But the greatest of these is love.
—*1 Corinthians 13:11–13*

The soul aggressively engaged in pursuing intimacy with Jesus is positioned to overcome temptation. On the other hand, the passive soul that wanders from fantasy to fantasy while living in a spiritual vacuum that lacks affection for God is much more vulnerable to fall to temptations that happen to come along. In our pursuit of intimacy with Jesus, we realize that feelings will come and go, sometimes swinging from the highs of holy passion to the lows of spiritual barrenness. We will have seasons of fervent longing and love for Jesus, times when we pray with great feeling and inspiration. But we will also experience seasons when we pray without any feeling of God's presence. Yet, as we persist, we will begin to realize that even in the dry, barren seasons our hearts are still growing in mature love toward Jesus.

PRAYER STARTER

*Your love protects my heart from yielding to temptation, dear God.
Even in the dry, barren seasons of my life, my heart wants only to mature in
You and to be all that You want me to be.*

**OUR FOCUS IS ON JESUS, NOT UPON FEELINGS THAT
COME AND GO.**

DAY 116

Put me like a seal over your heart,
Like a seal on your arm.
For love is as strong as death,
Jealousy is as severe as Sheol;
Its flashes are flashes of fire,
The very flame of the Lord.
—*Song of Solomon 8:6, NAS*

God's holy flame is relentless and consuming. It will eventually ignite one focused on Jesus with emotions of love for Him. However, if we are too busy to ask Him for this and to wait before Him for it, then this flame will be diminished. Even though our careless living causes this flame of the Spirit to die down, this does not mean God's love has decreased toward us. The flame we are referring to here does not represent God's love and affection for us; rather, it represents the passion and zeal that He imparts in us for His Son. We can lose our passion for Jesus without losing God's love for us.

PRAYER STARTER

Yes, Father, the fire of Your love has caused a flame to arise within me that seeks to love You more and to know You more.

WE MUST REFUSE TO BELIEVE THE SUBTLE LIE OF THE
ENEMY THAT SAYS GOD'S LOVE FOR US GOES UP AND DOWN
WITH OUR OWN VACILLATING SPIRITUAL FEELINGS
AND ATTAINMENTS.

DAY 117

Let them give thanks to the LORD for his unfailing love
and his wonderful deeds for men,
for he satisfies the thirsty
and fills the hungry with good things.
—*Psalm 107:8–9*

Intimacy with Jesus is the context in which the deep longing in our hearts for more of Him is progressively satisfied. People who are born again do not automatically have a sense of the nearness of God. Effective ministry produces a satisfaction that comes through helping others and being useful in God's kingdom, but it is not the same as the satisfaction that comes from encountering God in our inner man. The Holy Spirit may give spiritual gifts to believers and release His power through us, but these things do not ultimately satisfy the desire in our hearts for more of God. When our spiritual hunger is not being satisfied, we will experience frustrating spiritual boredom and restlessness.

PRAYER STARTER

You alone can satisfy the longing of my heart, Jesus. All I want is more of You. Let me live my life in intimacy with You.

> NOTHING BUT AN INTIMATE RELATIONSHIP WITH JESUS
> WILL SATISFY THIS INNER CRY BIRTHED
> BY THE HOLY SPIRIT.

DAY 118

I have set the LORD always before me.
Because he is at my right hand,
I will not be shaken.
Therefore my heart is glad and my tongue rejoices;
my body also will rest secure.
—*Psalm 16:8–9*

Intimacy with Jesus brings a deepened security and rest in our inner man. As we interact in a deeply personal way with Him, we grow in our knowledge that we are accepted and cherished by God. This knowledge progressively frees us from feelings of insecurity and the intimidating, paralyzing fear of others' opinions or actions against us. A focus on Jesus ultimately leads us to an increased knowledge of His heart of affirmation for us. This is absolutely vital. As important as human affirmation is, it is woefully inadequate without God's affirmation of us. When we are secure and confident in God's love, we grow out of our fears related to how people receive and treat us. When we know we are pleasing Him, the criticism that comes from others does not affect us nearly as much as it did in the past. "Proving" our value to others ceases to be the dominant drive in our emotional makeup. God's pleasure and His approving smile become the most powerful emotion that we have.

PRAYER STARTER

Father, as I learn to rest more and more in Your love, I am able to grow out of my fears and intimidation from others. Your approving smile is all I need.

IT IS THE KNOWLEDGE THAT WE ARE LOVED, ACCEPTED, AND VALUED BY GOD THAT GIVES US A GREATER SENSE OF VALUE AND TRUE SELF-WORTH.

DAY 119

Bless the LORD, O my soul, and forget not all his benefits:
Who forgiveth all thine iniquities; who healeth all thy diseases;
who redeemeth thy life from destruction; who crowneth thee with
lovingkindness and tender mercies; who satisfieth thy mouth with
good things; so that thy youth is renewed like the eagle's.
—*Psalm 103:2–5, KJV*

If we are to experience true, lasting wholeness and healing in the places of our wounding, we must encounter the Healer Himself and be encouraged to build a relationship of intimacy with Him. How are the inner wounds of the heart healed? We must give everything back to God, including all bitterness, self-pity, and desire for revenge. Our grief, anger, shame, and pride—even our hopes, ambitions, and dreams—must be laid on God's altar, along with our personal rights and the desire to run our own lives. Jesus must become the focus of our hearts—not our tragedies, our past, or all that might have been. Only Jesus can transform self-pity into victory or tears into triumph.

PRAYER STARTER

Father, show me the inner healing that I still need. Reveal to me my wounds so that I may lay them on the altar and allow Jesus to transform my self-pity into victory and triumph.

A FOCUS ON INTIMACY WITH JESUS IS ESSENTIAL IN HEALING THE INNER WOUNDS OF THE HEART.

DAY 120

In the beginning was the Word, and the Word was with God, and the Word was God. He was with God in the beginning. Through him all things were made; without him nothing was made that has been made. In him was life, and that life was the light of men. The light shines in the darkness, but the darkness has not understood it.

—John 1:1–5

We best combat spiritual darkness in our lives by receiving more spiritual light! Darkness is driven out of our hearts by the entrance of the light of the revelation of Jesus. Attempting to drive the darkness out of our hearts by ourselves is frustrating and futile, but when the person of Jesus is unveiled to our hearts, that is when His light enters our hearts and the darkness flees. The same is true of natural light in a room. It would be absurd to try to take buckets full of darkness out of a dark room. Rather, we simply turn the light switch on, and darkness is automatically overpowered. This principle applies to our spiritual lives as well. We will wear ourselves out by trying to remove darkness only by focusing on resisting it. Instead, we directly attack the darkness in our lives by focusing on receiving more light.

PRAYER STARTER

God, the darkness in my heart is totally gone when the reflection of Your love abides there. There is no dark recesses in my heart that are not overpowered by the light of Your love.

NO DARKNESS IN THE LIFE OF A SINCERE BELIEVER HAS THE POWER TO OVERPOWER THE EXPERIENCE OF GOD'S LIGHT OR REVELATION.

DAY 121

The weapons we fight with are not the weapons of the world.
On the contrary, they have divine power to demolish strongholds.
We demolish arguments and every pretension that sets itself up
against the knowledge of God, and we take captive every thought
to make it obedient to Christ.
—*2 Corinthians 10:4–5*

Satan is not intimidated by the boasts of believers who do not have an intimate relationship with Jesus. He knows that as long as darkness reigns unchallenged and unconquered in many areas of their own lives, those believers pose no real threat to his kingdom. Jesus is the One whom Satan fears. If believers are not filled with the reality and knowledge of Jesus, Satan knows it is only a matter of time until they will become victims of his attacks, not victors over darkness. Satan is troubled by believers who are undistracted from the purity and simplicity of devotion to Jesus. He flees before the sword of the Spirit when it is wielded by men and women who have a secret history in God of intimacy, faithfulness, and obedience.

PRAYER STARTER

Father, with Your strength and power, I will never be intimidated by the enemy again. I am a victor through Your love, not a victim of Satan's deceiving tactics.

THE WEAKEST, MOST IMMATURE BELIEVER WHO HAS A HEART FOCUS OF HOLY PASSION WILL BECOME A THREAT TO SATAN'S KINGDOM.

DAY 122

After this I looked, and there before me was a door standing open in heaven. And the voice I had first heard speaking to me like a trumpet said, "Come up here, and I will show you what must take place after this." At once I was in the Spirit, and there before me was a throne in heaven with someone sitting on it. And the one who sat there had the appearance of jasper and carnelian. A rainbow, resembling an emerald, encircled the throne. Surrounding the throne were twenty-four other thrones, and seated on them were twenty-four elders. They were dressed in white and had crowns of gold on their heads. From the throne came flashes of lightning, rumblings and peals of thunder. Before the throne, seven lamps were blazing. These are the seven spirits of God. Also before the throne there was what looked like a sea of glass, clear as crystal.

—*Revelation 4:1–6*

During my early years of seeking to establish a consistent prayer life, I felt as though I were praying into the air—to some nebulous being far beyond my grasp. I had a feeling of disconnectedness, with no real sense of praying to a real person. But over time, my prayer life has been greatly enriched through a simple devotional focus that I began some years ago. I call it "gazing on God's throne." John describes the scene in heaven into which our prayers ascend. This description of God's throne, the Lord Jesus, the four living creatures, and the twenty-four elders significantly changed my prayer life.

PRAYER STARTER

Father, may the vision of Your throne remind me daily that my prayers ascend unto that very place and are heard—and answered—each time I pray.

JOHN PAINTS A WORD PICTURE OF THE SETTING TO WHICH OUR REQUESTS AND PETITIONS COME.

DAY 123

In the center, around the throne, were four living
creatures...Day and night they never stop saying: "Holy, holy, holy is
the Lord God Almighty, who was, and is, and is to come." Whenever
the living creatures give glory, honor and thanks to him who sits on
the throne and who lives for ever and ever, the twenty-four elders fall
down before him who sits on the throne, and worship him who lives
for ever and ever. They lay their crowns before the throne.
—*Revelation 4:6–10*

This throne, filled with the grace of God, is the most awesome place
in all existence. It is the foundation of the entire created order. It is
the center of everything. It is the purpose for everything, for He who
created all things sits upon the throne, and all things exist for His
pleasure. When we stand before Him at the judgment seat, what He is
thinking about us will be the only thing that counts. When we lose the
awareness of God our Father on this throne with Jesus seated at His
right hand, then our problems become insurmountable in our thinking.
The despair can be unbelievable. We forget that everything else passes
away, and nothing has any significance and relevance outside the reality
of the person upon this throne.

PRAYER STARTER

*Jesus, it is incredible to me that from Your throne beside the Father in
heaven You watch over my life. Thank You for Your intercession on my behalf.
Let me please You with my life.*

**ALL ELSE IS TEMPORAL, EXCEPT THE THINGS THAT ARE
PLEASING TO HIM.**

DAY 124

And God raised us up with Christ and seated us with him in
the heavenly realms in Christ Jesus, in order that in the coming ages
he might show the incomparable riches of his grace, expressed in his
kindness to us in Christ Jesus.
—*Ephesians 2:6–7*

Do you ever imagine standing in heaven's throne room as you worship
and intercede? Picture a mighty throne, immersed in flames, standing
in heaven. Imagine an indescribably glorious person with hair and garments as white as snow, seated upon that throne. Picture twenty-four
lesser thrones surrounding the great thrones on the right and the left
and twenty-four elders clothed in white and wearing golden crowns sitting upon those thrones. Listen to the mighty roar of praise ascending
from the myriads and myriads of angels on every side of the throne.
Jesus is there at the right hand of His Father. His loveliness and His
splendor are beyond description. He is welcoming you to the throne of
grace, smiling and bidding you to come. As we come there, day after
day, year after year, our spiritual lives will surely be enriched. Our
spirits will be invigorated, and our minds will be renewed.

PRAYER STARTER

*Lord, the thought of standing with You before the Father's throne is
more than I can comprehend. Yet You welcome me to the throne of grace and
renew my being as I stand in that holy place.*

**OVER THE COURSE OF TIME WE ARE CHANGED—
TRANSFORMED—FROM GLORY TO GLORY.**

DAY 125

And we, who with unveiled faces all reflect the Lord's glory, are being transformed into his likeness with ever-increasing glory, which comes from the Lord, who is the Spirit.
—*2 Corinthians 3:18*

In Old Testament times, veiling the face was a way of signifying the great gulf between a person and God and the need for a mediator. God through Christ has invited us to come fearlessly to His throne of grace (Heb. 4:16). We come without a sense of condemnation or accusation because Christ took our penalty and gave us the gift of righteousness. We can open our hearts to the Lord and speak plainly of our failures, hurts, disappointments, fears, and frustrations.

PRAYER STARTER

Jesus, it is because of Your gift of righteousness that I can come boldly before the throne of grace. I pray that You continue to transform me into Your likeness and image.

WE BEHOLD THE GLORY OF JESUS WITH UNVEILED FACES.

DAY 126

> But we all, with open face beholding as in a glass the glory of the Lord, are changed into the same image from glory to glory, even as by the Spirit of the Lord.
> —*2 Corinthians 3:18, KJV*

There's a false notion among many Christians that the Word of God works only if you have ten hours a day to be shut up in a room all alone reading it. But the Word of God was written primarily to the 99 percent of the human race who will never be in "full-time," salaried positions of ministry. God's promises aren't just for paid preachers. They are also for the everyday person on the street, the stressed-out mother dealing with a toddler stuck in the "terrible twos," the truck driver, the clerk at Wal-Mart, the secretary, the businessman, the schoolteacher, and the courtroom lawyer. God's Word is for the believer who fell into sin and lost everything except a heart that still cries out for God. Every Christian—any Christian—can be progressively transformed from glory to glory.

PRAYER STARTER

Lord, I'm that everyday person for whom Your great promises were given. Teach me from Your Word the way to be transformed from glory to glory.

> **BEING TRANSFORMED FROM GLORY TO GLORY IS AN OPERATION OF THE HOLY SPIRIT ON THE INSIDE—IN OUR MINDS, WILLS, AND EMOTIONS.**

DAY 127

I thank my God every time I remember you. In all my prayers
for all of you, I always pray with joy because of your partnership in
the gospel from the first day until now, being confident of this, that
he who began a good work in you will carry it on to completion
until the day of Christ Jesus.
—*Philippians 1:3–6*

The glory of God is not limited to a burning-bush encounter with God.
It's not, as some people mistakenly think, either the full glory or no
glory at all. Being transformed from glory to glory is a promise made
to every believer. We can experience an ever-increasing measure of that
glory in the small, subtle dimensions that often go unnoticed. Never
underestimate the grace of God or despise the day of small beginnings.
We should not say, "I'll never be different. I will always be in bondage
to lust, anger, and covetousness. I'll never be free." The glory of God is
already at work in your life. Thank Him for the sincere desire you have
to break free from sinful habits and walk in the Spirit. Those small
beginnings are firm steps in the direction of full maturity.

PRAYER STARTER

*Holy Spirit, help me to see each tiny step I take as I grow more and
more like Christ. Teach me to recognize that each small step moves me closer
and closer to Your image that I may be spiritually mature.*

HAVE CONFIDENCE THAT EVEN NOW "HE WHO BEGAN A
GOOD WORK IN YOU WILL PERFECT IT."

DAY 128

*But by the grace of God I am what I am, and His grace toward
me did not prove vain; but I labored even more than all of them, yet
not I, but the grace of God with me.*
—1 Corinthians 15:10, NAS

Change is a difficult process. Here's the good news. Sanctification
and transformation come from beholding—not from *striving!* Part
of the Christian world has dived headlong into a never-ending cycle
of recovery, self-help, and how-to-do-it sermons, books, and tapes.
Transformation comes from beholding the glory and splendor of Jesus,
who is a real person. Unless God changes our hearts with His presence,
we will never change. We may drag ourselves into the prayer room on
a regular basis, but only God can change the heart. It happens by His
grace working in us.

PRAYER STARTER

*Whatever it takes, dear Lord, allow me to behold the wonders of Your
being so that I may be changed into Your image. Change me, Lord; empower
me by Your grace to be all that You created me to be.*

**TRANSFORMATION DOES NOT COME FROM STRIVING OR
FROM PSYCHOLOGICAL TECHNIQUES ALONE.**

DAY 129

He who has an ear, let him hear what the Spirit says to the churches. To him who overcomes, I will give some of the hidden manna. I will also give him a white stone with a new name written on it, known only to him who receives it.
—*Revelation 2:17*

Jesus Christ loves the world and He loves the church, but there's a special bread He feeds those who love Him in private. There's a divine manna He reserves for those who extravagantly waste themselves in His presence. How do you waste your life on Jesus? Easy. It's no secret. Make the decision in your mind, and your heart will catch up. Get in His presence. Reject sin. Cry out to Him in prayer. Lift your soul to Him in worship. Read and meditate on the Word until your heart is filled with the things that fill God's heart. Utterly abandon yourself to Him, for intimacy with God takes time, and there is no substitute for waiting in His presence. Allow yourself to be broken and spilled out for the priceless One whose body was broken and whose precious life's blood was spilled out for you.

PRAYER STARTER

Lord, I hunger for the divine manna You have reserved for those who desire to live in Your presence. Show me how to "waste my life for You." Let me abandon myself to You as you abandoned Your life for my salvation.

WE CAN WASTE OUR LIVES ON SERVING THE DEVIL AND END UP IN A FLAMING TRASH HEAP CALLED HELL, OR WE CAN WASTE OUR LIVES AND OUR RESOURCES ON JESUS.

DAY 130

For if, by the trespass of the one man, death reigned through
that one man, how much more will those who receive God's abundant
provision of grace and of the gift of righteousness reign in life
through the one man, Jesus Christ.
—*Romans 5:17*

Do you seek spiritual renewal? Do you desire divine satisfaction beyond
your greatest imaginations? Then focus on two things: First, focus on
the intimate knowledge of God's beauty, or what God looks like (in
terms of knowing His personality). Second, focus on the knowledge of what it means to be created in His image—in other words,
what we look like to God in Christ. These two arenas of truth will
invigorate your heart like nothing else. The truth of our beauty being
imparted to us by the beautiful God is a subject that will fascinate and
exhilarate our hearts throughout all eternity. Imagine, the beauty Jesus
possesses is the very beauty that He imparts to His bride in the gift
of righteousness.

PRAYER STARTER

*I desire to be renewed in You, dear Father. I long to be re-created in
Your image. Prepare me to be Your bride, adorned by Your righteousness.*

**A DEEPLY SATISFIED SOUL, A PERSONAL SENSE OF MEANING
AND SIGNIFICANCE, AND A RICH TREASURE STORE OF DIVINE
PLEASURE CAN ONLY COME THROUGH THE INTIMATE
KNOWLEDGE OF GOD HIMSELF.**

DAY 131

*...and have put on the new self, which is being renewed in
knowledge in the image of its Creator.*
—*Colossians 3:10*

We can draw a very important principle about personal renewal from
this verse. It is key to your own personal renewal and to ushering others
into wholehearted commitment to the Lord as well. A genuine understanding of the knowledge of the personality of God is probably the
area in which the church is most lacking. Something awakens inside of
us when we know what God is like. He designed us so that our spirits
will dull when we have a void of the knowledge of God's beauty. Our
spirits will become progressively more dull and callous if we are not
coming into regular, fresh contact with the Word of God where the
Holy Spirit reveals to us what God is like.

PRAYER STARTER

*Birth in me a genuine understanding of Your personality, God. I want
to know You, what You are like, what You desire, and what Your vision is
for my life and for this world.*

THE KNOWLEDGE OF THE PERSONALITY OF GOD—THE
KNOWLEDGE OF WHAT GOD IS LIKE—WILL WIN YOUR
FRIENDS AND LOVED ONES TO THE LORD.

DAY 132

Jesus answered, Verily, verily, I say unto thee, Except a man be born of water and of the Spirit, he cannot enter into the kingdom of God. That which is born of the flesh is flesh; and that which is born of the Spirit is spirit. Marvel not that I said unto thee, Ye must be born again. The wind bloweth where it listeth, and thou hearest the sound thereof, but canst not tell whence it cometh, and whither it goeth: so is every one that is born of the Spirit.

—John 3:5–8, KJV

Men and women in the kingdom of God who do not have a healthy revelation of the weakness of their own flesh are dangerous if God anoints them for leadership and ministry. They can wreak havoc in the kingdom of God through spiritual pride. Self-righteousness, spiritual abuse, and misuse of spiritual authority can all stem from this problem. A lot of crazy things happen outside the context of this twofold revelation. We are reckless with pride if we do not know that we have weak flesh. But when we see our weakness, we begin to despair if we do not know that we have a willing spirit. God wants neither reckless pride nor despairing condemnation. Rather, He wants us secure in love, secure that He enjoys us in love, and secure that our love, though weak, is still seen as genuine by God.

PRAYER STARTER

Lord, I also want to see myself as You see me. Show me the weakness of my flesh, and then reveal Your transforming love to me. Cause me to be secure in Your love.

THERE IS NOTHING MORE ABUSIVE THAN A LEADER ANOINTED IN MINISTRY WHO DOES NOT HAVE A HUMBLE REVELATION OF THE WEAKNESS OF HIS FLESH.

DAY 133

When they had finished eating, Jesus said to Simon Peter, "Simon son of John, do you truly love me more than these?" "Yes, Lord," he said, "you know that I love you." Jesus said, "Feed my lambs." Again Jesus said, "Simon son of John, do you truly love me?" He answered, "Yes, Lord, you know that I love you." Jesus said, "Take care of my sheep." The third time he said to him, "Simon son of John, do you love me?" Peter was hurt because Jesus asked him the third time, "Do you love me?" He said, "Lord, you know all things; you know that I love you." Jesus said, "Feed my sheep."
—*John 21:15–18*

So often when we fall and come up short, we want to shut out the grace of God. Our hearts are locked tightly with shame. We would never dare imagine that the God who knows all things actually knows that we are genuine lovers of Jesus. Instead, we become so focused on our stumbling that we are washed away by despair, losing sight of the fact that we are lovers of God and are loved by God. But when we do, we are placing our confidence in something other than the burning love of Jesus and the finished work of the Cross. If we fix our eyes and hearts on the finished work that was accomplished in His death, the Lord will then come to us and cause us to confess the truth of who we are before Him.

PRAYER STARTER

Jesus, I want to be a genuine lover of You. Help me to fix my eyes and heart on Your finished work at Calvary. Let me come into a realization of Your great sacrificial love for me.

THE LORD CAME BACK IN RESURRECTED POWER, LOOKED INTO PETER'S FACE, AND GAVE HIM BOLD NEW DEFINITION: "YOU ARE LOVED, AND YOU ARE A LOVER."

DAY 134

Your love, O LORD, reaches to the heavens,
your faithfulness to the skies.
Your righteousness is like the mighty mountains,
your justice like the great deep.
—*Psalm 36:5–6*

Sometimes my ministry has good cycles in which it goes well, and sometimes it has bad cycles when I cannot sense the anointing of God's presence and the people seem bored. Sometimes my circumstances have cycles of blessing, and sometimes I have life cycles where I can hardly see any blessing at all. Sometimes my health is very good, and sometimes it has been assaulted. Sometimes my most important relationships are healthy; sometimes they are being undermined. But none of these circumstances ever change the fact, the bedrock of truth, that I am loved and that I am a lover. When pressures come in all areas of life, the confession that brings me comfort, the confession that brings me out of despair, is this: I am loved. I am a lover. Therefore, I am successful.

PRAYER STARTER

Father, nothing compares in life to the fact that You utterly and unconditionally love me! As long as I remember Your love, I know that I will be successful before You.

**IN THE MOST ABSOLUTE SENSE, I AM SUCCESSFUL
BEFORE GOD.**

DAY 135

Why are you downcast, O my soul?
Why so disturbed within me?
Put your hope in God,
for I will yet praise him,
my Savior and my God.
—*Psalm 43:5*

You do not have to listen to the voice of the accuser that may come through your spouse, your children, your parents, or your best friends. In fact, they may call you everything else. They may even define you by your weaknesses, flaws, and failures, but remember, you are not defined by the areas with which you struggle. You are defined as one who loves God and one whom God loves. That is the essential definition of your life. This powerful definition will bring forth lifelong repentance that grows stronger and mightier in the inner man. You could lose your health and ministry, have relationships broken, and be overwhelmed and assaulted by spiritual attack, but if you truly know you are loved, and if you seek to be a lover, you will be successful in the sight of God.

PRAYER STARTER

Father, I know that the people around me often define me by my weaknesses, but You define me by Your strength and love for me.

THE KNOWLEDGE OF WHO HE IS AND THE KNOWLEDGE OF WHO WE ARE IN HIM BRING LASTING RENEWAL TO OUR OWN SPIRITS, AFFECTING EVERY PERSON WE ENCOUNTER.

DAY 136

Though he slay me, yet will I hope in him;
I will surely defend my ways to his face.
Indeed, this will turn out for my deliverance,
for no godless man would dare come before him!
—Job 13:15–16

I speak this confession to God when I face pain and pressure: "I am loved, and I love You; therefore, I am successful. I love You even when my love is only in seed form and is still immature. Even though my love is weak, the position of my soul is to be a lover." The pain of pressure drives our souls into the secret place. When circumstances are difficult, many individuals hold to their confession that the circumstances will improve in a certain way. But a higher confession is this: I am loved, and I am a lover; therefore, I am successful. Pain will drive you to the only place of comfort—to that confession—the confession that delivers our hearts from despair.

PRAYER STARTER

Father, with Mike Bickle, help me to confess daily: "I am loved, and I love You. Even though my love is weak, it is my position and desire to be a lover of You. Therefore my life is a success."

ONE REASON WHY GOD ALLOWS PRESSURE IS BECAUSE IT
REFOCUSES OUR SOULS ON REALITY.

DAY 137

Keep me as the apple of your eye;
hide me in the shadow of your wings
from the wicked who assail me,
from my mortal enemies who surround me.
—*Psalm 17:8–9*

When the pressure comes into my life, I hide in that secret place—in that posture of refocusing my soul. There I find the Spirit of life, and I am quickened inside. It is like a muscle that is worked over and over. My heart keeps enlarging in the absolute truth that I am loved, I am a lover, and therefore, I am successful. Because the Son of God, the eternal, heavenly Bridegroom, has chosen us as the delight of His heart, it is inconceivable that we would ever be insignificant. He has chosen us to rule and reign in that vast, eternal, expanding empire that is called the kingdom of God. We are what His heart pulsates for. We are what He longs for. We are what He waits for as His inheritance. Knowing this, it is inconceivable that we would languish in the despair of insignificance. If only we could see who we are because of Him!

PRAYER STARTER

Hide me in the secret place, dear God, and quicken me there with Your Spirit. Because of You, I can find true significance in this fact—I am loved by God.

I CAN NEVER BE INSIGNIFICANT AGAIN—AND NEITHER CAN YOU!

DAY 138

After he had said this, Jesus was troubled in spirit and testified, "I tell you the truth, one of you is going to betray me." His disciples stared at one another, at a loss to know which of them he meant. One of them, the disciple whom Jesus loved, was reclining next to him. Simon Peter motioned to this disciple and said, "Ask him which one he means." Leaning back against Jesus, he asked him, "Lord, who is it?"
—*John 13:21–25*

King David is just one example of a man who was impacted by a life of deep intimacy with God. However, the one who had the greatest revelation of the Bridegroom and the bride was the apostle John. Consider John's life. He rebuked people who cast out demons because they were not in his group. He asked Jesus to let him sit at His right hand forever. Imagine, he wanted to be the main guy over everyone forever at the right hand of Jesus in eternity. At times, this apostle rebuked people, but he was also the man who put his head on the Lord's breast. To be a man who lays His head on the Lord's breast and receives His embrace will set your heart ablaze.

PRAYER STARTER

Lord, teach me to love You as David loved You. Help me to seek Your embrace as John did. Give me a revelation of Your glory, and set my heart ablaze in Your love.

THE LORD JESUS ENTRUSTED THE REVELATION OF THE BRIDE TO THE APOSTLE JOHN.

DAY 139

Yet the LORD longs to be gracious to you; he rises to show you compassion. For the LORD is a God of justice. Blessed are all who wait for him!
—*Isaiah 30:18*

Most of us can believe that when we get to heaven, God will enjoy us there. Others picture a God who will enjoy them after they've experienced a significant spiritual transformation. But I have something stunning, radical, and necessary to tell you: God enjoys you even now in your weakness. Whether you're up in victory or down in defeat—He still enjoys you, because His enjoyment of you is not based on your achievements but rather upon His own heart and your sincere response to Him. As a matter of fact, feeling enjoyed by God on a regular basis will directly result in greater spiritual growth and maturity. This is not something for you to strive to achieve, but it is an awesome key that can unlock an amazing source of power in your life.

PRAYER STARTER

Even when I am defeated and discouraged, Lord, You love me. Your enjoyment of me is not based on what I do—it is based on how You love me.

WHETHER YOU ARE STRUGGLING WITH DIFFICULTIES OR RIDING HIGH, YOU ARE ENJOYED BY GOD ALMIGHTY.

DAY 140

The LORD appeared to us in the past, saying:
"I have loved you with an everlasting love;
I have drawn you with loving-kindness."
—*Jeremiah 31:3*

Many believers have a distorted view of God. If you press the average believer, he will say, "I know that God has total authority, and I know He means well, but I do not know how He feels. He seems a little distant in His emotions." God is often viewed as a strict coach who is trying to discipline us by calling us to hard things and by letting difficult things happen to us. Others view Him as an exacting judge, always trying to catch us in our sin and never getting emotional until we fail—and then He gets angry. Many look at God as a type of army sergeant who will sacrifice us for the sake of the cause. They see Him saying, "Oh, well, it's OK if I lose a few along the way, so long as the cause goes forward." Beloved, this distortion is very different from the God of the Bible.

PRAYER STARTER

Father, like so many others, I often have had a distorted picture of who You are. Remove my distorted thinking, dear God, and allow me to see You as You are revealed in Your Word.

WE THINK HE CALLS US TO BE DISCIPLES JUST SO HIS CAUSE
WILL BE PROMOTED, NEVER REALIZING THAT HIS HEART
BURNS WITH DESIRE FOR US.

DAY 141

If a man would give for love all the wealth of his house, it
would be utterly despised.
—*Song of Solomon 8:7, NKJV*

Picture a young couple with five million dollars in the bank who own
a five-million-dollar house. One day this couple learns that their five-
year-old daughter has a terminal illness. The doctor informs them that
it will cost everything they have to successfully treat their child—their
entire bank account, their home, their stocks—everything. So they
liquidate their home and belongings and use all ten million dollars,
and their daughter is saved. The apostle Paul said that he considered
his sacrifice for Christ as rubbish compared to the excellency of experiencing the beauty of Jesus. (See Philippians 3:8.) Why? Because it was
the sacrifice of love. When men and women are so preoccupied with
the love and beauty of Jesus, the power to respond in wholehearted
love toward God is the only reward they want. Martyrs will gladly give
their lives and see their act of supreme devotion as God's gift of grace
to them, which enables them to operate in supernatural love under
pressure. The power to love is our great reward.

PRAYER STARTER

*Holy Spirit, teach me to be so preoccupied with the love and beauty of
Jesus that I have the power to respond to His love with wholehearted devotion to Him.*

THE REWARD OF A TRUE LOVER IS THE POWER TO LOVE.

DAY 142

Let us rejoice and be glad and give him glory! For the wedding
of the Lamb has come, and his bride has made herself ready.
Fine linen, bright and clean, was given her to wear.
—*Revelation 19:7–8*

When God called me to begin seeing myself through the revelation
of the bride of Christ, I protested. How could the son of a tough
boxer focus on proclaiming to the body of Christ about being a bride?
Confused, I said, "Lord, that does not make sense!" Now I understand
that I will never enter into a more radical posture as a warrior than as
a bridal warrior, a romanced warrior against the kingdom of darkness.
We will have power to sustain us in the battle. Other warriors will
burn out, they'll get injured, and the passion in their hearts will be
lost. It is so easy to get your heart wounded in the heat of battle. But
romanced warriors' hearts are more protected and empowered because
they carry their primary reward (which is the power to be exhilarated
in love and fascinated with beauty) within their hearts. Though they
may even die as martyrs, their hearts die aflame with the passion of
Christ's love.

PRAYER STARTER

*I want to be Your bridal warrior, dear Savior, and to fight the good
fight of faith in Your power and strength. Let my heart be strong in the fire
of Your love.*

> **IN THE POSTURE OF A BRIDAL WARRIOR, WE WILL BE
> SECURE, AND OUR HEARTS WILL BE PROTECTED.**

DAY 143

For I am jealous for you with godly jealousy. For I have
betrothed you to one husband, that I may present you as
a chaste virgin to Christ.
—*2 Corinthians 11:2, NKJV*

The revelation of the Bridegroom was preached by the apostle Paul.
Paul saw his ministry as betrothing unbelievers through conversion to a
Bridegroom God and presenting them as a pure bride. In this ministry
identity, namely, as friends of the Bridegroom, we operate very differently than those without this revelation. We get our identity through
the power of relationship with God Himself. When I consider God the
Bridegroom, I first think about His desire for us. Oh, to be exhilarated
with God's love! Nothing is more invigorating than the revelation
of the God filled with pleasure, the God who has intense desire for
human beings, and the God who woos us through spiritual pleasures.

PRAYER STARTER

*God, give me a new revelation of Yourself as the Bridegroom awaiting
me, His bride. Draw my heart to You, and allow me to help prepare the way
for others to become Your bride as they accept the sacrifice of Your Son.*

FRIENDS OF THE BRIDEGROOM ARE FEARLESS BECAUSE
WE ARE CONNECTED TO SOMETHING FAR BIGGER
THAN OURSELVES.

DAY 144

I delight greatly in the LORD;
my soul rejoices in my God.
For he has clothed me with garments of salvation
and arrayed me in a robe of righteousness,
as a bridegroom adorns his head like a priest,
and as a bride adorns herself with her jewels.
—*Isaiah 61:10*

A Bridegroom God is a God who has indescribable desire and delight in human beings. He is a God in whom we feel liked, enjoyed, wanted, pursued, and delighted. Both the Father and the Bridegroom desire us. The Holy Spirit, on the other hand, mediates this revelation and imparts love to our hearts so that we might respond wholeheartedly to the Father as children and to the Son of God as a bride. Whether our hearts are focused on the Father God or the Bridegroom God, we experience burning desire. Something profound happens in us when even in our weakness and brokenness we feel wanted, longed for, and rejoiced in. Our response is to abandon our hearts to God. When we see Him as our Bridegroom, our need to feel enjoyed by God is met. Our lives and personalities are completely changed by the realization that God not only likes us and enjoys us in heaven, but He also actually enjoys us and takes pleasure in us while we are here on the earth.

PRAYER STARTER

How incomprehensible it is that Your love causes me to feel liked, enjoyed, wanted, pursued, and delighted. Your love causes me to give my heart back to You, and to live my life only to bring You pleasure.

SOMETHING RESONATES IN US WHEN WE FEEL THE BURNING DESIRE OF GOD'S HEART.

DAY 145

This powerful statement from the very lips of Jesus describes what we will inherit. Here the Lord tells how He desires for us to sit on His throne with Him. Beloved, you have married into indescribable wealth and power and into the aristocracy of the eternal city. One day soon you will instantly be in the midst of it in full power. Giving our hearts to Him as voluntary lovers is the only purpose God has for us. Therefore, that should be the summation and summary of all that we are and all that we do. When we receive our crown on the last day, we will then say, "We have loved You because we so enjoyed loving You. We were not forced to love You. This is how we long to live. We did not serve out of some sort of mandatory decree of obedience. We are voluntary lovers of God. We want to be lovers because of the beauty of God."

PRAYER STARTER

Father, I give my heart unreservedly to You. I want nothing more than to love You all the days of my life and to spend eternity as Your bride.

DEVELOPING OUR RELATIONSHIP WITH THE BRIDEGROOM GOD IS THE BEST WAY WE WILL KNOW THE FULLNESS OF HIS PLAN FOR US.

DAY 146

As long as it is day, we must do the work of him who sent me.
Night is coming, when no one can work.
—*John 9:4–5*

God wants you to be a working lover. Who you are is the lover, and what you do is the work. You are not to be only a worker who struggles to love God. Instead, you are a lover of God. Being lovers is our very identity. It's who we are. We are lovers of God who happen to work, not the other way around. In a fallen world, we want to do something in order to be someone. With God, exactly the opposite is true. God wants us to be lovers so that we do work. It is extremely important that what we do flows out of who we are. It is also important that we do not live from the self-centered motivation of trying to be something and seeking to achieve more. With minds that are not renewed, we work to feel important and to appear significant in the eyes of others. God expects just the opposite of that. We are not first warriors; we are first a bride. We are first lovers, and then we do the acts of war.

PRAYER STARTER

Lord, it is an understanding of Your great love that motivates me to war against the enemy for the souls of the lost. My love compels me to bring others to You.

GOD WANTS US TO BE SOMETHING BEFORE HE WANTS US TO DO SOMETHING.

DAY 147

Therefore, my dear brothers, stand firm. Let nothing move you.
Always give yourselves fully to the work of the Lord, because you
know that your labor in the Lord is not in vain.
—*1 Corinthians 15:58*

God wants us to be relationally oriented first and achievement oriented second. Yes, we are to do the Great Commission, but who we are in Him is far more important than what we do for Him. Christ's kingdom is established in this way. He does indeed want us to sow spiritual seed and cultivate a spiritual garden. To know we are loved, to actually feel God's affection, is more vital to our growth to be a wholehearted lover of God. This is our life source. This is the essence of true success. When we are relationally oriented first, we do not work in ministry because of a need to feel successful. We already feel successful because of our relationship with Jesus. We launch out and do the work of the Great Commission from a foundation of success. This sense of success equips us to continue working even when we face adversity. But if we work because we are trying to achieve success, we will burn out quickly through added temptation and strife.

PRAYER STARTER

Father, I want to continue growing in my relationship with You. My relationship with You is the focus of my life. Knowing You love me and desire to be with me empowers me to work to fulfill Your Great Commission.

ONCE WE ARE SUCCESSFUL IN THIS SPIRITUAL SENSE,
THEN WE CAN SERVE HIM IN MINISTRY WITH DEEPER
OBEDIENCE AND PERSEVERANCE.

DAY 148

Now it happened as they went that He entered a certain village; and a certain woman named Martha welcomed Him into her house. And she had a sister called Mary, who also sat at Jesus' feet and heard His word. But Martha was distracted with much serving, and she approached Him and said, "Lord, do You not care that my sister has left me to serve alone? Therefore tell her to help me." And Jesus answered and said to her, "Martha, Martha, you are worried and troubled about many things. But one thing is needed, and Mary has chosen that good part, which will not be taken away from her."
—*Luke 10:38–42, NKJV*

Of course, it's absolutely essential for us to embrace Christ's mandate to reach out to people and to touch the nations. But this heart of service must be secondary, not primary. The reversal of these priorities was Martha's problem. When Mary and Martha were in their little conflict, Martha was not wrong because she wanted to be a servant. However, her priorities were upside down because her natural self, her natural abilities and interests, compelled her to be a worker before she was a lover. In fact, her work distracted her from being a lover (v. 40). When I **see** a worker I say to myself, "Well, he's halfway there." But I also understand that such an individual will be a much more effective worker if he or she first becomes a lover.

PRAYER STARTER

Father, so often in my spiritual service to You I respond like Martha, focusing on the work of the ministry. Help me never to forget that I am first to be a "lover," then to be a "worker."

> **MANY INDIVIDUALS ARE SO FOCUSED ON ENRICHING THEIR EARTHLY CIRCUMSTANCES AND PURSUING PERSONAL COMFORTS THAT THEY NEVER GET SERIOUS ABOUT BECOMING A WORKER, LET ALONE A LOVER.**

DAY 149

Oh, how I love your law!
I meditate on it all day long.
Your commands make me wiser than my enemies,
for they are ever with me.
I have more insight than all my teachers,
for I meditate on your statutes.
I have more understanding than the elders,
for I obey your precepts.
—*Psalm 119:97–100*

Are you a student of the Bible? It is important for us to remember that although it is good to study the Word of God, we are not called to be students first. I love to study the Scriptures, but I am not first called to be a student. I am first called to be a lover. Oh, the glory of being a lover of God! I love to love Him! Therefore, I study in a way that produces love in my heart and produces love in the hearts of the people I impact. Depending on an individual's heart, being a student can either help or hinder a person to fulfill this first priority. On this same note, we are not called primarily to be debaters or fighters for truth. Some people think that their mandate in life is to preserve the truth. They do not realize that we are first called to be lovers.

PRAYER STARTER

Loving You should be the focus of my life. Let me never forget that I have first been called to be a lover. Teach me to love first, then to serve.

GOD WANTS US TO FIGHT FOR TRUTH, BUT NEVER BEFORE WE WRESTLE WITH THE IDEA OF BEING LOVERS OF GOD.

DAY 150

Therefore, my dear brothers, stand firm. Let nothing move you.
Always give yourselves fully to the work of the Lord, because you
know that your labor in the Lord is not in vain.
—*1 Corinthians 15:58*

We are also not called to be religious. We are not called primarily to
jump through the hoops of our religious systems and political struc-
tures, or to dot the *i* and cross the *t* according to a particular doctrine
or policy. The Great Commission was spoken from the heart of our
Father God to a bride who is ordained to partner with the Son of God.
It was spoken to the church to be a lover partner, whose work would
flow out of the energy of divine romance through hearts energized
with love. The Great Commission is often seen through the paradigm
of a worker. It is seen as a mandate of great sacrifice. But by the end of
the age, evangelism will be accomplished as the overflow of a lover in
partnership with her Bridegroom God. We won't consider it sacrifice,
but a privilege. We will work in the fields of harvest with hearts that
are absolutely lovesick with desire for the Lord of the harvest.

PRAYER STARTER

*Father, whenever religious systems or policies have taken first place in
my life, remind me that I have been called to be in relationship as a lover with
the Bridegroom God.*

GOD HAS CALLED US FIRST TO BE LOVERS.

DAY 151

> I love you, O LORD, my strength.
> The LORD is my rock, my fortress and my deliverer;
> my God is my rock, in whom I take refuge.
> He is my shield and the horn of my salvation, my stronghold.
> I call to the LORD, who is worthy of praise,
> and I am saved from my enemies.
> —*Psalm 18:1–3*

Many Christians who reach out to others burn out quickly because they launch out into ministry before they establish in themselves the foundations of being lovers of God. Discouragement, despair, boredom, and frustration will inevitably occur if we do not recognize that we are first called to be lovers. The reward of our labor is that we get to enjoy being a lover as the primary preoccupation of our lives. It's a pleasure beyond compare. As a lover first, now when I experience attacks from other people, when I am undermined, when things don't work out, when disappointment comes while I am laboring for the gospel, I can always run back to the secret place. I still have a secret place of pleasure where I am immersed in the knowledge that God loves me. This is where God imparts back to me a little bit of the Father's love for His Son. This is true spiritual pleasure!

PRAYER STARTER

> *Lord, You have privileged me to share Your intimacy as Your bride. It is that love relationship that allows me to fulfill Your will for my life. I am Your loved one.*

GOD FASHIONED US TO RECEIVE LOVE AND TO BE VESSELS THROUGH WHICH HIS AFFECTION FLOWS BACK TO HIM.

DAY 152

But I will sing of your strength,
in the morning I will sing of your love;
for you are my fortress,
my refuge in times of trouble.
—Psalm 59:16

God has ordained many pleasures for believers. But no pleasure is more intense than the pleasure that comes when God communicates Himself to the human spirit. Such tender moments with God cause life and spiritual vitality to resonate deep within. As God pours His love into me, that same love flows through me back to Him. As I am loving Him back, greater revelation of His affection and beauty comes to me, and the cycle just gets richer and richer. Feeling loved—a little bit—and feeling love for God—a little bit—has a powerfully dynamic impact upon the human spirit. I don't cry out this message because I want to be a noble soldier for God. I'm committed to sharing this message, to crying out the necessity of putting the first commandment first because I've experienced a reality that the body of Christ has within its reach. But we must refocus our souls; we must put first things first to realize the awesome spiritual pleasures of walking in a love relationship with Christ.

PRAYER STARTER

Lord, I love You—help me to love You more. Let my love for You grow daily; let it be the focus of all I do and all I am.

BURNOUT OCCURS WHEN WE DO NOT EXPERIENCE THE
PLEASURE OF THE CHRISTIAN LIFE FOUND IN A LOVE
RELATIONSHIP WITH GOD.

DAY 153

For whether we be beside ourselves, it is to God: or whether we be sober, it is for your cause. For the love of Christ constraineth us; because we thus judge, that if one died for all, then were all dead: And that he died for all, that they which live should not henceforth live unto themselves, but unto him which died for them, and rose again.
—*2 Corinthians 5:13–15, KJV*

The word *constrain* means "to grip tightly." Paul was motivated by Christ's love working in him and through him. God's love became a driving force in all he did. It is the very power of living in godliness. I encourage people to focus on enjoying God more, not trying harder to overcome sin. Many people are driven by fear instead of by affection for God. In fact, I often recognize fear in many of my friends. I even see it in my own heart at times. When fear comes, we must respond by throwing ourselves into the first commandment. I become far more stable on the second commandment and the Great Commission when the first commandment is first in my life. The wonder, freedom, power, and pleasure of this is within the reach of every Christian, because it is the work of the Holy Spirit in the human spirit.

PRAYER STARTER

Holy Spirit, constrain my heart in love that I may experience the wonder, freedom, power, and pleasure You desire to put within my life.

AS WE POSITION OUR SOULS TO MAKE THE FIRST COMMANDMENT FIRST, WE WILL BE LOVERS BEFORE WE ARE WORKERS.

DAY 154

As for you, the anointing you received from him remains in you, and you do not need anyone to teach you. But as his anointing teaches you about all things and as that anointing is real, not counterfeit—just as it has taught you, remain in him.
—1 John 2:27

Secondary rewards on the earth are very important. They include an anointed ministry, a breakthrough of finances, a couple of good friends, health, and strength. All of these are very important rewards, but they are secondary. I love the secondary rewards. We need them, and they are God's will. When the first commandment is seen as a task of labor—as a sacrifice—the secondary rewards often become primary to us. In other words, our main concern becomes how much anointing is on our ministry, how much money we have, the condition of our health, and the number of deep and loyal friendships we have. These secondary rewards become our primary focus when we see ourselves as making sacrifices for God. However, such rewards become secondary when Jesus is our magnificent obsession, because our highest level of purpose is fulfilled.

PRAYER STARTER

Father, may loving You never become a task of labor or a difficult sacrifice to me. Your Son, Jesus, has become my magnificent obsession.

WE BECOME POWERFUL AND FEARLESS IN THE GRACE OF GOD WHEN THE PRIMARY PURPOSE OF LOVE FOR WHICH WE WERE CREATED BEGINS TO BE FULFILLED.

DAY 155

Give thanks to the LORD, for he is good; his love endures
forever. Let Israel say: "His love endures forever." Let the house
of Aaron say: "His love endures forever." Let those who fear the
LORD say: "His love endures forever."
—*Psalm 118:1–4*

We are loved by Him, and therefore, we are lovers of Him. That is
our primary identity. From this perspective, life looks totally different
because no matter what happens, a song fills our hearts, our spirits are
stirred, and our inner man becomes tender toward God. I have set out
to do risky ministry endeavors that the Lord called me to and have
unexpectedly hit many brick walls. During such times the Lord makes
clear to me that He does not want ministry or financial success to be
our primary reward. He wants His Son to be our magnificent obsession, not the fact that we might preach to a stadium of one hundred
thousand people and lead ten thousand to the Lord. The great news is
that when your primary reward is in place, you can be in prison and
still be successful. You can have the disappointments of a lifetime in
your ministry and have people in the local church misunderstand you
and write you off, but you will still be successful in your heart if loving
Him and being loved by Him are your primary reward.

PRAYER STARTER

*Loving You and being loved by You are all the reward I need. Keep me
from allowing achievements or successes to be more important than Your love.*

> I KNOW ABOUT MINISTRY ENDEAVORS IN WHICH I FELT
> AS IF I HAD LOST GROUND, EVEN THOUGH I KNEW I WAS
> IN THE WILL OF GOD.

DAY 156

The Spirit and the bride say, "Come!"
—*Revelation 22:17*

In this passage of Scripture the people of God see the Son of God, the Son of Man—fully God and fully man. They see Him in a way that they have never before understood Him. They see Him as a heavenly Bridegroom. And from the overflow of that revelation, they see themselves in an entirely new light as a cherished, lovesick bride. This new spiritual identity changes our emotional chemistry. It changes everything about us. When the Holy Spirit and the church are in unity in a bridal identity, together we will cry out, "Come!" As the Holy Spirit reveals to God's people the attributes and character of the Bridegroom, lovers will rise up to wholehearted devotion. This revelation of the Bridegroom God will empower, sustain, shield, and protect the bride during the difficult times that lie ahead.

PRAYER STARTER

Father, as the Bridegroom God is revealed in greater measure to my life, I long more and more for the day when He will come and claim me as His bride for all eternity.

THE HOLY SPIRIT IS AT WORK TODAY REVEALING THE BRIDEGROOM GOD TO US.

DAY 157

Place me like a seal over your heart,
like a seal on your arm;
for love is as strong as death,
its jealousy unyielding as the grave.
It burns like blazing fire,
like a mighty flame.
—*Song of Solomon 8:6*

There is nothing more compelling or attractive than desire that goes above and beyond. Hollywood has made billions of dollars from the craving of the human heart to experience deep, abiding love. The love stories through the ages are very similar. They are the stories of the man who sells all to win the love of his lady. People flock to the theater to see the same story line over and over. Why? Because something in us longs for love that knows no boundaries, love that knows no sacrifice in pursuit of the one it loves. Shakespeare's timeless classic *Romeo and Juliet* touches the deep chord within. It cries out that life itself is only worthwhile if the heart burns with love. There is no sacrifice too great when the heart is set on fire.

PRAYER STARTER

So much of the world is searching for love in all the wrong places, Father. Help me to reveal the love of Father God to others, so that sharing a revelation of Your love becomes my highest goal.

> WHEN YOU UNDERSTAND THE REVELATION OF THE FIRE OF GOD, EXPERIENCING HIS BURNING DESIRE FOR HIS SON AND FOR OTHER HUMAN BEINGS WILL RADICALLY CHANGE YOUR LIFE.

DAY 158

But as it is written, Eye hath not seen, nor ear heard, neither have entered into the heart of man, the things which God hath prepared for them that love him.
—*1 Corinthians 2:9, KJV*

Something is on the horizon for Planet Earth for which the church is completely unprepared. An unprepared church cannot possibly prepare an unprepared world. It is wise, excellent, and necessary to be totally given to God right now. That Someone who is coming is not a comet. He who is coming measures the universe with the span of His hand. Beloved, He is coming in fierceness to terrify the nations. (See Revelation 19.) No evolutionary philosophy, no technology of man, no training or education will stop His judgments. My friend, the world is completely unprepared for what lies ahead. The day of the Lord is a day of fire. (See 2 Peter 3:7.) And a Bridegroom who is a consuming fire will burn passionately with both love and judgment.

PRAYER STARTER

Father, the day of Your appearing draws ever closer, and so much of the world is totally unprepared for Your return. Let my life be consumed with a passion for making the love of God known to my world.

GOD'S MERCY TO THE GLOBE IS A PREPARED CHURCH, A PREPARED BRIDE.

DAY 159

And when Jesus was in Bethany at the house of Simon the leper,
a woman came to Him having an alabaster flask of very costly fragrant
oil, and she poured it on His head as He sat at the table. But when His
disciples saw it, they were indignant, saying, "Why this waste? For this
fragrant oil might have been sold for much and given to the poor."
—*Matthew 26:6–9, NKJV*

I really like the heart of Mary of Bethany. She was not an apostle. She
was never famous, never wrote a book, never did a conference, and never
said much. Her passionate love was in secret—she just loved the Lord
ferociously in secret. She took all she had, her earthly treasure—an alabaster box filled with spikenard, worth thirty thousand dollars—and
she lavishly, extravagantly poured it upon the One she loved. All the
apostles were mad, not just Judas. In fact, everyone was mad about
this. But Jesus ignored their reactions. He silenced their accusations by
honoring this adoring worshiper. Jesus knew that she would never write
a book or speak at a conference or do anything of worldly significance,
but despite her obscurity, no one would ever forget how she moved the
heart of Christ with her love. Something magnificent happens when
human beings recognize the gold of the pleasure of this romance and
choose it instead of the sawdust of this world.

PRAYER STARTER

*Lord Jesus, Mary had so little to give You, yet she gave all she had.
She lavished her love upon You through her sacrificial gift of perfume. Help
me to give You everything I have, everything I am, and everything I know
for Your love.*

SOMETHING SUPERB HAPPENS WHEN WE FALL IN LOVE WITH
JESUS AND PUT OUR OWN GOLD IN THE DUST.

DAY 160

If you return to the Almighty, you will be built up; you will remove iniquity far from your tents. Then you will lay your gold in the dust, and the gold of Ophir among the stones of the brooks. Yes, the Almighty will be your gold and your precious silver; for then you will have your delight in the Almighty, and lift up your face to God.

—*Job 22:23–26, NKJV*

In His mercy, God will reward forever those who consider Him gold—who are overwhelmed by the precious Savior's unfathomable value. God just looks for ways to bless us. He honors us so much more greatly than our simple responses to Him deserve. He honors us disproportionately and beyond measure just because we choose Him over the sin that will result in our judgment. It is unbelievable that He responds in this way just because we see who He is.

PRAYER STARTER

It amazes me, Father, that You look for ways to bless my life. I lay all I have on the altar before Your throne, and I grab hold of the promise of Your blessings to me.

**PERSONALLY, I AM GOING TO GRAB HOLD OF
THIS HOLY INVITATION.**

DAY 161

> ✒ But from everlasting to everlasting
> the LORD's love is with those who fear him,
> and his righteousness with their children's children—
> with those who keep his covenant
> and remember to obey his precepts.
> —*Psalm 103:17–18*

The first longing of the human heart is to have the assurance that we are enjoyed by God while still spiritually immature. To be enjoyed by God is a necessary part of living right. You cannot repent of or get free from this longing of the human spirit because God Himself placed it within you. The idea of being enjoyed by God is difficult for some to receive. Some say, "Maybe God will enjoy me in heaven, but never while I am on Earth." Others admit that God may enjoy them on Earth, but only if they are as spiritually mature as the apostle Paul. But the truth is that God will enjoy us while we mature. The knowledge of this is a vital key to turning sincere desire into spiritual maturity.

PRAYER STARTER

✒ *Is it possible, dear God, that You enjoy me just as I am? That you enjoy my feeble attempts to become more like You, and that You actually could not love me more?*

GOD ENJOYS US EVEN WHEN WE ARE IN THE MIDST OF OUR IMMATURITY AND WEAKNESS.

DAY 162

Remember, O LORD, how I have walked before you faithfully and with wholehearted devotion and have done what is good in your eyes.
—*Isaiah 38:3*

The second longing that I associate with the bridal paradigm is a desire to be wholehearted and passionate. Our hearts were created as the seat of great desire and passion; therefore, experiencing this desire is also very important for spiritual health. It is not enough to know that God wants us. We also need to know that we are giving ourselves to Him with all of our hearts. If we have nothing to die for, we'll have nothing to live for. We enjoy loving Jesus with all our hearts. Living in a state of spiritual passivity and boredom makes us vulnerable to Satan's attacks. Loving and serving with a whole heart pleases the Lord, but there is more to it than that. Many believers attempt to live in the grace of God without abandonment to God. We need to experience grace that leads us to the joy of wholehearted living and loving.

PRAYER STARTER

Move me from wholehearted service to You, dear Father, into a passionate desire to abandon myself to Your will and purposes for my life.

A WHOLEHEARTED GOD DESIGNED ME TO NEED AND TO LONG TO BE WHOLEHEARTED!

DAY 163

One thing I have desired of the LORD, that will I seek: that
I may dwell in the house of the LORD all the days of my life,
to behold the beauty of the LORD, and to inquire in His temple.
—*Psalm 27:4, NKJV*

This was the number one theme of King David's life. He had a desire
to be fascinated, to be filled with wonder, to be awestruck, and to
marvel. Our fascinating God created us with a need to be fascinated.
The Word promises that the *Branch of the Lord*, which is a term for the
Messiah in His humanity, will be seen in His beauty throughout the
entire earth. The Father will use the beauty of Jesus at the end of
the age to fascinate the end-time church with Jesus. The Holy Spirit
searches the deep things of the beauty of God, and the Father has
granted Him permission to impart aspects of this revelation to you and
me. A billion years from now in heaven we will still be discovering new
dimensions of the vast ocean of God's beauty.

PRAYER STARTER

*Like David, I long to be fascinated by Your glory. Your beauty fills
me with wonder and marvel. I will never stop being motivated by Your love
to become more and more like You.*

To LIVE BEFORE GOD WITH EVEN A BEGINNING MEASURE OF
AWE COMPLETELY CHANGES THE WAY WE LOOK AT SIN.

DAY 164

The fourth longing that I identify as expressing the bridal paradigm
is the desire to possess beauty. We as members of the bride of Christ
long to receive the impartation of the Bridegroom's beauty in our
own lives. When we feel beautiful before God because of the glory of
His presence, something powerful is released deep within our hearts.
Jesus Christ's resurrected body is the most beautiful body imaginable!
Philippians 3:21 declares that the same resurrected body will be given
to the saints. When our longing to be beautiful is fulfilled in God,
then our hearts enlarge in power. Although only a measure of spiritual
beauty is released in this age, a little goes a long way. It is powerful to
feel spiritually beautiful before God—at least a little bit. I am well
aware of my sins, struggles, and weaknesses, but I also understand
who I am as the bride. So I come before the Lord knowing that He
enjoys me and fascinates me with His beauty. I feel genuinely beautiful
before Him.

PRAYER STARTER

*Lord, the beauty of Your resurrected body fills me to overflowing with
a desire to please You in everything I do. You make me feel beautiful in You,
and all I want is to live for You.*

THIS ROMANCE OF THE GOSPEL FREES US FROM THE
ENSLAVEMENT OF INFERIOR PLEASURES, AND THE
DOMINATION OF SINFUL PLEASURE BEGINS TO BE BROKEN.

DAY 165

Behold, I stand at the door and knock. If anyone hears
My voice and opens the door, I will come in to him and dine
with him, and he with Me. To him who overcomes I will grant to
sit with Me on My throne, as I also overcame and sat down
with My Father on His throne.
—*Revelation 3:20–21, NKJV*

The bride of Christ has a desire to be great, noble, and successful. This deep human longing is answered by God as He enthrones us as His bridal partner throughout eternity. As the bride of Christ we have the highest position of honor and authority in eternity, a position far above all the angels. The highest position of honor for all of God's creation is reserved for the bride who will partake of the wedding table of Revelation 3:20. The bride who sits at the table feasting with Christ is the one who sits with Him in the position of government and authority as well. The bride of Christ is the queen of heaven because she is married to the King of kings. Believers are priest and kings. As priests we are wholehearted lovers, but as kings we are indeed in the government of the city of God.

PRAYER STARTER

Lord, Your desire for me to be Your bride satisfies the deep longing of my heart to be great, noble, and successful. I am great in You and will rule and reign with You in glory forever.

> **GREATNESS IN GOD IS NOT DEFINED BY EARTHLY CIRCUMSTANCES—GREATNESS IN GOD FOCUSES UPON HIS GREATNESS.**

DAY 166

A second time they summoned the man who had been blind. "Give glory to God," they said. "We know this man is a sinner." He replied, "Whether he is a sinner or not, I don't know. One thing I do know. I was blind but now I see!"
—*John 9:24–25*

As the bride of Christ, we desire to impact others, to feel significant, and to exhilarate others with good news of the gospel. For example, when one of the blind men was healed at Jesus's meeting, imagine his joy in telling his blind friends about the meeting the following day. How exhilarating to bring that news to them! Imagine the joy as he informs his friends that another healing meeting is scheduled for the following evening. The ability to make an impact on others is something that was given to us by God.

PRAYER STARTER

Father, let my life impact others because of the wonderful transformation You have brought to me. May I never lose my joy or enthusiasm in telling others of Your miraculous grace.

WHEN WE DO NOT HAVE AN IMPACT ON ANYBODY, OUR SPIRITUAL LIVES LOSE THEIR JOY AND FRESHNESS.

DAY 167

For I delight in your commands
because I love them.
I lift up my hands to your commands, which I love,
and I meditate on your decrees.
—*Psalm 119:47–48*

Picture walking up to a homeless little boy and handing him a ticket for a wonderful vacation by the sea. The dirty little youngster takes the ticket from you and places it among other collected items in a corner of the large box where he sleeps at night to shelter himself from the rain and cold wind. Instead of eating hamburgers and fries, apple pie and ice cream, he curls up on a door stoop and eats spoiled meat he has gathered from the trash. He plays in the dirt, making mud pies and eating them as his dessert. That's the choice we make every time we are confronted with a decision to say yes or to say no to this world. The pleasures of God are a banquet set before us, a table of spiritual delights that once tasted deliver us from the emptiness of seeking earthly pleasures. The way to free the heart from the domination of sin is by delighting in God.

PRAYER STARTER

I choose You, Father. In every circumstance, in every decision, I choose to say yes to Your plans and purposes for my life. Nothing compares to the wonder of Your acceptance of me.

> **HOLINESS IS A SUPERIOR PLEASURE THAT TRANSCENDS ANYTHING THAT SIN CAN OFFER US.**

DAY 168

Put off, concerning your former conduct, the old man which
grows corrupt according to the deceitful lusts...lest any of you
be hardened through the deceitfulness of sin.
—*Ephesians 4:22; Hebrews 3:13*

Have you ever thought about why we sin? Sin produces immediate pleasure. It gives a physical, spiritual, and emotional rush. We do not sin
out of obligation. We sin because we believe that it will provide a pleasure that is superior to the pleasure of obedience to God. The power
of temptation rests on a deceptive promise that sin will bring more
satisfaction than living for God. The Word of God calls this promise
the deceitfulness of sin or the deceitful lusts. We will only win the
battle of temptation as we enjoy God. The Holy Spirit is setting forth
the beauty of God in Jesus Christ so that we might become enticed by
a holy affection whose power rivals the power of our sin.

PRAYER STARTER

*Father, remove from me the desire for instant gratification. Keep far
from me the temptation for giving in to the pleasures of the moment. My only
pleasure is in doing the will of my Father God.*

THE SECRET TO CONQUERING SIN IS SATISFACTION IN GOD.

DAY 169

By faith Moses, when he became of age, refused to be called the son of Pharaoh's daughter, choosing rather to suffer affliction with the people of God than to enjoy the passing pleasures of sin, esteeming the reproach of Christ greater riches than the treasures in Egypt; for he looked to the reward.
—*Hebrews 11:24–26*

Moses had experienced the pleasures of the flesh that accompanied the riches and power of his position in Egypt, but he chose greater riches. He experienced something more pleasurable and beautiful than Egypt, something supernaturally attractive and altogether satisfying. God does not call us to holiness to keep us from a life of pleasure. Holiness is not drudgery. Instead, God calls us to a holiness that fully releases infinite and perfect pleasure to us forever. We do not glorify God when we arrogantly presume that we can give God what He doesn't have. He is most honored when we come to Him with an attitude that recognizes that all He does for us is intended to increase our satisfaction in Him.

PRAYER STARTER

Father, whether You choose to send me pain or pleasure, I choose to honor You with my life of obedience and love. Call me into holiness and purity, and allow me to live my life in the fullness of holiness.

AS YOU PRESS INTO THE PLEASURES OF HOLINESS, LIKE MOSES, YOU WILL DISCOVER THAT NONE CAN FILL THE SOUL LIKE JESUS.

DAY 170

> Can the friends of the bridegroom mourn as long as the bridegroom is with them? But the days will come when the bridegroom will be taken away from them, and then they will fast.
> —*Matthew 9:15, NKJV*

Have you ever felt that you just could not stand to go on living without more of Jesus Christ in your life? I have. It's for such seasons of spiritual hunger that God has given us the Bridegroom fast. It is a fast that enlarges our capacity to receive freely from the Spirit of God. Instead of having an external purpose such as averting a crisis, this kind of fasting changes us on the inside. When you cannot live without something in God, some place of depth of communion in His love, then it is God's will for you to cry out for it with a new resolve and intensity. If you absolutely cannot live without a new depth in your intimacy with God, the Lord will usually increase your portion of it over the following months and years.

PRAYER STARTER

> *Lord, sometimes my heart is filled with intense longing for more of You. Sometimes I feel as though I cannot go on without a fresh revelation of Your love. Draw me into a new and higher level of intimacy with You.*

WE RECEIVE SPIRITUAL TENDERNESS AND NEW DISCOVERIES OF INTIMACY WITH GOD MORE QUICKLY AND MORE DEEPLY WHEN WE FAST.

DAY 171

Paul and Barnabas appointed elders for them in each
church and, with prayer and fasting, committed them to the Lord,
in whom they had put their trust.
—*Acts 14:23*

Jesus knew that His disciples' hearts had become accustomed to His physical presence as He gazed into their eyes and communicated His affection, beauty, and stunning wisdom to them every day. He knew that once He had died and ascended, fasting would help them recover some of the wonderful reality that they had experienced with Him in His physical presence with them. Christ knew that once He was gone, the disciples' desire, longing, and lovesickness for Him would cause them to mourn to be close to Him as in the days that He walked with them. That hunger to recover that same sense of closeness to Him would prove to be a key to their intimacy, power, anointing, and the fellowship of the Holy Spirit. Only Jesus could have thought of the unique paradigm to respond to spiritual lovesickness. Jesus combined the two seemingly divergent ideas into one.

PRAYER STARTER

Jesus, I cannot imagine the emptiness Your disciples felt when You left them to return to heaven. But that emptiness drew them into a new experience of fellowship with Your precious Holy Spirit. Let that experience be mine, Lord, and reveal Yourself through Your Spirit to my longing heart.

**NO OTHER RELIGION IN THE WORLD HAS EVER LINKED
FASTING TO LOVESICKNESS.**

DAY 172

> While they were worshiping the Lord and fasting, the Holy Spirit said, "Set apart for me Barnabas and Saul for the work to which I have called them." So after they had fasted and prayed, they placed their hands on them and sent them off.
> —*Acts 13:2–3*

While Jesus was still walking the earth, the disciples felt the Lord's love for them, they experienced His embrace, and they sensed His deep desire for them. They were the Lord's for life. When the Bridegroom ascended into heaven, the ache of desire and the remembrance of intimacy stung their hearts with pangs of love's desire. Jesus knew the disciples would long for the opportunity to look into the eyes of Jesus and to feel the warmth of His nearness as in former times when they walked the hills of Galilee. However, God had a new plan to satisfy their longing. By the Holy Spirit, the Lord would release the fulfillment of their hearts' desire. As they would seek His comfort, they would again experience the previous satisfaction they had when He was so near to them. This would come about through the Holy Spirit revealing Christ through the Word. At that point, they would add fasting to the longing in their hearts, and their spirits would become tender in love. This is fasting in the grace of God. Fasting is absolutely essential for developing a deeper experience of devotion for Christ.

PRAYER STARTER

Lord, Your Holy Spirit can satisfy the longing of my heart. Teach me to experience a deeper devotion for You through the Bridegroom fast.

THE BRIDEGROOM FAST TENDERIZES OUR SPIRITS, HELPING US TO RECEIVE FREELY AND DEEPLY.

DAY 173

They said to him, "John's disciples often fast and pray, and so do the disciples of the Pharisees, but yours go on eating and drinking." Jesus answered, "Can you make the guests of the bridegroom fast while he is with them? But the time will come when the bridegroom will be taken from them; in those days they will fast."
—*Luke 5:33–35*

The Bridegroom fast will be used by the Holy Spirit to unlock deep places of our hearts in spiritual intimacy. Fasting enables us to see spiritual things that we normally could not see. The increase will not happen overnight. In fact, it may not even happen much in the first months, but our level of intimacy with the Lord will grow over years and seasons. We will see more this year than we did last year, and more next year than we did this year. Fasting increases the tenderizing of our hearts by removing the spirit of dullness and deadness off of us so that we feel the presence of God and His love in a more discernable way. When you embrace the fasted lifestyle, you will feel Him more than you do now. I can assure you of that.

PRAYER STARTER

As I fast before You, Father, unlock the deep places of my heart so that I may experience a deeper intimacy with You. Tenderize my heart so that I can feel Your love in a greater way.

YOUR SPIRITUAL COMMITMENT AND INTENSITY WILL GROW
AS A RESULT OF FASTING.

DAY 174

But God chose the foolish things of the world to shame the
wise; God chose the weak things of the world to shame the strong.
He chose the lowly things of this world and the despised things—
and the things that are not—to nullify the things that are, so that no
one may boast before him. It is because of him that you are in Christ
Jesus, who has become for us wisdom from God—that is,
our righteousness, holiness and redemption.
—1 Corinthians 1:27–31

Fasting in fellowship with the Holy Spirit helps protect us from
discontentment, coveting, and fleshly cravings. Fasting will lead to a
change of your emotional chemistry. You will, for the most part, no
longer desire to have the things that you once wanted. This is because
fasting intensifies your detachment from worldly concerns. The strange
thing about fasting is that it requires doing nothing instead of doing
something, for when you fast you don't eat, don't work, don't talk, and
so on. This is the ultimate state of the foolish and weak things of this
world confounding the so-called wise things of the world. Fasting literally begins to unlock and release those negative feelings that have been
ruling our hearts and ruling us. The presence of God released through
fasting also helps to break the bondages of self-absorption so common
in today's world.

PRAYER STARTER

Father, remove my fleshly cravings and concerns so that I can fast
unimpeded by the cares of this world. Strengthen my spiritual identity in You
so that I will no longer desire the things of this world.

**FASTING IS A POWERFUL SPIRITUAL TOOL THAT
STRENGTHENS YOUR SPIRITUAL IDENTITY IN GOD AND
WEAKENS YOUR FLESHLY IDENTITY.**

DAY 175

There was also a prophetess, Anna, the daughter of Phanuel,
of the tribe of Asher. She was very old; she had lived with her
husband seven years after her marriage, and then was a widow until
she was eighty-four. She never left the temple but worshiped
night and day, fasting and praying.
—Luke 2:36–37

Anna and Mary of Bethany were two full-time watchmen set upon the Jerusalem wall. Anna speaks of the spiritual warfare, intercession, and fasting. These are people whose main focus is to open the windows of blessing and tear down the spiritual walls of resistance. They are full-blast intercessors and spiritual warriors who are committed to fasting. The Marys of Bethany will enjoy great grace for prayer and worship and will change the atmosphere of the cities and churches that they are a part of by being extravagant lovesick worshipers. God has placed them in the midst of the people as a tender fragrance of the beauty of the Lord.

PRAYER STARTER

Make me a watchman on the wall of Your glory like Anna and Mary of Bethany. I want to give myself to intercession so that I might influence the atmosphere of my city and church to a higher level in You.

EVEN IF THE ANNAS AND MARYS NEVER SPEAK TO ANYONE,
THEIR VERY PRESENCE CREATES A TYPE OF GRACE THAT
PRESERVES THE CHURCH.

DAY 176

And this woman was a widow of about eighty-four years,
who did not depart from the temple, but served God with
fastings and prayers night and day.
—*Luke 2:37, NKJV*

Anna—what an interesting woman! She served the Lord (ministered
to the Lord) with fasting and prayer night and day. The word *ministered*
is often exchanged with the word *serve*. What an unusual idea for a
woman to minister to the Lord in prayer and fasting. Anna was probably about seventeen or eighteen years old when she was married, and
after seven years she was widowed. So beginning in her early twenties
she began ministering to the Lord night and day. At eighty-four years
old, sixty years later, Anna was still faithful in this! She was constantly
in prayer in the temple. What a woman! This calling is not reserved
only for Catholic monks. The Protestant church must call the Annas
forth, find a place for them, honor them, and find ways of releasing
them into their calling.

PRAYER STARTER

Father, I may not be remembered for sixty years of faithful intercession, but I pray that I will be remembered as a faithful intercessor—no
matter how many years I have left to live for You.

BELOVED, IN THIS VERY HOUR THE LORD IS WOOING THE
ANNAS OF THE END-TIME CHURCH, AND HE PERSONALLY IS
SETTING THEM INTO THEIR PLACE.

DAY 177

But they will have to give account to him who is ready to judge
the living and the dead. For this is the reason the gospel was preached
even to those who are now dead, so that they might be judged
according to men in regard to the body, but live according to God
in regard to the spirit.

—1 Peter 4:5–6

Three faces of Jesus Christ—Bridegroom, King, and Judge—will be
revealed and emphasized in the unprecedented end-time activities of
the Holy Spirit. The revelation of the Bridegroom is what God will
use to restore the first commandment to first place. Seeing the passionate Lover will make us passionate lovers of God. The revelation
of the King will cause us to operate in the power of God as we go out
to meet the great harvest. The revelation of the Judge will cause us to
participate with Him in loosing His judgments. As you reach your
heart toward Him, be encouraged that a powerful new dimension of
His presence is waiting to unfold; it is the mystery of eternal ages, the
heavenly Bridegroom and you—His beloved. The explosive power of
this revelation will change you and make you ready to meet the challenges of holiness, compassion, and beauty that await you in the glorious age in which you live.

PRAYER STARTER

*Jesus, You have awakened a passionate love for You within me. I pray
that You will fill me with Your power to win the lost to You. I loose Your
judgment in this world and pray that You enable me to bring a harvest of
souls into Your kingdom.*

> OPEN UP YOUR HEART TO THE PASSIONATE LOVER WHO IS
> EXHILARATED AND THRILLED ABOUT YOU EVEN WHILE YOU
> ARE MATURING IN HIM.

DAY 178

After this, God gave them judges until the time of Samuel the prophet. Then the people asked for a king, and he gave them Saul son of Kish, of the tribe of Benjamin, who ruled forty years. After removing Saul, he made David their king. He testified concerning him: "I have found David son of Jesse a man after my own heart; he will do everything I want him to do."

—Acts 13:20–22

King David has been a puzzle, a mystery, a holy conundrum for thousands of years. His life perplexes, maddens, and humbles students of the Bible. To many, it doesn't make sense that this man who was so prone to personal weakness was able to "get away with" so much and still have God treat him with special favor. He was many things: a shepherd, a psalmist, a king, a liar, a murderer, and an adulterer. But most important of all, he was the only person in the entire span of the Bible to be called a man after God's own heart. Can you think of four more stunning words in all of creation? A man—lowly and often full of doubts and sin, like all of us—and yet God singled him out and called him a man after His own heart. What an awesome, almost unfathomable compliment! But in saying those words, God threw open the door to every person on the planet to be, like David, a man or woman after God's own heart.

PRAYER STARTER

Father, like David, there are many who wonder how You could possibly love me as You do. I too am full of doubts and sin, yet you allow me to become a man or woman after God's own heart.

WE ALL HAVE THE SAME OPPORTUNITY TO EMBODY IN OUR OWN PERSONALITY AND IN OUR OWN WAY THE KIND OF HEART THAT REFLECTS THE VERY HEART, EMOTIONS, AND PERSONALITY OF GOD.

DAY 179

After this, God gave them judges until the time of Samuel the prophet. Then the people asked for a king, and he gave them Saul son of Kish, of the tribe of Benjamin, who ruled forty years. After removing Saul, he made David their king. He testified concerning him: "I have found David son of Jesse a man after my own heart; he will do everything I want him to do."
—*Acts 13:20–22*

One of the toughest questions throughout Christian history has been, "Why did David get this special distinction from God? What set him apart from so many other godly men and women?" The answer has the power to revolutionize the way you see God, the way you relate to Him, and how you view yourself and your destiny in Him. What set David apart as a man after God's heart was his unrelenting passion to search out and understand the emotions of God. This, I believe, is the distinguishing factor in the life of any person—you or me or anyone else—who sets out to have a heart after God's. In fact, someday the church worldwide will be like David in this regard. We will be a massive group of people who worship, serve, and love God with ever-increasing understanding of His emotions and passions. Like David, we will understand and reflect the heart of God in a way humanity has rarely seen.

PRAYER STARTER

I want nothing more than to be a person after God's own heart. I want to worship, serve, and love You with an ever-increasing awareness of Your great love for me.

YOU CAN BE A PERSON AFTER GOD'S OWN HEART, JUST AS DAVID WAS.

DAY 180

Jesus replied, "If anyone loves me, he will obey my teaching.
My Father will love him, and we will come to him and make our
home with him. He who does not love me will not obey my teaching.
These words you hear are not my own; they belong to
the Father who sent me."
—*John 14:23–24*

Jesus equated obedience with love. Let's not deceive ourselves: it's critically important to obey God. David was tenacious, determined, and sincerely devoted to following hard after God's commands. This desire chiseled and shaped his heart over many years. But he was far from a model of obedience. There was often a yawning gap between his sincere resolve and his actions. In other words, he blew it from time to time, sometimes in spades. Yet he was still a man after God's own heart. That should flutter your heart a bit! What does this tell us? That there's more to being a person after God's heart than obedience. There is also the posture of your heart before God. God counted the sincere intentions of David's heart even when his great weakness led him to wrong decisions. God sees us the same way. Our sincere intentions to obey are very significant to God. He notices our desires, not just our outward actions.

PRAYER STARTER

Father, search my heart and show me where I have failed to walk in obedience to Your will. Keep my heart pure before You, and help me to walk in ever-increasing obedience to Your plans and purposes.

**A SINCERE DETERMINATION TO LOVE JESUS EVEN IN THE
MIDST OF YOUR WEAKNESS IS A HUGE PART OF BEING A MAN
OR WOMAN AFTER GOD'S OWN HEART.**

DAY 181

Teach me your way, O LORD,
and I will walk in your truth;
give me an undivided heart,
that I may fear your name.
—*Psalm 86:11*

David went beyond a determination to sincerely obey; he became a student of God's emotions. He wanted to know what wonders, pleasures, and fearsome things filled God's heart. He had many responsibilities and challenges as warrior and king, but he spent his best energies trying to understand what emotions burned in the personality of God. He had a remarkable hunger to understand the emotions and heart of God, and as a result he had a unique grasp of the emotions, intentions, and passions of God's heart. This is the one key, the single motivation that empowered David. And if we are to follow in his footsteps toward an understanding of God's heart, we must have the same motivation. We must yearn to know how God feels, how the passions of His heart move. As we discover the same truths about God's heart, we will find ourselves living the way David lived and fulfilling the call of God on our generation.

PRAYER STARTER

Father, motivate me to desire to understand Your emotions, intentions, and passions. I want to know what You feel, what makes Your heart respond to me in love.

BY THE ANOINTING AND THE GRACE OF GOD, WE MUST BECOME SCHOLARS OF GOD'S HEART.

DAY 182

Show me your ways, O LORD,
teach me your paths;
guide me in your truth and teach me,
for you are God my Savior,
and my hope is in you all day long.
—*Psalm 25:4–5*

The Holy Spirit is impressing this upon people across the earth. He is taking what David saw in the heart of God, combining it with all that Jesus revealed about the Father's heart in the New Testament, and causing an explosion of revelation about the emotions of God's heart to come into the body of Christ. People are listening to this message and developing rock-solid resolve to be scholars of God's emotions, as David was. This explains the deep, worldwide hunger people have to experience God in a way that goes beyond what many churches are accustomed to. We must fix it in mind that David was a man after God's heart primarily because he sought to understand the emotions of God—and we must do the same.

PRAYER STARTER

Father, I confess that I do not understand all that I should know about You and Your great purposes. Let me discover more about You daily; teach me Your ways, and show me Your path of righteousness.

OUR ATTAINMENT OF MATURE LOVE HAPPENS OVER MONTHS, YEARS, AND DECADES, AND THE RESULTS WILL BE SEEN IN DUE TIME AS WE BEAR FRUIT.

DAY 183

I have not departed from your laws, for you yourself have
taught me. How sweet are your words to my taste, sweeter than
honey to my mouth! I gain understanding from your precepts;
therefore I hate every wrong path. Your word is a lamp to my feet
and a light for my path.
—*Psalm 119:102–105*

David refused to live with less than the very highest God would give him
in his day. He never let himself feel disqualified by his weaknesses, but
he contended mightily for the release of God's power during his generation. He caught a glimpse of God's zeal for His people and became
convinced that the Lord would release His power for the benefit of the
entire nation of Israel. In David's generation, God's power was often
expressed in military feats. Therefore, entering into all that God would
give his generation translated into military conquest of enemies. The
principle today is the same, though not expressed in military terms.
But like David, we must refuse to draw back until we experience God's
full power for our generation. When we get caught up in the glorious
emotions that burn within God's heart as David did, we begin to see
the tremendous, unprecedented blessing and power God has planned
for this hour in history. We lose our ability to settle for same ol', same
ol'. We burn like torches with strong vision as our fuel.

PRAYER STARTER

*God, what is Your plan for my generation? What are You doing in
my world today? Reveal to me the path I am to take to be a part of Your
great plan.*

**WE BECOME PEOPLE WHO CONTEND FOR THE POWER OF
GOD AVAILABLE TO OUR GENERATION.**

DAY 184

Your love, O LORD, reaches to the heavens,
your faithfulness to the skies.
Your righteousness is like the mighty mountains,
your justice like the great deep.
—*Psalm 36:5–6*

I don't think it's possible to outgrow the thrill, the wonder, the overwhelming certainty of being loved and enjoyed. It is the single experience all humans grope for and cling to in human relationships and with God. Knowing you are loved by another person fills your days with endless marvels, no matter what's going on outside your heart. You go through problems as if they're cotton candy. Your car breaks down and you think, "Big deal," because somebody loves you. You lose your wallet, get caught in traffic, and forget the milk in the trunk all in the same day, but you don't even care because in your heart is that lamp lit with the strong power of love. You know that, should all else fail, you have this most important thing. God created us to be this way. He put deep longings to be loved inside of us. We were designed down to our DNA to live in spiritual pleasure of being enjoyed not just by other humans but also by Him.

PRAYER STARTER

Loving You, and knowing how much You love me, has transformed my life into a wondrous adventure of pleasing You. I was born to praise You, I was born to love You, and I was born to fulfill Your purpose for my life.

MERE KNOWLEDGE OF LOVE MAKES LIFE A LITTLE MORE
BEARABLE IN THE MIDST OF THE WORLD'S MADNESS,
BUT FEELING LOVE TURNS LIFE INTO AN UTTERLY
PLEASURABLE ADVENTURE.

DAY 185

The earth is filled with your love, O LORD;
teach me your decrees.
Do good to your servant
according to your word, O LORD.
Teach me knowledge and good judgment,
for I believe in your commands.
—*Psalm 119:64–66*

Most believers are so disconnected from the reality of God's astonishing, frightfully lavish love for us that they totally miss out on 99 percent of what they could experience in their everyday walk with Christ. They treat God like an employer, a business partner, a judge, a traffic cop—anything but a lover. They rarely feel His passion, love, or pleasure. Perhaps they tell themselves that feeling it is not all that important, as long as they are obeying His commands, reading the Bible, and keeping up the spiritual disciplines. But as a consequence of this dryness, they rarely feel love or pleasure of any kind. Most believers put prayer in the "sacrifices-I-make-for-God" category, but that only happens when you live with a total misconception of who God is. When we look into His heart, He reveals to us what He looks like emotionally and what we look like to Him. The result turns our brains and hearts inside out. You can't get over it! It's like falling in love for the first time. He absolutely burns with love for you!

PRAYER STARTER

Father, I don't want to miss one fraction of 1 percent of what You have planned for me. I'm ready, O God, to do or be whatever You want me to do or be.

YOU HAVE TO UNDERSTAND: GOD IS NOT A BORING FUDDY-DUDDY WHO WEARS SLIPPERS AND PUTTERS AROUND HEAVEN FEELING CONSTANTLY PERTURBED.

DAY 186

Test me, O LORD, and try me,
examine my heart and my mind;
for your love is ever before me,
and I walk continually in your truth.
—*Psalm 26:2–3*

Imagine this great tragedy: A woman walks with God for forty years, fully saved, redeemed, and following Christ. She comes before the throne in the resurrection, and for the first time, she realizes what she's missed. She feels wave upon wave of pleasure flowing from the Son of God, and she says to herself, "I could have drunk from this well of spiritual delight every day on Earth. I just had to encounter Your heart and Your beauty. Life would have been so much better! Everything would have changed, and I would have accomplished so much more." Beloved, we don't have to wait to experience the deep pleasures! God has ordained for the human heart to experience them even in this life. It's not optional for us to go on as generations have, without a transforming revelation of God's heart. We desperately need hearts anchored and sustained by an outrageous love that comes from another world.

PRAYER STARTER

Father, I don't want to come to the end of my life with regrets for holding back on giving You all there is of me. Anchor my heart in You, and then pull out all the stops and let me soar with You.

**BELOVED, YOU AND I CANNOT PRODUCE A GOOD ENOUGH
ARGUMENT TO CHANGE GOD'S EMOTIONS TOWARD US.**

DAY 187

I will give you shepherds according to My heart, who will feed
you with knowledge and understanding.
—*Jeremiah 3:15, NKJV*

After God gives a beckoning call to return to Him because He is
married to us, inviting us to come near to Him in confident love and
wholeheartedness, He then, in effect, says, "I am going to raise up men
and women who will experience the spiritual reality of God's heart
as a Bridegroom God. That revelation will flow like a river on the
inside of those shepherds, and they will live in the mighty power of
this revelation. Then they will feed the church from it." The Lord is
now raising up men and women after His heart, like David, and He
will give them as a gift to the backslidden church to win her back to
wholeheartedness. They will speak it with deep, undeniable revelation
and feed the people with the knowledge of God's heart. Their mandate
will be to equip the people of God to understand what it means to be
married to God.

PRAYER STARTER

*Let me be a person who captures Your heart, dear God. Raise me up
to be a part of the army who is winning back Your church to wholehearted
devotion to You.*

THE HOLY SPIRIT IS RAISING UP SHEPHERDS TO TEACH
GOD'S PEOPLE TO LIVE AFTER HIS OWN HEART.

DAY 188

"I myself will gather the remnant of my flock out of all the
countries where I have driven them and will bring them back to
their pasture, where they will be fruitful and increase in number.
I will place shepherds over them who will tend them, and they
will no longer be afraid or terrified, nor will any
be missing," declares the Lord.
—*Jeremiah 23:3–4*

The Holy Spirit is raising up shepherds to teach God's people to
live after His own heart. They will feed others from the reality they
encounter through their own unyielding personal pursuit of God.
They will only be able to shepherd others because they have given
themselves wholly to the great Shepherd. Some of these shepherds will
lead through preaching and some through writing, singing, or other
skills and talents. Some will do it through one-on-one discipleship and
spending time nurturing younger believers' faith in a spiritual relationship. Some will do it in the context of their business or workplace.
I encourage you to pray specifically about this. You can't afford to miss
your appointment in these end times.

PRAYER STARTER

*Allow me to become one of Your shepherds, Father. Let me lead Your little
lambs to a personal encounter with the God who loves them unconditionally.*

PERHAPS YOU ARE CALLED TO BE A SHEPHERD, TO
AGGRESSIVELY PURSUE THE KNOWLEDGE OF HIS
PERSONALITY IN YOUR OWN LIFE SO YOU CAN FEED OTHERS
WITH THE TRUTHS YOU DISCOVER.

DAY 189

The watchman opens the gate for him, and the sheep listen to his voice. He calls his own sheep by name and leads them out. When he has brought out all his own, he goes on ahead of them, and his sheep follow him because they know his voice. But they will never follow a stranger; in fact, they will run away from him because they do not recognize a stranger's voice.

—*John 10:3–5*

As individual believers, we stand in two positions in regard to God's invitation to us. We first must feed our own spirits on the truths of this Bridegroom God's heart and personality, and then we will arise as shepherds in the body of Christ to feed others. Therefore we must become people with a clear focus on personally discovering who Jesus is in all of these dimensions of His Bridegroom heart. At some point in this process we will be equipped to lead other believers who are entrenched in compromise. We'll take them by the hand and show them into the freeing and empowering encounter of what our God is like. It's not enough to tell people that God is a Bridegroom and we are His bride. It must come from our hearts. It is transformation by personal revelation. Shepherds will train people and feed them on specific parts of God's emotions and personality, and then, little by little, like a flower in spring, the listeners' spirits will open up and be transformed.

PRAYER STARTER

Feed my spirit, Father, that I may be counted worthy of feeding Your flock. Help me to bring Your message of transformation to the lost around me.

WE CAN'T FEED OTHERS IF WE DON'T FEED OURSELVES FIRST.

DAY 190

"Return, faithless people," declares the LORD, "for I am your
husband. I will choose you—one from a town and two from a clan—
and bring you to Zion. Then I will give you shepherds after my own
heart, who will lead you with knowledge and understanding.
—*Jeremiah 3:14–15*

God intimately understands the human heart, which He formed. He
knows perfectly how to motivate His people toward holiness. This very
revelation is the highest and most effective motivator for calling people
to abandon all else for Him. Great desire for human beings is the secret
weapon in God's arsenal. The power of this revelation when we grab
on to it is simply unmatched by any other revelation in the universe. It
is not built on shame or fear but on strong desire. He says in essence,
"Turn to Me because I am married to you and because I desire you."
He is not negating all of the other types of biblical motivation, but He
is making it clear what the superior motivation is. This will become
the single most important impulse toward holiness in the final hour of
natural history as the Lord raises up a bride with a heart after God's.

PRAYER STARTER

*Lord, You are my Bridegroom, my husband, my eternal Lord and
master. Let Your holiness flood over my soul so that I am prepared to be a
holy, consecrated bride to You forever.*

**THE HIGHEST AND BEST WAY OF MOTIVATING THE HUMAN
HEART TO RIGHTEOUSNESS IS THROUGH FASCINATION AND
EXHILARATION IN LOVE.**

DAY 191

"Return, faithless Israel," declares the LORD, "I will frown on you no longer, for I am merciful....I will not be angry forever. Only acknowledge your guilt—you have rebelled against the LORD your God, you have scattered your favors to foreign gods under every spreading tree, and have not obeyed me," declares the LORD.
—Jeremiah 3:12–13

Hell is a true reality. And we experience real loss in our spiritual lives and in the fullness of our earthly ministry by not fully responding to the Holy Spirit during revival. Shame and embarrassment lead to genuine pain when sin is exposed. All these arguments have their place. There is a time to warn people of hell or to warn them that they may lose out and be disqualified in terms of their earthly mandate and ministry. There is a time to exhort people to leave their ungodly ways because of the public and private humiliation they will taste if they don't. Yet the primary and most effective method is the way that the Lord Himself spoke through the prophet Jeremiah. The Lord is crying out "Return! Return!" to the backslidden children who have found their pleasures elsewhere. He is calling to the redeemed who have lost their way and whose hearts have grown cold. He is ready to "wow" them with a revelation of His heart that will cause true holiness to spring up like a geyser from within their spirits.

PRAYER STARTER

Father, I long for a new revival of Your holiness and power upon this broken world. I want to warn others of the realities of hell and tell them of the wonders and majesty of Your heaven.

THE LORD BECKONS US TO DO AWAY WITH COMPROMISE
AND LEAVE OUR BACKSLIDING BECAUSE HE WANTS US
AND DESIRES US.

DAY 192

I have revealed you to those whom you gave me out of the world. They were yours; you gave them to me and they have obeyed your word. Now they know that everything you have given me comes from you. For I gave them the words you gave me and they accepted them. They knew with certainty that I came from you, and they believed that you sent me. I pray for them. I am not praying for the world, but for those you have given me, for they are yours.

—*John 17:6–9*

Modern and "pop" psychology, which is pervasive in the world and even in the church, emphasizes self-discovery, or "discovering who I really am." This is an important thing to do, but it's out of sequence. The answer doesn't lie within yourself or your surroundings or your past. The secret to who you are lies in the heart of one Man alone. He is the Bridegroom God. Only by gazing in His eyes and understanding who He is will you know who you are. All other searching is in vain. How many hours, years, and lifetimes have been wasted as people gaze at their own hearts and come up empty? How many good people have fallen for theories and philosophies that put self-discovery at the top of the totem pole, only to leave them with no clue who they really are? The answer is in the other direction.

PRAYER STARTER

You alone, dear Father, can show me who I am. Help me to discover who You are, and in the process You will teach me who I am in You.

> YOU WILL NEVER DISCOVER "WHO YOU ARE" BY EXAMINING YOUR ENVIRONMENT, YOUR JOB, YOUR FAMILY HISTORY, OR THE PEOPLE YOU KNOW.

DAY 193

May they be brought to complete unity to let the world know
that you sent me and have loved them even as you have loved me.
Father, I want those you have given me to be with me where I am,
and to see my glory, the glory you have given me because you loved
me before the creation of the world.
—John 17:23–24

You shouldn't concern yourself at the beginning of the journey with finding out who you are. That will come in time. God will reveal you to you in a deeply meaningful, life-transforming way. But, like John the Baptist, you need to first discover who Jesus is as a Bridegroom and to feed your spirit on what His personality is like. When that knowledge begins to come alive in your mind and spirit, you will inevitably discover His affections, His desires, and His tender dealings with you in your weaknesses. You will see that you are indeed a cherished bride. The real you will emerge and blossom in light of who He is.

PRAYER STARTER

Lord Jesus, reveal Yourself to me. Help me to see myself as You see me—as Your cherished bride. Allow me to emerge and blossom in Your image so that I might be prepared to be Your bride.

THE SECRET TO WHO YOU ARE LIES IN THE HEART OF ONE MAN ALONE. HE IS THE BRIDEGROOM GOD.

DAY 194

"Let not the wise man boast of his wisdom or the strong man boast of his strength or the rich man boast of his riches, but let him who boasts boast about this: that he understands and knows me, that I am the LORD, who exercises kindness, justice and righteousness on earth, for in these I delight," declares the LORD.
—*Jeremiah 9:23–24*

When we come before this passionate Bridegroom as His cherished bride, Jesus progressively reveals certain aspects of His heart to us. Typically, He begins with His tenderness and mercy. This is the same tenderness and mercy that encounter us at salvation, when we feel utterly weightless and free and jubilant—and rightly so. Jeremiah tells us God delights in showing us loving-kindness. God knows we can bring nothing to the bargaining table to motivate Him to deal kindly with us. He is fully motivated within Himself to be merciful. But this is an extremely difficult message for people to receive. When sincere lovers of Christ stumble due to weakness or immaturity, they often hold it against themselves for months or even years. The truth is, when we ask for forgiveness, the Lord forgives us instantly. His tenderness toward us far surpasses our own. Oh, the tender dealings of the Bridegroom's heart!

PRAYER STARTER

Lord, in Your tenderness and mercy You have offered me Your glorious salvation. Your loving-kindness has bestowed on me the blessings of Your inheritance. Your forgiveness has freed me from my sins, and in gentleness You are preparing me to spend eternity with You in heaven.

WE ARE OFTEN TOO HARD ON OURSELVES, THINKING THAT CONDEMNING OURSELVES WILL SOMEHOW MAKE IT ALL BETTER OR WILL HELP GOD TO LOVE US.

DAY 195

Then Jesus told them, "This very night you will all fall away on account of me, for it is written: 'I will strike the shepherd, and the sheep of the flock will be scattered.' But after I have risen, I will go ahead of you into Galilee." Peter replied, "Even if all fall away on account of you, I never will." "I tell you the truth," Jesus answered, "this very night, before the rooster crows, you will disown me three times."
—*Matthew 26:31–34*

The only reason we are shocked when we stumble is because of our own religious pride. God is never surprised, disillusioned, or confused by our failings. At the Last Supper, when Jesus said, "All of you will stumble tonight," Peter slammed his hand down on the table and said, "Wait a minute! I will never stumble." Like many of us, Peter had more confidence in his own dedication to the Lord than he had in the Lord's dedication to him. His relationship with Jesus was based on misplaced confidence in his own devotion. For this reason, Peter was probably the only one shocked when the rooster crowed and the sound of his third denial was still echoing off the walls. Though every believer's personal dedication to God is absolutely crucial, we must understand that our dedication to the Lord is only an outcome of His dedication to us.

PRAYER STARTER

Lord, it is my intention to live a sinless life before You. But in my own strength that is impossible. It is only through Your powerful gift of righteousness that I can stand before You, clothed in Your righteousness, and none of my own.

THE STRENGTH OF OUR COMMITMENT AND OBEDIENCE IS IN THE DRAWING POWER OF JESUS'S TENDER LEADERSHIP.

DAY 196

"Their leader will be one of their own; their ruler will arise
from among them. I will bring him near and he will come close to
me, for who is he who will devote himself to be close to me?" declares
the LORD. "So you will be my people, and I will be your God."
—*Jeremiah 30:21–22*

It is the Lord who causes us to draw near to Him. God knew we would
mess up. He saw it way in advance and made provision for it from the
very beginning. He knows our frailty, both physical and emotional.
He recognizes the limited capacity of our hearts. He sees the yes in
the hearts of His people and says, "I understand your weakness, and
yet I recognize your willingness to be wholly Mine." He looks at the
agreement in our hearts and calls forth our budding virtues into full
maturity. You see, we are dealing with a loving Bridegroom, the Man
Christ Jesus. He is fully God, but He is also fully man. He has intense
affections filled with tenderness. Even while we grow and falter on
our way to full maturity, He enjoys us, and His heart flows with
extravagant compassion, the likes of which the world will never know
without Him.

PRAYER STARTER

*Lord, how awesome the knowledge that You allow me to present myself
in sin and weakness before You, and then in love You raise me up to spiritual
maturity because You love me.*

**HE DOESN'T WIELD A BIG HAMMER, HOPING HE CAN FIND A
GOOD REASON TO SMASH US FLAT.**

DAY 197

Worship the LORD with gladness;
come before him with joyful songs.
Know that the LORD is God.
It is he who made us, and we are his;
we are his people, the sheep of his pasture.
—*Psalm 100:2–3*

God is a God of gladness. Not only does He have unfathomable mercy, but God also possesses powerful pleasures beyond our comprehension. His rejoicing emotions are infinite in measure and eternal in duration. Experiencing God is like riding a roller coaster that never ends but gets better with each curve. He smiles with delight and enjoyment when He gazes on each one of us. This strikes many people as strange. They are accustomed to relating to a God who is mostly mad or mostly sad when they come before Him. They imagine that He is either mad because they have rebelled, or sad and grieved all the time because His people are not dedicated enough.

PRAYER STARTER

Father, show me Your gladness. Let me see You smile with delight as You gaze upon me. Let me experience the exhilaration of joy that comes from living my life in Yours.

WHEN THE FATHER FINDS US IN THE STRUGGLE OF OUR WEAKNESS, IN SOME SHABBY PLACE OF SIN AND SELF-LOATHING, HE LIFTS US OUT OF IT WITH GREAT ENJOYMENT.

DAY 198

But only the redeemed will walk there, and the ransomed of
the LORD will return. They will enter Zion with singing; everlasting
joy will crown their heads. Gladness and joy will overtake them, and
sorrow and sighing will flee away.
—*Isaiah 35:9–10*

God is the God of gladness, a happy God of infinite joy. In the billions
of years that we will relate to Him, His anger will only be for a brief
moment, and the other 99.9999999 percent of our experience and relationship with Him will be based on the gladness of His heart toward
us. He is a God of happy holiness, without any contradiction between
those words. His holiness flows from abundant joy that cannot be
imagined. This does not deny His anger with rebellion. He is fierce to
remove what hinders the love between you and Him. But in the life of a
sincere believer, there is an important distinction between rebellion and
immaturity. They are entirely different things. God hates rebellion, but
He sees immaturity as something other than outright sin. He is smart
enough to separate the individual from the sin. He can enjoy us and
still disapprove of things we do or believe, like a parent who disciplines
and enjoys a child from one moment to the next.

PRAYER STARTER

*Father, I want to experience the happy, abundant joy that will permeate
eternity. Reveal Your exuberant Father heart to me, Your child. Raise me up
to share Your eternal joy.*

**THE GOD OF AFFECTION—THIS IS THE FOUNDATIONAL
TRUTH THAT YOU EXPERIENCE IN YOUR INTIMACY
WITH JESUS.**

DAY 199

Yet the LORD longs to be gracious to you; he rises to show
you compassion. For the LORD is a God of justice.
Blessed are all who wait for him!
—*Isaiah 30:18*

Our Bridegroom God burns with fiery affections. This fact is separate
and distinct from His tenderness and great gladness. Most people have
a hard time thinking of God as desiring or wanting anything. After
all, He owns everything. His pantry is always stocked. He can create
creatures and worlds and galaxies to bring Him pleasure. He could
entertain Himself endlessly. But the fact is deeply rooted in Scripture
that He is also full of intense desire and burning love for each of us.
This God of affection is what so many are longing to encounter, even
though they may not be aware that the encounter will radically transform their heart. This is what makes you great. This is what makes you
special and unique in all the universe. This provides each of us with the
primary definition for our lives.

PRAYER STARTER

*Father, You own this universe and those in the world unknown to me.
You hung the stars in space and caused the oceans to stay in place. When You
spoke a word, the earth came into being. Yet You know me, and You desire to
have a personal relationship with me. This is far beyond my understanding.*

**HE LONGS TO BE NEAR EACH ONE OF US PERSONALLY, IN THE
WAY FRIENDS AND LOVERS WANT TO BE TOGETHER.**

DAY 200

Who is a God like you, who pardons sin and forgives the transgression of the remnant of his inheritance? You do not stay angry forever but delight to show mercy. You will again have compassion on us; you will tread our sins underfoot and hurl all our iniquities into the depths of the sea.
—*Micah 7:18–19*

Our success and value are not based on our level of production; our financial worth; our talent in sports, music, or academics; or anything else. These are all sideshows. What gives us true meaning in the vast, complex world in which we find ourselves is that the eternal One, the uncreated God, pursues us with passionate desire. This is what crowns our lives with meaning and power. This is what makes us great. We did nothing to become born, and since then we have stumbled and fallen in so many ways. Yet Jesus, our Bridegroom God, says, "I want you!" And that confers upon us eternal significance. Though every other circumstance be unstable, and though we mess up in myriad ways, we walk in grace before an audience of One with profound success and contentment simply because He longs for us and declares Himself the lover of our souls.

PRAYER STARTER

Father, it doesn't matter to You that I am an insignificant nobody in this vast, complex world in which I live. Still You love me . . . want me . . . and call me into Your presence.

WE ARE THE ONES GOD DESIRES.

DAY 201

For true and righteous are His judgments, because He has
judged the great harlot who corrupted the earth with her fornication;
and He has avenged on her the blood of His servants shed by
her....And I heard...the voice of a great multitude...saying,
"Alleluia! For the Lord God Omnipotent reigns! Let us be glad and
rejoice...for the marriage of the Lamb has come,
and His wife has made herself ready."
—*Revelation 19:2, 6–7, NKJV*

The essence of God's judgment is His commitment to remove all that
hinders love in our lives. This passage describes a scene in heaven related
to the marriage of Jesus to His church, which takes place immediately
after Jesus releases His terrifying judgments on the world system at
the time of His Second Coming. As a Bridegroom God preparing His
people for the great wedding day, the focus of God's jealous anger is
directed in judgment of two things: first, those who gave themselves
to immorality; second, those who persecuted His people. Both issues
cause harm to His bride. The principle underlying His jealous anger is
this: whatever harms His bride's preparation as His eternal companion
will be judged.

PRAYER STARTER

*Lord, I long for the great marriage feast to join with You in eternity as
Your bride, and You as my Bridegroom. Thank You for protecting me from
harm and for preparing me for that great wedding day in heaven.*

> GOD WILL NOT ALLOW ANYTHING TO CONTINUE IN OUR
> LIVES THAT HINDERS THE DEVELOPMENT OF OUR LOVE.

DAY 202

The sun will no more be your light by day, nor will the brightness of the moon shine on you, for the LORD will be your everlasting light, and your God will be your glory. Your sun will never set again, and your moon will wane no more; the LORD will be your everlasting light, and your days of sorrow will end.
—*Isaiah 60:19–20*

One day we will gaze upon our Bridegroom God for billions of years at a stretch. This description and any other will seem pitiful in its attempt to convey the reality of Him, but we must understand as well as we can that our Bridegroom possesses a beauty that transcends any other in the created realm. He is far above all other magnificence and pleasure. His endless splendor shines forth from His tenderness, gladness, and desire for us. (Indeed, it's impossible to understand His beauty without first understanding His tenderness, gladness, and desire, for His beauty radiates from them.) As we encounter it through Scripture and by His revelation in our spirits, His beauty fascinates and captivates our hearts. He woos and wows us with magnificence.

PRAYER STARTER

Father, a billion years will seem as nothing when I stand before You and gaze into Your endless splendor. Teach me about Your tenderness, gladness, and desire so that I may fully comprehend Your beauty.

BEING CONFIDENT IN GOD'S LOVE FOR YOU IS NECESSARY TO SEEING GOD'S BEAUTY.

DAY 203

You have made known to me the path of life;
you will fill me with joy in your presence,
with eternal pleasures at your right hand.
—*Psalm 16:11*

This fascination with the God of beauty is easily the greatest source of pleasure in heaven and the earth. Above all things that give the human heart pleasure, one is paramount: God revealing Himself to us personally and individually. David was saying, in a way, "When I discover more of Your beauty, my spirit is completely exhilarated!" He experienced the highest pleasure known to the human heart. This was the single greatest attribute of his life. He drank from the well of God's endlessly unfolding beauty. King David gave insight into his heart's obsession when he testified, "One thing I ask of the LORD, this is what I seek: that I may dwell in the house of the LORD all the days of my life, to gaze upon the beauty of the LORD" (Ps. 27:4). This must also become our obsession if we are to be people after God's own heart, fulfilling our destiny in this generation.

PRAYER STARTER

Lord, with the psalmist, I ask only for the privilege of dwelling in the house of the Lord all the days of my life. Let me gaze upon Your beauty as eons of time flow endlessly before us.

> **DAVID LIVED WITH A FASCINATED HEART THAT CONTINUALLY DISCOVERED NEW DIMENSIONS OF GOD'S MAGNIFICENCE.**

DAY 204

I have loved you with an everlasting love;
I have drawn you with loving-kindness.
—Jeremiah 31:3

Beloved, we will have divine satisfaction forever, discovering more of His beauty through endless ages. And we can begin now! Indeed, we must begin now, for the sake of what God would have us be. He wants us to be always caught up in fascination and to become confident in love before Him; then and only then does He reveal more of His sublime beauty to us. Take one step into this realm, and you find it's impossible to exhaust His store of surprises; they unfold as you perceive more of His heart and as He reveals Himself to you in progressively greater measure. It's like a walk through an endless garden of flowers, each kind more resplendent and inventive than the one before, each path leading to waterfalls and vistas ever more breathtaking to behold. All beauty on Earth is merely a reflection of Him; even the most beautiful thing you can think of will one day be swallowed up by the beauty of His heart like the beam of a flashlight in the intensity of a thousand suns.

PRAYER STARTER

Father, what awesome wonder awaits Your children in eternity. I cannot wait for You to take me by the hand and walk me through Your heaven. Your beauty will radiate forever, and I long to begin eternity with You.

THE HEART OF GOD IS A WONDERLAND, A UNIVERSE OF BEAUTY LIKE NO PLACE MANKIND COULD DREAM UP.

DAY 205

What is more, I consider everything a loss compared to the surpassing greatness of knowing Christ Jesus my Lord, for whose sake I have lost all things. I consider them rubbish, that I may gain Christ and be found in him, not having a righteousness of my own that comes from the law, but that which is through faith in Christ— the righteousness that comes from God and is by faith.

—*Philippians 3:8–9*

Are you surprised at this new approach to holiness? It will change the very face of Christianity. It's nothing like the legalistic straitjackets of yesterday. It's rooted in strong desire, not shame; beauty, not bashing. By understanding that God desires us as His bride, our generation will arise in beauties of holiness yet unknown, with hearts ripe and sweet with passion and love. We will gladly choose Him over everything else that competes for our attention. We will deny our flesh not primarily because of fear but out of the overflow of lovesick hearts, captured by the Man Christ Jesus, beauty incarnate. This intimacy will be motivated most of all by the astonishing revelation that He wants to marry us and have us share His gladness, pleasure, and beauty for time and beyond.

PRAYER STARTER

God, the knowledge of Your desire for me causes me to desire to be holy as You are holy. Your love captures my heart and causes me to long to share Your gladness, pleasure, and beauty forever.

WE WILL COUNT ALL THINGS LOST FOR THE EXCELLENCE OF KNOWING JESUS CHRIST OUR LORD.

DAY 206

Send forth your light and your truth, let them guide me; let them bring me to your holy mountain, to the place where you dwell. Then will I go to the altar of God, to God, my joy and my delight. I will praise you with the harp, O God, my God.

—*Psalm 43:3–4*

It sounds romantic to us now, but as a shepherd boy watching the flocks, David was the equivalent of a night watchman sitting in a booth and making sure nobody breaks into a storage facility. Anybody who has held a job in security knows there is nothing special about it. It's boring, unglamorous, mundane work. You sit there filing your nails, listening to the radio, counting the crickets chirping outside. You don't even want to admit to your friends that you have a job like that. I can picture David, a young teenager sitting in the fields behind his house, playing his guitar, and biding his time. Nobody cared to hear the songs he composed on his nondescript, homemade harp. But as he wandered those back hills of Bethlehem and looked up at the stars, something caught his attention, and he began to sing, "I don't know You very well, but I love You. I want to know You. What are You like? Who are You? What is my life about?" What did David see? What did God whisper to his heart that became the foundation of who he was to become?

PRAYER STARTER

Father, like David, the little shepherd boy who spent his hours isolated and alone, teach me to spend my life in discovering who You are and what You want my life to be.

WHAT DID DAVID FIND IN THE LONG HOURS OF GAZING ON GOD'S BEAUTY IN THE STARS AND THE SUNSETS?

DAY 207

Whom have I in heaven but you?
And earth has nothing I desire besides you.
My flesh and my heart may fail,
but God is the strength of my heart
and my portion forever.
—*Psalm 73:25–26*

Behind that ruddy face, deep inside that boy's frame, was a heart unlike any the world had seen. It drew God's attention away from the cosmos, away from the majesty of the cities and oceans and natural wonders of the world. Wouldn't you love to feel His attention focused squarely on you? It happened to David. One day the Spirit of the Lord came upon the prophet Samuel and whispered in his ear, "I am replacing Saul, the rebellious king of Israel. I have found a young man who has a heart for Me. He wants the same things I want. He's a young guitar player, and I really like him. He doesn't even know I've heard his love songs in the night, but he has a heart that's hungry for the things that fill My heart. I hear his voice, and I have taken note of him. I want you to tell him what I think about him." In those sun-scorched, no-name fields behind Bethlehem, even before Samuel arrived, David was becoming a picture of the end-time church.

PRAYER STARTER

Do You see my heart, O God? It longs to hear Your voice, to see Your face, and to spend time in Your presence. All I want is You, Lord…just to be with You and to experience Your love for me.

> **WOULDN'T YOU LOVE FOR YOUR HEART TO CATCH GOD'S EYE AS HE LOOKED UPON CREATION?**

DAY 208

Show me your ways, O Lord,
teach me your paths;
guide me in your truth and teach me,
for you are God my Savior,
and my hope is in you all day long.
—*Psalm 25:4–5*

People often ask me after I teach on David's life, "How do I get a heart like David's, consumed with love for God?" I tell them that if they behold and study God's fiery love for them, their hearts will become fiery with love for God. As we behold the inner life of the Godhead, we receive divine information about what God feels about human beings, about you and me individually, about our destinies, our personalities, our likes and dislikes, our places in history. We connect with and behold the emotions of God. But more than that, we begin to change.

PRAYER STARTER

Teach me Your ways; show me Your personality; let me feel Your emotions, Father. Knowing You in this way will change me from corruptible to incorruptible, from hopelessness to destiny.

WHAT DOES IT MEAN TO BE A STUDENT OF GOD'S EMOTIONS?

DAY 209

And we, who with unveiled faces all reflect the Lord's glory,
are being transformed into his likeness with ever-increasing glory,
which comes from the Lord, who is the Spirit.
—*2 Corinthians 3:18*

The apostle Paul referenced this spiritual principle: "But we all…
beholding as in a mirror the glory of Lord, are being transformed into
the same image from glory to glory." As we behold the glory of the
Lord we become transformed. This very basic principle is foundational
to Paul's theology of heart transformation, and it's what made David
a man after God's own heart. Simply stated, whatever we behold or
understand about God's heart toward us—that's what we become in
our hearts toward God. If we behold a mean and stingy God, we will
become mean and stingy. But if we behold His glory, as Paul wrote, the
Holy Spirit transforms us into something glorious. David was a student, a Rhodes scholar, a PhD of God's emotions. He was so consumed
by this high endeavor that he made it his primary preoccupation "all
the days of [his] life" (Ps. 27:4). As a result, he had more insight into
the things that burn in God's heart than any other man in the Old
Testament. He became different.

PRAYER STARTER

*Lord, I want to gaze unafraid into Your passionate heart and experience
Your transformation from glory to glory. All I want is to be more like You!*

DAVID CREATED HIS OWN CATEGORY OF INTIMACY WITH
GOD BECAUSE HE DARED TO GAZE, UNAFRAID, AT THE
PASSIONATE HEART OF GOD.

DAY 210

Let the morning bring me word of your unfailing love,
for I have put my trust in you.
Show me the way I should go,
for to you I lift up my soul.
—*Psalm 143:8*

Gazing at the heart of God is what made David a man after God's heart. That's what brought intimacy with God—intimacy that captivated him his entire life. Beholding and becoming does the same for us. By pressing into God's heart through study and a personal pursuit of our relationship with Him, we become men and women after His heart. We experience what David experienced when he gazed upon the almost indescribable heart of God. I'm convinced that if we beheld what David beheld about God, we would live as he lived, and we would carry our hearts before God as he did. We would become different as a result. Without even thinking about it much, we would follow in the footsteps of this ancient, yet very modern, king. You see, David was no superman. The things he beheld in God's heart are still there, available to you and me as they have been available throughout history for men and women who cared to pursue Him with all their might.

PRAYER STARTER

When I read the story of David, at times I feel inadequate to experience friendship with You as David experienced it. But that is the yearning of my heart. Let me be a person who lives in intimacy with You.

GOD INVITES YOU AND ME, RIGHT NOW, TO BEHOLD THE VERY THINGS DAVID DID.

DAY 211

I will sing of the LORD's great love forever;
with my mouth I will make your faithfulness known
through all generations.
I will declare that your love stands firm forever,
that you established your faithfulness in heaven itself.
—*Psalm 89:1–2*

When we begin to understand God's emotions for us, a corresponding emotion is quickened in our hearts. For example, when we behold the passion in God's heart for us, our own hearts start to feel passion toward Him. We enjoy Jesus—why? Because we finally "get" that He enjoys us. We pursue Jesus because we grasp that He is pursuing us. The point is that our gazing into the emotions of God transforms us from the inside out. If you want to become a fiery lover of God, then you must understand God as the fiery lover of all the ages. The secret to having more love—or peace or joy or faith or any fruit of the Spirit—is enjoying God more. Wow! What a revelation! Trying harder will get you nowhere.

PRAYER STARTER

God, I finally "get" it—You are pursuing me, You are seeking ways to bring me into a relationship with You. Here I am, Lord; overtake me and overwhelm me with Your glory.

WE ARE COMMITTED AND DEDICATED TO JESUS BECAUSE IT HITS US THAT HE IS COMMITTED AND DEDICATED TO US.

DAY 212

> He who dwells in the shelter of the Most High will rest in the
> shadow of the Almighty. I will say of the LORD, "He is my refuge
> and my fortress, my God, in whom I trust."
> —*Psalm 91:1–2*

Churches are full of people who spend Monday through Saturday
trying harder in their walk with the Lord. They wake up early so
they can read through the Bible in a year; they make promises to
themselves to invite a neighbor to church or pray for the ailing child
a few doors down. They try to show the light of Christ at work and
hold their tongues when angered by their spouse. Then on Sunday
they cringe in the pew during worship and feel somehow that they've
spent another week failing to be a good Christian. But if you experience God's enjoyment of you, then you will begin enjoying God, and
this whole cycle changes. Transformation happens as naturally as the
changing of seasons. You will live in much greater holiness, and you
will be truly happy. You won't be so concerned about not doing bad
things because your heart will find no pleasure in them anyway. This
process of transformation never ends. We will be always gazing, always
discovering, always changing, always enjoying, always reflecting more
of His glory and passion.

PRAYER STARTER

> *Day by day You are changing me into Your likeness, Jesus. The things
> that used to hinder me no longer appeal to me. The wonder of Your presence
> is all I want. Let me reflect Your glory and passion.*

**WE ENJOY GOD MORE BY SEARCHING OUT AND CONVINCING
OURSELVES OF GOD'S ENJOYMENT OF US.**

DAY 213

Put to death, therefore, whatever belongs to your earthly
nature.... You used to walk in these ways, in the life you once lived.
But now you must rid yourselves of all such things as these: anger,
rage, malice, slander, and filthy language from your lips. Do not lie
to each other, since you have taken off your old self with its practices
and have put on the new self, which is being renewed
in knowledge in the image of its Creator.
—*Colossians 3:5, 7–10*

Paul taught the Colossian believers to seek renewal by receiving knowledge
of the image of God. Spiritual renewal and that durable transformation
of the mind we all seek will only happen through the knowledge of God's
heart bursting into our own hearts. That only happens when we come
into contact with God and the truth about God in His Word. Nothing
holds greater power to transform your inner life than that moment when
God's voice touches your spirit with personal revelation of who He is, who
you are in light of that, and what He would have you do. It might be nothing more (and nothing less) than the revelation that He really enjoys being
with you. That alone can change your life, if you make it a foundation of
your walk with God. When you witness that, you are transformed—you
behold and become. Such an experience can never be neutral. It awakens
you to who you are, who He is, and who you will be.

PRAYER STARTER

*What You think about me, the way You feel about me, is all that
matters to me, Father. All else seems far away when I behold Your awesome
beauty and discover Your marvelous love for me.*

**WHAT GOD THINKS AND FEELS ABOUT YOU IS WORTH FAR
MORE THAN THE BEST ADVICE FROM THE MOST IMPORTANT
PEOPLE IN YOUR LIFE.**

DAY 214

Though you have not seen him, you love him; and even though
you do not see him now, you believe in him and are filled with an
inexpressible and glorious joy, for you are receiving the goal of your
faith, the salvation of your souls.
—1 Peter 1:8–9

You may have discovered in this life that you don't have the power to
change your emotions directly. You can't say, "Joy!" and elicit joy from
your soul. You can't demand, "Gladness, rise up within me now!" It
will never happen. You might get a jolt of adrenaline, but long-lasting
emotions are not awakened by determination. That's God's part of the
division of labor, and it's a supernatural work of the Spirit in us. But
here's the good news: all our emotions are linked to thoughts or ideas.
Correct thoughts about God bring wonderful emotions. This is why
the truth sets us free (John 8:32). You can indirectly change your emotions by flooding your thoughts with the truth about God.

PRAYER STARTER

*I choose to think about Your truth, O God. I choose to harness my
mind and focus it on Your grace and goodness to me. Complete Your work in
me through Your Holy Spirit.*

**BEHOLDING GOD'S EMOTIONS IS SOMETHING ONLY YOU CAN
DO IN YOUR OWN SECRET LIFE IN GOD.**

DAY 215

Therefore, I urge you, brothers, in view of God's mercy, to offer your bodies as living sacrifices, holy and pleasing to God—this is your spiritual act of worship. Do not conform any longer to the pattern of this world, but be transformed by the renewing of your mind. Then you will be able to test and approve what God's will is—his good, pleasing and perfect will.
—*Romans 12:1–2*

In the early days of my Christian life, my friends and I read Romans 12:2 in the negative sense. We thought it meant, "You will be transformed mostly by staying away from sinful movies," and we had a whole list of bad things to stay away from so that we would end up transformed. But there is much more to this principle than clamping down on ourselves and staying away from bad things. Your mind is not renewed primarily by staying away from bad things but by filling your mind with the truth about God. You don't need better sin-avoidance techniques but a new vision of what God's heart looks like. Flowing from that vision will be a new vision of what you look like to God. When I fill my mind with what God's emotions look like, I experience new dimensions of grace to stay away from the "bad things."

PRAYER STARTER

Give me a vision of Your heart, O God, and the things of this world that used to defeat me and cause me to sin will no longer have any appeal to me. Flood over my heart and mind with Your presence.

YOU DON'T NEED BETTER SIN-AVOIDANCE TECHNIQUES BUT A NEW VISION OF WHAT GOD'S HEART LOOKS LIKE.

DAY 216

And we, who with unveiled faces all reflect the Lord's glory,
are being transformed into his likeness with ever-increasing glory,
which comes from the Lord, who is the Spirit.
—*2 Corinthians 3:18*

Transformation will not happen simply by hearing a teaching or reading a book. It has to be more than a sermon, more than a class you attend, and more than a video series you watch. You will not find the fire of love for Him by only hearing teachings that exhort you to be a fiery lover. Exhortation to action does not equip your heart to carry out that action. Have you noticed that? Exhortations to "love harder" never awaken love in your heart. A good teaching or book will arouse spiritual desire and give you the vision to go find the food for yourself. It makes you say, "I want it!" But hunger and vision are all books and sermons can offer. In and of themselves, books and sermons will never equip your heart to actually love. That change requires a lifestyle of being in the Word. If you want passion or love for God, then fill your time and your mind with the revelation of God's passion and love for you.

PRAYER STARTER

More and more I long to spend time in Your presence and to behold the beauty of Your being. Develop in me a lifestyle of studying Your Word and spending time in Your presence.

BECOMING IS GOOD, BUT GOD'S SEQUENCE SAYS WE MUST FIRST BEHOLD THE REALITY WITHIN HIS HEART.

DAY 217

May the God of hope fill you with all joy and peace as
you trust in him, so that you may overflow with hope by
the power of the Holy Spirit.
—*Romans 15:13*

Beloved, I tell you, studying the heart of God is absolutely crucial if we are to have healthy families and careers. The most practical thing you can do to take care of your family or business is to cultivate an over-flowing heart. As you regularly behold the happy God in the Word, you will be progressively filled with happiness. You will take care of your family far better than if you were grouchy. Have you noticed that the blessing is much smaller for the people around you when you go about your God-ordained responsibilities with a spirit of depression, heaviness, anger, and bitterness? But if you invest time in understanding the happiness of God's heart for you, your heart is gloriously awakened. You become powerful and effective in your duties in the kingdom of God and in all aspects of life. Don't buy the argument that spending time on this is not realistic or practical. In truth, there is nothing more practical we can do.

PRAYER STARTER

Remove any spirits of depression, heaviness, anger, and bitterness from my heart. I do not want them there. I want to experience Your abundant joy and have a heart that is filled with happiness and power.

GRUMPY, DUTY-BOUND SERVICE IS BETTER THAN NOTHING,
BUT IT IS NOT GOD'S BEST WAY.

DAY 218

Who is wise? He will realize these things.
Who is discerning? He will understand them.
The ways of the LORD are right;
the righteous walk in them,
but the rebellious stumble in them.
—*Hosea 14:9*

If there is even one area of rebellion against God in your life, then your heart won't flow in the way God promises. Declare war on any area of compromise in your life. You may stumble in that area, but if you are sincerely warring against it, you will still gain ground. After all, the flowing heart is what empowers you to get free from besetting sin. God doesn't require that you be free from all struggles before He releases His power in your heart. Just the opposite; the power of God helps you get free. It is the wisdom of God and the will of God that we obey Him when we don't feel like it. I believe in obedience when I don't feel like obeying. When I'm depressed and feeling horrible, I still need to obey God. However, I obey a lot more and with greater strength when my emotions are touched by the revelation of God's emotions. Lovers have always made better workers. When desire and enjoyment, even in their beginning stages, are in place, obedience seems like the only reasonable option.

PRAYER STARTER

Father, reveal any hidden rebellion in my heart. Touch my emotions with a revelation of Your emotions so that I can follow You in obedience and joy.

DISCIPLINE, WORK, AND EFFORT FOLLOW MUCH EASIER AFTER YOU HAVE TOUCHED AT LEAST THE BEGINNINGS OF ENJOYMENT.

DAY 219

The fruit of righteousness will be peace; the effect of
righteousness will be quietness and confidence forever. My people
will live in peaceful dwelling places, in secure homes,
in undisturbed places of rest.
—*Isaiah 32:17–18*

You must cultivate confidence in God's affection toward you even when you stumble. If you lack this confidence, then you close your spirit toward Jesus. The revelation that God enjoys you in your weakness transforms you. In my experience, this is the hardest revelation for people to enter into and the place on the spiritual journey where most people stall and stop. The reason? You will never enjoy God more than your revelation of God enjoying you in your weakness. But when you do see that He enjoys you in weakness, then you bear fruit. You begin to enjoy God all the time. Your heart responds in affection. You hear the Godhead, the Three in One, say, "We like you." Your heart answers, "I like You, then." Who doesn't enjoy being with people who like him? So when you understand that God likes you all the time, you respond by liking Him. You start smiling just thinking about God. It happens automatically.

PRAYER STARTER

I rest in the fact that You like me, Lord. You want to spend time with me, and You enjoy me just as I am. What an incredible thought, dear Lord, and it fills me with confidence in Your love for me.

YOU WILL NEVER ENJOY GOD MORE THAN YOU EXPERIENCE HIS ENJOYMENT OF YOU IN YOUR WEAKNESS.

DAY 220

I have set the LORD always before me.
Because he is at my right hand,
I will not be shaken.
Therefore my heart is glad and my tongue rejoices;
my body also will rest secure.
—*Psalm 16:8–9*

When you know that God enjoys you, then another miraculous thing happens: you begin to enjoy yourself. You begin to like you. You prefer to be yourself over any other person on Earth. This is a revolutionary change for most people. A woman prayed earnestly, "Lord, I want to love my neighbor as I love myself." The Lord surprised her with His answer: "That's the problem—you do. You despise yourself; therefore, you despise your neighbor." God wants you to inhabit the place of personal enjoyment and satisfaction. It's a position where, in the secrecy of your own heart, you would rather be who you are than anybody else. That gives you incredible confidence and desire to enjoy and love others. Fireworks go off inside you; streams of life touch your being. There's nothing like waking up in your own skin and thinking, "I'm glad I am who I am. Thank You, Lord!"

PRAYER STARTER

Yes, God, because You love me just as I am, I am glad that You created me to be me. I like being loved by You, and Your love prepares me to love You in return.

IT IS GOD'S WILL THAT YOU WOULD COME TO THE
TRANSFORMING SUMMIT OF SELF-ACCEPTANCE
ON YOUR JOURNEY.

DAY 221

If you spend yourselves in behalf of the hungry
and satisfy the needs of the oppressed,
then your light will rise in the darkness,
and your night will become like the noonday.
The LORD will guide you always;
he will satisfy your needs in a sun-scorched land
and will strengthen your frame.
You will be like a well-watered garden,
like a spring whose waters never fail.
—Isaiah 58:10–11

The prophet Isaiah said that if we extend our souls for others, then our hearts would be like a well-watered garden. Some of God's people carefully guard their lives from all inconvenience and only contribute as long as their comfort zone isn't disturbed. But we must give ourselves away to God's people as servants of God's purpose. Jesus said the greatest among us would be the servant of all. We can't gaze into the heart of God and retain a "me first" attitude.

PRAYER STARTER

Others, Lord, others. Let me reach out with Your love to others. Let me tell them of the miracle of salvation through Your sacrifice on Calvary. Make me a soulwinner, Lord. Let me share in the harvest of souls before You return.

WE BECOME DEVOTED TO THE THINGS AND PEOPLE HE IS DEVOTED TO.

DAY 222

You will again obey the LORD and follow all his commands
I am giving you today. Then the LORD your God will make you most
prosperous in all the work of your hands and in the fruit of your
womb, the young of your livestock and the crops of your land. The
LORD will again delight in you and make you prosperous, just as
he delighted in your fathers.

—*Deuteronomy 30:8–9*

Here's a question: How does God feel most of the time? Is He bored?
Worried? Blasé? Happy? Concerned? Detached? Engaged? Mad, glad,
or sad? It sounds lighthearted, but it's one of the most important
questions of our entire spiritual journey. How does God feel when He
looks at you? I have asked many people this question over the years,
and they usually respond in one of two ways: God is mostly mad, or
God is mostly sad. And in both cases, they think it's their fault. Many
Christians believe very strongly that God is angry and grieved with
each of us. It's one of those under-the-surface, sinister opinions everybody holds but nobody talks about. God is viewed as distant, angry,
sitting on the throne, and spending the bulk of His emotional energy
being disappointed in mankind. We picture a weeping God who beats
His breast and turns His eyes away from us in shame. But Scripture
tells us the very opposite. Our God smiles and rejoices. His emotions
fall into a third category: God is mostly glad.

PRAYER STARTER

*Father, You have revealed to me that when You look at me I make You
glad. Let me see Your smile of approval and hear You rejoicing over me. It
fills my heart with love for You and overwhelms my soul.*

**GOD WILL REVEAL HIMSELF TO US AS THE GLAD GOD WHO
OVERFLOWS WITH DELIGHT AND ENJOYMENT.**

DAY 223

For the LORD takes pleasure in His people;
He will beautify the humble with salvation.
—*Psalm 149:4, NKJV*

If at the center of your theology is a God who smiles, then it is not hard to understand this next truth about Him: He is smiling at you as you respond to Him in willing obedience. His infinite smile extends over His creation. He is delighted in Himself and in the overflow of that delight, but He especially enjoys humans who respond to the grace He offered freely in Christ Jesus. This applies to each of us individually and uniquely. God has affection and enjoyment for you even at your weakest point. He actually enjoys you! What a powerful concept! Not only does He smile, but He also smiles when He looks at you!

PRAYER STARTER

Your smile warms my heart and thrills my soul. It is beyond my comprehension that You could smile about me, but I know You do, and I will focus on that smile as long as I live.

**THIS MUST BE THE FOUNDATION OF OUR THEOLOGY:
OUR GOD IS A GOD WHO SMILES.**

DAY 224

I was filled with delight day after day,
rejoicing always in his presence,
rejoicing in his whole world
and delighting in mankind.
—*Proverbs 8:30–31*

Jesus describes Himself as One rejoicing in the inhabited world and experiencing delight in the sons of men. Though His delight in us is so clearly stated in Scripture, we find ourselves like the prodigal son who was confused by his father's overwhelming delight: we stand at a distance, not knowing how to receive it. It's more logical and comfortable for us to bring our list of failures and then plead for a low position in His kingdom. Yet instead of negotiating with us, He embraces us with unabashed affection and covers us with the royal robe of righteousness. This is the God we serve. This is who He is regardless of what we do.

PRAYER STARTER

Just as You did for the prodigal son, O Lord, You cover me with Your robe of righteousness. You throw a party in my honor, and You welcome me into Your presence.

HE CELEBRATES YOU OR ME AS HIS CHILD AND THROWS A PARTY IN OUR HONOR.

DAY 225

Therefore my heart is glad and my tongue rejoices;
my body also will rest secure,
because you will not abandon me to the grave,
nor will you let your Holy One see decay.
You have made known to me the path of life;
you will fill me with joy in your presence,
with eternal pleasures at your right hand.
—*Psalm 16:9–11*

David had this incredible revelation that the atmosphere around the throne of God was full of gladness. Around the throne of God is an atmosphere saturated with gladness and rejoicing. The closer you get to the person of God, the more gladness you experience. King David, the great theologian of the pleasure of God, described this joyful environment around God's throne in one of his songs: "Honor and majesty are before Him; strength and gladness are in His place" (I Chron. 16:27, NKJV). He testified first of God's majesty and power and then of the gladness that surrounds the throne. In His presence is fullness of joy. Happiness prevails everywhere in heaven. Jesus referred to this joy as being His at Creation (Prov. 8:30). The One seated on the throne is glad, and all those that stand near Him are swept up in joyful contagion of His gladness.

PRAYER STARTER

I can only imagine the joy around Your throne in heaven. Your happiness is contagious, and even the angels explode in joyous song when one of Your children accepts the gift of salvation. I can't wait to share that atmosphere of joy with You.

**THE CLOSER WE GET TO HIS THRONE IN HEAVEN,
THE HAPPIER WE BECOME.**

DAY 226

Where were you when I laid the earth's foundation? Tell me, if you understand. Who marked off its dimensions? Surely you know! Who stretched a measuring line across it? On what were its footings set, or who laid its cornerstone—while the morning stars sang together and all the angels shouted for joy?

—Job 38:4–7

Job said that when God was creating the world, the angels, "the sons of God" (NKJV), were filled with happiness as they sang. They were over-the-top exhilarated. God even created angels with a capacity for happiness—a phenomenal reality! I see Jesus smiling and asking, "Well, Father, what kind of servants should We create for My bride?" The Father replies, "Happy servants." So God placed the capacity for happiness in their very design. In Luke 2, these very angels appeared in the heavens to tell people that God had supplied a remedy—a Savior—to bring us back into fellowship with Him. The choirs of heaven and the angels appeared and were almost unable to contain their glee. They sang it loud and long, "Hosanna! Glory to God in the highest!" They trumpeted the good news that God was removing the barriers so people could come into one-heart fellowship with Him. This wasn't a one-time celebration but a lifestyle of heaven being revealed for a moment to citizens of Earth.

PRAYER STARTER

How I would have loved to have heard the angel choir singing, "Hosanna! Glory to God in the highest!" on the night of Your Son's birth. And someday I shall join with the angelic host as we celebrate eternity with You.

IN MY IMAGINATION I CAN SEE THE FATHER LOOKING AT THE SON WITH A BIG GRIN AS THEY PLANNED CREATION.

DAY 227

And the twenty-four elders, who were seated on their thrones
before God, fell on their faces and worshiped God, saying:
"We give thanks to you, Lord God Almighty,
the One who is and who was,
because you have taken your great power
and have begun to reign."
—*Revelation 11:16–17*

What kind of God would put happiness at the very core of the servants
of the house? Only a God who is happy Himself. If God were always
angry, surely His servants would always be angry. If God were vengeful,
surely His servants would be a vengeful army, not a singing choir that
suddenly appears in the heavens. Angels have happy hearts because God
has a happy heart. And the angels aren't the only ones. In my mind's eye
I can see the elders who sit before Him falling down to worship as they
are caught up in awe with gladness before God's throne. I imagine that
one day I'll get to approach one of them and inquire, "Excuse me, I know
you are worshiping, but I want to know one thing: how are you feeling?"
I imagine he will rise and respond, "The closer we get to the throne, the
more joy we feel! It's fantastic! I can't get enough." The angels in His presence are full of joy. The elders are overcome with bliss. Jesus, at the right
hand of the Father, brims and overflows with happiness. The Father
loves His kingdom, His angels, and His people! He is a happy God!

PRAYER STARTER

*In Your presence is joy forevermore. I can only imagine the excitement
and bliss that surround Your throne. What a glorious environment to look
forward to as I anticipate eternity in heaven.*

IN GOD'S PRESENCE, AROUND HIS THRONE IS THE FULLNESS
OF JOY, AND ONE DAY WE WILL WITNESS IT FOR OURSELVES!

DAY 228

Both high and low among men
find refuge in the shadow of your wings.
They feast on the abundance of your house;
you give them drink from your river of delights.
For with you is the fountain of life;
in your light we see light.
—*Psalm 36:7–9*

Wonder of wonders—God calls us to partake of this joy. In Psalm 36:8, David says to God the Father, "You give them drink from the river of Your pleasures" (NKJV). By giving us drink, David means God shares the pleasure of His Being with us. There is simply no greater pleasure than when God reveals Himself to the human spirit. It happens now on Earth to a certain degree for those of us who are His children, and it will happen in heaven in exponentially greater measure. When we see Him face-to-face we will voluntarily rejoice.

PRAYER STARTER

God, I don't know what my heavenly body will look like, but I know I'll need a lot of smile muscles. Prepare me to rejoice forevermore.

SMILING IN HEAVEN IS NOT REQUIRED—IT'S INEVITABLE.

DAY 229

Because you did not serve the Lord your God with joy
and gladness of heart, for the abundance of everything,
therefore you shall serve your enemies.
—*Deuteronomy 28:47–48, NKJV*

This doctrine of God's gladness isn't a theological curiosity meant to entertain us. It is foundational to helping our hearts grow into spiritual maturity. When we enter into God's joy and gladness, the door to much of Satan's activity slams shut in our lives. The joy of serving God keeps us from compromise. A glad heart is a strong heart. The Bible says the joy of the Lord is our strength (Neh. 8:10). And don't get the wrong idea about the above verse from Deuteronomy. God is not acting out of spite. He's not pouting and saying, "I was glad, and you would not enter into My gladness, so forget it. You're going to serve your enemies. Now you're really going to hurt." Rather, He is laying out the only two options that exist. Either we enter into His gladness with whole hearts, or we will eventually come under the influence of the enemy, giving in to his accusations, becoming offended at God.

PRAYER STARTER

Lord, that's exactly what I want. I want You to realign my heart, transform my spirit, and strengthen, mature, and renew my life. I will not give way to the enemy, but I will accept the joy of the Lord as my strength.

GOD WOULD HAVE US EXPERIENCE HIS HAPPY HEART
SO OUR HEARTS MIGHT BE REALIGNED, TRANSFORMED,
STRENGTHENED, MATURED, AND RENEWED.

DAY 230

Therefore judge nothing before the appointed time; wait till the
Lord comes. He will bring to light what is hidden in darkness and
will expose the motives of men's hearts. At that time
each will receive his praise from God.
—*1 Corinthians 4:5*

Paul described this aspect of God: the glad-hearted Judge. Paul was
addressing the Corinthians, the most carnal church we know of in the
first century. Only the Laodiceans in the next generation rivaled them
in carnality. Paul exhorted the Corinthians, "Do not judge anything
before the time when the Lord comes." In other words, "Don't make
final evaluations toward people or even yourselves." He distrusted his
inability to accurately judge even his own heart. Then he dropped a
bomb by telling the Corinthians that God will someday reveal the
things hidden in darkness and in the secret counsels of their hearts.
You can almost hear the gasp: "Oh no! We're in for some big-time
punishment." Yet they had not heard Paul's full message. In the next
sentence he zigged when they thought he was going to zag.

PRAYER STARTER

*How amazing that when I stand before You in judgment You will
reveal the hidden things of my heart. It's amazing because Your Word tells me
that You will rejoice over me with gladness, not punish me in anger.*

**WHEN GOD JUDGES US, HE DOESN'T FUME WITH
FRUSTRATION AND ANGER.**

DAY 231

Therefore judge nothing before the time, until the Lord comes,
who will both bring to light the hidden things of darkness and
reveal the counsels of the hearts. Then each one's praise
will come from God.
—1 Corinthians 4:5, NKJV

When we think about God revealing the dark things and the hidden counsels of our hearts, we think rebuke and immediately recoil. "Oh no, not the hidden counsels!" we say, assuming that hidden things are dark and ungodly. But God says the opposite. Hidden within our hearts are not just shameful things but many good things, like the deep cry to be totally God's. Deep inside we fight to be fully His against all opposition of the enemy. Only God fully perceives the depth of this longing of our heart. And the good news is that on the last day He will reveal it and give us praise for it. The yes in our spirit is an imperfect yes, but it is a yes. It is the very work of God Himself in us. It is His supernatural activity in our inner man. He perceives our willing spirit in the struggle. While we may define ourselves by our failures, God defines us through His grace and by the sincere movements of our hearts, which we may not even fully understand.

PRAYER STARTER

I am defined by Your awesome grace, dear Jesus. You see the deep cry of my heart to be like You, and You will someday praise me for it. Thank You for Your grace and mercy to me.

**GOD IS PLEASED WITH THE LONGINGS OF SINCERE
BELIEVERS TO BE FULLY HIS.**

DAY 232

Suppose a woman has ten silver coins and loses one. Does she not light a lamp, sweep the house and search carefully until she finds it? And when she finds it, she calls her friends and neighbors together and says, "Rejoice with me; I have found my lost coin." In the same way, I tell you, there is rejoicing in the presence of the angels of God over one sinner who repents.

—*Luke 15:8–10*

In Luke 15, Jesus addressed angry Pharisees who were miffed at Him for eating with and fellowshiping with sinners. In reply, Jesus said His Father rejoiced and the angels that did His bidding were glad; therefore, we ought to be glad. Over and over in this chapter Jesus revealed the joyous atmosphere around the throne. In verse 10, He said, "I say to you, there is joy in the presence of the angels of God over one sinner who repents" (NKJV). He was speaking of the repenting sinner who is still very immature. If the sinner repents at 3:00 p.m., the angels are singing and rejoicing by 3:01 p.m. That sinner is still profoundly immature in his faith, but the angels are abundantly glad. His repentance is absolutely sincere though his maturity is nonexistent. The yes in his spirit is imperfect, but it is eternally significant.

PRAYER STARTER

Give me Your understanding in regards to the immaturity and insincerity I see in others—and in myself at times. Let me look at others through Your eyes and see the potential for spiritual maturity and genuine love.

LOVE IS SINCERE AND GENUINE MANY YEARS BEFORE IT BECOMES MATURE AND STRONG.

DAY 233

> My son, do not despise the LORD's discipline
> and do not resent his rebuke,
> because the LORD disciplines those he loves,
> as a father the son he delights in.
> —*Proverbs 3:11–12*

God does not say to the sinner, "You have sincerely repented, but look at all these unsettled issues in your life. We will see how you do. Come on in, I guess, but We will be keeping a close eye on you." We think God is this way because we ourselves are this way. People clap with excitement the day a man gets saved and testifies of his desire to leave his old ways and follow the Lord. They cheer and shout, "Praise the Lord! It's real! It counts!" But within a few months, the same crowd is ready to censure him for issues of immaturity they see in his life. Within days their theology changes, and they no longer delight over his growing faith. They turn into grumpy Pharisees, saying, "Bah humbug! Get it right. We're keeping our eye on you now." The Lord says the opposite: "I delight in you when you have zero maturity." If His gladness were based on our performance, He would be a sad God indeed!

PRAYER STARTER

> Father, how grateful I am that You delight in me regardless of my immaturity. You love me while You gently lead me into spiritual maturity. Help me to love others in their immaturity and to encourage them to grow instead of discouraging them with my criticism.

REMEMBER, GOD CAN ENJOY YOU EVEN WHILE DISAPPROVING OF AN AREA OF SIN IN YOUR LIFE.

DAY 234

The older brother became angry and refused to go in.... "My son,"
the father said, "you are always with me, and everything I have is yours.
But we had to celebrate and be glad, because this brother of yours was
dead and is alive again; he was lost and is found."

—*Luke 15:28, 32*

Our own patience is so insufficient. We spot one thing we disapprove
of in another believer's life, and then we struggle to enjoy him. Why?
Because we secretly believe that God does that to us. This is not the
heart of God. When the Lord finds something about our character that
bothers Him, He doesn't cut us out of His heart. Rather, He is filled
with patience and is slow to anger. Luke 15 is often called the parable
of the prodigal son, but it's primarily about a father who lost his son
and what he did when his son returned. Jesus was teaching His church
how to respond to those brothers or sisters who stumble. We all know
what to do when a new convert comes into the kingdom. We rejoice and
throw a party. Yet we don't easily enter into God's gladness when one
of our brothers stumbles or, far worse, when we ourselves stumble. And
yet our ability to enter into God's patience and loving-kindness when we
stumble is determined by how much patience and loving-kindness we
have toward a brother or sister who stumbles.

PRAYER STARTER

Holy Spirit, empower me to exhibit Your patient love toward a fellow
believer who has stumbled. Give me the courage to stand alongside and encourage and strengthen that person through Your love and power.

GOD DOES NOT REJECT US WHEN SOMETHING AWFUL IN
OUR CHARACTER COMES TO LIGHT.

DAY 235

After this I heard what sounded like the roar of a great multitude in heaven shouting.... The twenty-four elders and the four living creatures fell down and worshiped God, who was seated on the throne.... Then I heard what sounded like a great multitude, like the roar of rushing waters and like loud peals of thunder.... Then the angel said to me, "Write: 'Blessed are those who are invited to the wedding supper of the Lamb!'"
—*Revelation 19:1, 4, 6, 9*

I often wonder what Jesus was thinking the days before His crucifixion. How did He stay focused? What was on His mind? What mattered to Him in those moments? The Bible answers this for us in part. When Jesus came into Jerusalem for the last time, He carried a message in His heart. I believe He had waited three and one-half years to share this message. It was one of the deepest things on His heart. The essence of His last public sermon was, "There is a King—My Father—who is preparing a wedding for His Son." (See Matthew 22:2.) His heart was caught up in that glorious future day, the great bridal feast. Emotion must have surged in His heart as He opened the treasury of this parable to the crowds. He was revealing one of the primary reasons for the cross, which would secure the inheritance His Father had promised Him—an equally yoked companion, a bride.

PRAYER STARTER

It is beyond my comprehension, dear Lord, that You chose me to be Your bride, to be Your eternal companion, and to share Your glory in heaven. Prepare me for that great wedding day, I pray.

JESUS LOOKED TOWARD ONE OF THE GREATEST EVENTS OF ALL HISTORY: THE WEDDING SUPPER OF THE LAMB.

DAY 236

Go forth, O daughters of Zion, and see [the King]…on the day
of his wedding, the day of the gladness of his heart.
—*Song of Solomon 3:11, NKJV*

What Jesus accomplished on the cross is exceedingly powerful. But why
He did what He did is just as stunning. What motivation beat in His
heart as He endured the cross? What burned in His emotions? What
was the divine logic behind the event? Simply put, He longed to be
united with His bride. He burned with desire for human beings. Any
bridegroom who plans a wedding knows the feeling. The Bible even
gives us a glimpse into the gladness of Jesus's heart on His wedding day
in the Song of Solomon. This natural love song depicting the beauty of
married love is an excellent picture of the spiritual love between Jesus
and His church. The cross was motivated by a God who had great gladness about His wedding day. The cross became a reality because, from
before the beginning of time, He desired to marry us.

PRAYER STARTER

*Jesus, it amazes me that while You hung in agony on the cross of shame
to redeem me for Your own, You were anticipating that great coming day when
You will return from heaven and claim Your bride for eternity. How I love
You for Your inexplicable love for me.*

**THE PLAN OF REDEMPTION FLOWS FROM A GOD WHO
EAGERLY ANTICIPATES THE INTIMACY HE WILL HAVE WITH
HIS PEOPLE FOR ETERNITY.**

DAY 237

Jesus, full of joy through the Holy Spirit, said, "I praise you, Father, Lord of heaven and earth, because you have hidden these things from the wise and learned, and revealed them to little children. Yes, Father, for this was your good pleasure."
—*Luke 10:21*

Imagine, if you can, what it was like when Jesus entered a village of Israel during His earthly ministry. I see the kids making a beeline to Him, invited by His smile and His eyes alive with pleasure. They adored the carpenter from Nazareth, the new preacher in town. You can't fool kids. If you are mean, they avoid you, even if you try to act nice. Jesus wanted those kids around Him. They bypassed the sacred boundary lines and ran straight into His embrace. What I would give to see the Son of God overflowing with happiness and delight like that! How great is His joy when immature people receive revelation.

PRAYER STARTER

Lord, I can only imagine the wonderful joy and anticipation little children felt as they watched You come into their midst. They crowded around you and welcomed Your smile and gentle caress. Lord, I am also Your little child, and I long to bring a smile to Your face and feel Your gentle touch.

JESUS LOVES TO SHOCK HIS BABES WITH HOW GOOD HE WILL BE TO THEM!

DAY 238

Lift up your eyes and look about you:
All assemble and come to you;
your sons come from afar,
and your daughters are carried on the arm.
Then you will look and be radiant,
your heart will throb and swell with joy;
the wealth on the seas will be brought to you,
to you the riches of the nations will come.
—*Isaiah 60:4–5*

A great company of billions of believers will gather together on the sea of glass for the long-awaited wedding day. It's significant that human history ends with the marriage supper of the Lamb, one of the very few corporate responses of the church to Jesus described in the Word of God. On that last day we will have fully understood Jesus's leadership over history. His perfect leadership will have produced a bride that says with a glad tongue, "Rejoice and be glad, for the marriage of the Lamb has come!" We will rejoice with absolute gladness. We will erupt with joy. Under the leadership of Jesus, the human heart always erupts with joy. This is His desire for us even on this side of eternity.

PRAYER STARTER

Father, Your Word teaches me that the wedding day of Your Son and His bride will be a glorious celebration beyond my human comprehension. My heart is filled with longing and anticipation, and I'm overwhelmed with love for my Bridegroom, Your precious Son.

WHEN JESUS HAS HIS WAY, HE MAKES HEARTS GLAD.

DAY 239

To him who is able to keep you from falling and to present you before his glorious presence without fault and with great joy—to the only God our Savior be glory, majesty, power and authority, through Jesus Christ our Lord, before all ages, now and forevermore! Amen.
—*Jude 24–25*

Can you believe this? Jesus has the ability and intention to present you with exceeding joy before the Father. On that final day I can imagine an angel greeting me and saying, "So, what do you think? It's Judgment Day. Any nerves?" I'll answer, "Nerves? Nah, I love being here!" How about you? Do you cringe when you think of that day? Do you fear that God will rebuke you publicly, before all the saints? What is your dominant emotion when you envision that day? If it is fear or dread, what does that say about your image of God? Have you fallen for lies of the devil and accepted a false view of a vindictive, unsmiling Savior? Or do you picture yourself running and embracing the Lord? Does your heart skip a beat with anticipation? Do you picture His goodness outweighing and outlasting His anger? Do you see the judgment as revealing the good motives of your heart, too?

PRAYER STARTER

My heart is filled with unspeakable joy as I think about the moment I will stand before You in heaven. I long to see Your smile of approval and see Your arms outstretched in welcome. Because of Your gift of righteousness I am ready, and I cannot wait!

DO YOU WISH YOU COULD FIND SOME BROOM CLOSET AND WAIT OUT THE JUDGMENT, COMING OUT WHEN THE DAY OF RECKONING HAS PASSED?

DAY 240

"For my thoughts are not your thoughts,
neither are your ways my ways,"
declares the LORD.
"As the heavens are higher than the earth,
so are my ways higher than your ways
and my thoughts than your thoughts."
—*Isaiah 55:8–9*

When God the Holy Spirit reveals the heart of God to the human spirit, it is the most exhilarating experience in this age and the age to come. It is the ultimate pleasure in created order. But that pleasure is not just for eternity; it's for this age as well. He gives us tokens of that pleasure now. He wants to motivate us, empower us, and protect us by letting us experience those pleasures as a down payment for what's coming. That strong pleasure turns to strong motivation. When the enemy comes to accuse God in my presence, I latch on to what I know to be true. I remind him, "It is written, 'His heart rejoices, His tongue is glad.' Even in my weakness, He is filled with joy when He looks at me." The enemy tries to tell me I'm a hopeless hypocrite, that Christianity is not working for me, and that I am uniquely messed up compared to everybody else. These are the same old lies he tells everybody. I respond with what is written in the Word about His rejoicing heart and His glad tongue. I speak these words of God against the attack of the enemy and fill my heart and mind with truth.

PRAYER STARTER

Father, when Satan tries to intimidate me with his lies and accusations, help me to remember Your love and to hear Your voice speaking words of love and truth. Give me courage to confront the enemy with Your love for me and to send him packing.

GOD IS THE AUTHOR OF REAL PLEASURE. IT SPRINGS FROM HIS VERY PERSONALITY.

DAY 241

Brothers, I do not consider myself yet to have taken hold of it.
But one thing I do: Forgetting what is behind and straining toward
what is ahead, I press on toward the goal to win the prize for which
God has called me heavenward in Christ Jesus.
—*Philippians 3:13–14*

For most of us, life presents dozens of options for career, lifestyle, passions, and hobbies. In our pursuit of pleasure and meaning we run here and there, trying one job or recreational activity after another, collecting experiences but never devoting ourselves to one direction. But today, the call of God to the church is to dismiss ourselves from chasing hither and thither and to cultivate a heart of unwavering devotion. He wants us to love Him, first and foremost, with all of our hearts. When your heart is conquered by the One who is fascinating, then no other captivation will satisfy. You will refuse to dwell anywhere but in this position of waiting on Him. You will pursue Him alone, not allowing yourself to be distracted by anything less. Your hunger will be fixed on a single source. There will be no going back to what used to bring satisfaction. Secondary pleasures will fade away.

PRAYER STARTER

Father, like Paul I want to run to the goal to win the prize of eternity with You. Keep me from getting sidetracked in the pursuit of anything but Your love, Your destiny for my life.

GOD WANTS US TO BE A PEOPLE OF ONE THING.

DAY 242

> Then three of the thirty chief men…came to David at the cave
> of Adullum….And David said with longing, "Oh, that someone
> would give me a drink of the water from the well of Bethlehem,
> which is by the gate!"
> —2 Samuel 23:13, 15, NKJV

The Bible gives this compelling illustration of extravagant devotion as a model for becoming people of one thing. David had been anointed king, but he was not king yet. Jealous King Saul was chasing him from cave to cave. About six hundred men joined David, and they made the cave of Adullum their main headquarters. It was probably late one night, and David was saying with longing, "Oh, that someone would give me a drink of the water from the well of Bethlehem!" Hearing David's longing, his mighty warriors said, "Let's go get him some of that water." They knew it might cost them their lives, but they loved David with extravagance, and it thrilled their hearts to answer his request. They went far beyond the call of duty to answer the longing in their king's heart. Of all the stories that could have been told of David and his men, this story became famous as one of the most extravagant acts of devotion toward the king. For us, this becomes a picture of devotion to King Jesus. It's a pattern for becoming people of one thing, with hearts after God's.

PRAYER STARTER

> *Jesus, the example of David's mighty men shows me the depth of loyalty and devotion I want to have for You. Let me love You with that level of extravagance and live my life in the pursuit of all that makes You pleased with me.*

DAVID'S MIGHTY MEN WERE A PICTURE OF THE PASSIONATE LOYALTY WE SHOULD HAVE TO CHRIST JESUS.

DAY 243

But what things were gain to me, these I have counted loss for Christ. Yet indeed I also count all things loss for the excellence of the knowledge of Christ Jesus my Lord, for whom I have suffered the loss of all things, and count them as rubbish, that I may gain Christ…that I may know Him and the power of His resurrection, and the fellowship of His sufferings, being conformed to His death.
—*Philippians 3:7–8, 10, NKJV*

Paul gave an autobiographical look at what motivated him. Without apology, Paul pointed us to the necessity of fierce abandonment for the sake of one thing. Paul was not saying that he suffered these things to earn Jesus's approval, but that in forsaking them, he removed what hindered his ability to experience Jesus to the fullest possible degree. He purposely narrowed his options. He willingly became a man of one thing. In verse 12, Paul revealed the inner activity of his soul: "I press on to take hold of that for which Christ Jesus took hold of me." The Lord Jesus laid hold of each one of us for a very specific reason. God had something in mind for you when you were born and when you were born again. Beloved, we will not accidentally lay hold of the highest things God has called us to. We must press into them, knowing that the devil will press back. We must lay hold of the prize, and the only way to accomplish that is by being individuals and churches of extravagant devotion to Jesus. No other kind of devotion will survive the onslaught of the enemy.

PRAYER STARTER

Lord, when my life draws to a close, may I be able, like Paul, to say I counted all things loss as I spent my life in learning how to know You more, to experience a greater intimacy with You, and to love You more.

PAUL ACTUALLY GLORIED IN THE PRIVILEGE OF HAVING INTIMACY WITH JESUS IN SUFFERING, WHICH IS A NECESSARY DIMENSION OF THE KINGDOM OF GOD.

DAY 244

Brothers, I do not consider myself yet to have taken hold of it.
But one thing I do: Forgetting what is behind and straining toward
what is ahead, I press on toward the goal to win the prize for which
God has called me heavenward in Christ Jesus.
—*Philippians 3:13–14*

Beloved, this prize will not automatically fall at our feet. There is a pressing in. We reach for the one thing, the exceedingly great reward. There is a forgetting of what came before, both success and failure. Part of our offering to the Lord is forgetting our dedication and personal sacrifice. Paul counted them as nothing. We do not stand before the Lord and calculate how much we have given Him in prayer, fasting, finances, and persecution. We forget all that because our glory is not found in anything we can give. We also should forget our accomplishments. God doesn't look at spiritual résumés. We should discount them, let them go. God will reckon them in proper balance when we get to heaven, but for us there is nothing so valuable as simply knowing God. For this reason we should also let our failures go. These can distract us more than our accomplishments. We want to be a people of one thing, forgetting what is behind and pressing to what is ahead. That's how we become men and women after God's own heart.

PRAYER STARTER

Father, I know I have a long way to go to reach the level of spiritual maturity You desire for me. Teach me to forget everything, to discount all my efforts, and to focus only on knowing You better.

> **OUR GLORY IS IN BEING LOVED BY HIM AND IN THE
> ANOINTING TO LOVE HIM. THAT ALONE GIVES US VALUE.**

DAY 245

Then he turned toward the woman and said to Simon, "Do you
see this woman? I came into your house. You did not give me any
water for my feet, but she wet my feet with her tears and wiped them
with her hair. You did not give me a kiss, but this woman, from the
time I entered, has not stopped kissing my feet. You did not put oil
on my head, but she has poured perfume on my feet. Therefore, I tell
you, her many sins have been forgiven—for she loved much. But he
who has been forgiven little loves little."

—*Luke 7:44–47*

Mary loved Jesus extravagantly. Knowing that He was about to give His
life—an extravagant gift unmatched in all history—she determined to
give all that she had as a suitable response (Mark 14:8). Her moment
came when all were gathered at Simon the leper's house for a supper prepared in Jesus's honor. Without warning and without a word, she rushed
into the room, broke open the precious bottle of perfume, and poured
it on Jesus's head. Her entire inheritance was gone in a moment. In our
day, the Holy Spirit is emphasizing the anointing that was upon Mary
of Bethany, which is the anointing to "waste" our lives on one thing:
extravagant devotion to Jesus Christ. It is the anointing to linger long
with an engaged spirit in the presence of the Lord. This is impossible
to do with religious self-determination and the power of the flesh. The
abandonment flows out of a lovesick heart.

PRAYER STARTER

*Father, when I am tempted to withhold myself from giving all to You,
or begin to criticize the extravagance of one of Your children, remind me of
Mary's loving devotion and her gift to Your Son. Make me like her, Father.*

THE LORD ESTABLISHED MARY'S LIFE AND THIS ONE
MOMENT AS A PICTURE OF GOD'S DELIGHT IN OUR
EXTRAVAGANT DEVOTION.

DAY 246

What is more, I consider everything a loss compared to the surpassing greatness of knowing Christ Jesus my Lord, for whose sake I have lost all things. I consider them rubbish, that I may gain Christ and be found in him, not having a righteousness of my own that comes from the law, but that which is through faith in Christ— the righteousness that comes from God and is by faith.
—Philippians 3:8–9

Mary of Bethany, the apostle Paul, and David's mighty men all found the secret of a focused life. They tapped into the glory and pleasure of giving themselves to one thing. God invites each of us to do the same and to give ourselves wholeheartedly to Him. We can stand with these so-called giants of the faith. The key to sustaining our intense desire to be fully given to God is to have fresh encounters with His heart. We must equip or train our hearts to actually walk out the wholehearted-ness that we so intensely desire. This equipping of the heart is best found in intimacy. Our intense desire to be radical for God will be sustained with regular experiences of God's heart—intimacy sustains intensity.

PRAYER STARTER

Give me a heart of extravagant devotion to You, like Mary. Let me count everything as loss in my pursuit of You, like Paul. Let me be a person after Your own heart, like David. Let me live in intimate fellowship with You, dear Lord.

WE CAN BE PEOPLE AFTER GOD'S OWN HEART!

DAY 247

I will surely gather the remnant of Israel...They shall make
a loud noise because of so many people. The one who breaks open
will come up before them; they will break out...with
the LORD at their head.
—*Micah 2:12–13, NKJV*

Micah prophesied about a future day when the Messiah would lead
Israel with such an anointing. In other words, He would help Israel
break out of the old way and break open new dimensions of the purpose of God. Jesus is the ultimate expression of the breaker anointing,
one who breaks open new dimensions of the Spirit for others to enter
into. It's high time to break free from the fear of being considered too
fanatical. Beloved, we are so easily enslaved by the opinions of people.
We shouldn't feel the need to apologize for our lifestyle in God. We
don't have to look respectable to other Christians. Many religious
paradigms we hold dear today will be shattered by the Lord Himself.
We should follow Him and embrace the breaker anointing He is giving to many of us. As we break out, God will use us to break open
new dimensions in the Holy Spirit to the spiritually stagnant Western
church. He will make the end-time church a dwelling place of God's
power. The Holy Spirit is raising up forerunners today who will break
out and break through because they are people of one thing, contending for the power of God and the fullness of the apostolic faith.

PRAYER STARTER

*Holy Spirit, anoint my life with a "breaker anointing." Let me break
through my fear of being considered too radical, too fanatical, too "heavenly
minded" in my pursuit of You. Let me be a forerunner for God.*

**WE NEED MEN AND WOMEN WHO HAVE A
"BREAKER ANOINTING."**

DAY 248

The LORD is gracious and righteous;
   our God is full of compassion.
The LORD protects the simplehearted;
   when I was in great need, he saved me.
Be at rest once more, O my soul,
   for the LORD has been good to you.
—*Psalm 116:5—7*

It was the Lord's idea to be gracious to us, not our own. He longs to be gracious far more than we long for Him to be. But that grace must establish His relationship with us, not undermine it. Therefore He will not release it in fullness until He hears the great cry of His people, signifying our readiness. Though He will release a certain administration of grace no matter what, He's looking forward to giving more than that introductory dimension of the kingdom of God. He convinces us of what is in His heart as we cry out to Him day after day. We do not earn anything by crying out. We cannot sing or shout and earn power. Rather, the Lord's plan is that when we lift our voices to Him, our hearts become receptive and connected to Him. When that happens, we enter a realm where God's blessing and grace actually establish and enhance intimacy with God instead of diminishing it. The process of prayer has surprised, tenderized, and drawn us into intimacy with Him.

PRAYER STARTER

Lord, my heart cries out with a desire to experience the fullness of Your glory. Let me abide with You in the spiritual realm of blessing and grace and experience a deeper relationship with You.

THE LORD LONGS TO BE GRACIOUS TO US, BUT HE WON'T BE WHEN IT THREATENS TO ALIENATE US FROM HIM.

DAY 249

This is what the LORD says: "In the time of my favor I will answer you, and in the day of salvation I will help you; I will keep you and will make you to be a covenant for the people, to restore the land and to reassign its desolate inheritances, to say to the captives, 'Come out,' and to those in darkness, 'Be free!'"
—*Isaiah 49:8–9*

Our prayer meetings will not force God to answer us. We cannot in any way do anything to deserve supernatural power. The economy of heaven never works that way. We are in a time of preparation. God is preparing a root system and a foundation for what He will give us in His grace. The longer the time of delay, the greater the joy when the answer comes. More than that, the change that happens to us in the process will protect us when the answer comes. God desires more than our endurance and patience in prayer. He wants us to open our mind and spirits to Him in all the seasons of life. It can be difficult at times, but the Lord desires people of one thing, contending for the fullness of God in every season.

PRAYER STARTER

Whatever comes my way, dear Father, whatever season of life in which I find myself, still I long to experience your grace and mercy in abundant fullness. I will seek You with my whole heart, and will await Your loving response with joy.

THE LONGER THE TIME OF DELAY, THE GREATER THE JOY WHEN THE ANSWER COMES.

DAY 250

Incline your ear, and come to Me....I will make an everlasting
covenant with you—the sure mercies of David. Indeed I have given
him as a witness to the people.
—*Isaiah 55:3–4, NKJV*

David was a lot like many Christians today. He didn't just want to be
a man of obedience and intimacy. He wanted to see the power of God
released in his nation and in his personal life. This pursuit pleases God.
The Lord at this very moment is searching for men and women whose
hearts can be fully His. He is looking for that capital *Yes* in people's
spirits. Some mistakenly believe that they must be without weakness
in order to contend for and receive God's power. They imagine some
perfect, totally righteous person being endued with the power of the
Holy Spirit, but they never picture themselves doing great works of
power for God. They know their own faults too well. The good news
from David's life is that not only does God allow us to draw close to
Him in intimacy in spite of our failings, but He also encourages us to
pursue His power even when we are weak.

PRAYER STARTER

*Father, give me Your eyes to see myself as Your mighty warrior. Let me
confront the Goliaths in my life with David's confidence, saying, "You come to
me with human strength, but I come before you in the strength of my God."*

**DAVID'S LIFE IS A WITNESS THAT WEAKNESS DOES NOT
DISQUALIFY US FROM EXPERIENCING GOD'S POWER.**

DAY 251

Lord, remember David and all his afflictions; how he swore to the Lord, and vowed to the Mighty One of Jacob: "Surely I will not go into the chamber of my house, or go up to the comfort of my bed; I will not give sleep to my eyes or slumber to my eyelids, until I find a place for the Lord, a dwelling place for the Mighty One of Jacob."
—*Psalm 132:1–5, NKJV*

It was not enough for David to seek the Lord privately and experience the pleasures of gazing on His beauty. He wanted a demonstration of God's power in Israel for all the nations to see so they would fear the Lord. So intensely did this zeal burn within him that he swore to the Mighty One that he would not pursue his own personal comfort until there was a habitation of the power of God in Israel. Does this describe you? Will you do whatever it takes to see a spiritual breakthrough in your city that results in a long-term habitation of God? David was willing to make sacrifices to see that habitation established. You and I should also yearn to see the habitation of God—a place where God lives and manifests His glory and power over the long term, not just for short seasons of revival.

PRAYER STARTER

Father, give me the zeal of David for my city. I long to see my church, my community, my city become a place where You can inhabit with Your presence and dwell. Manifest Your power and glory in my city, I pray.

TO BE PEOPLE AFTER GOD'S OWN HEART, WE MUST PURSUE GOD'S POWER UNTIL IT IS ESTABLISHED ON THE EARTH.

DAY 252

"He [Jesus] who has the key of David, He who opens and no
one shuts, and shuts and no one opens"...I have set before you an
open door, and no one can shut it.
—*Revelation 3:7–8, NKJV*

Jesus quoted this prophecy and applied it to His church. Jesus has the
authority of David, and He will release it to His servants in the church.
This is a promise for people after God's own heart. When we seek Him
and His power in obedience and intimacy, Jesus releases the authority
to open and shut doors in the Spirit. This is how He interacts with
you and me. Jesus prophesied that His disciples would experience an
open heaven, speaking of opening a doorway of blessing in the Spirit.
Jesus said, "Most assuredly, I say to you, hereafter you shall see heaven
open, and the angels of God ascending and descending upon the Son
of Man" (John 1:51, NKJV). We are invited to live under that open
heaven! When God finds a corporate people wholeheartedly pursuing Him with the heart of David, He will open and shut doors in the
spirit and in the natural. Doors of darkness will be shut in the spirit,
and evil things in the natural will dry up. Positive doors of light and
righteousness will be opened in the spirit, and righteous things in the
natural will flourish.

PRAYER STARTER

*I thank You, Father, for the miraculous privilege of living under Your
open heaven. Open the doors You desire to be opened in my city and nation,
Lord, and flood us with Your light. Shut the doors that allow Satan and his
darkness to creep in and deceive Your people.*

**WE ARE TO BE A PEOPLE OF POWER, OPENING AND SHUTTING
DOORS ACCORDING TO THE WILL
AND POWER OF THE LORD.**

DAY 253

Guard my life, for I am devoted to you. You are my God; save
your servant who trusts in you. Have mercy on me, O Lord, for I call
to you all day long. Bring joy to your servant, for to you, O Lord,
I lift up my soul.
—*Psalm 86:2–4*

Like Jesus many years later, David was born in Bethlehem, the youngest
of eight sons of Jesse and the lowest in rank and privilege in the family
structure. In his early years, he became a shepherd. David lived for several
years in what amounted to solitary confinement in a desert environment.
His flock was small, so he was the only one needed to do the tiresome
work (1 Sam. 17:28). He was very much alone in harsh terrain. You have
to wonder what God saw in David that He didn't see in his brothers, who
are little known except as scoffers. The key is in these Bethlehem years.
David was too young to have done anything extraordinary. He hadn't
cast out demons, healed the sick, or preached anointed sermons. His
great exploits all lay in the future. We might think of him as a gas sta-
tion attendant or a janitor. His life was filled with menial tasks nobody
wanted to do, yet he did them with a spirit of devotion toward the Lord.
That was David's first victory. He had a heart that sought God when
seeking God seemed the least obvious thing to do.

PRAYER STARTER

*Father, I often wonder what You saw in me that qualified me for Your
work of grace and gift of righteousness. I devote my life to You, and say yes to
whatever You desire for me to do. I love You with my whole heart.*

> **DAVID HAD A YES IN HIS SPIRIT, EVEN IN
> HIS ROUTINE, BORING JOB.**

DAY 254

His master replied, "Well done, good and faithful servant!
You have been faithful with a few things; I will put you in charge of
many things. Come and share your master's happiness!"
—*Matthew 25:23*

In our own lives, the small days will make us faithful in small things so we can be trusted later with big things. This is also the place where we learn to find our satisfaction not in the prophecy or promise but in God. He must be the sole source of our identity. Each of us starts in Bethlehem, finding our identity in God and becoming faithful in small things. It would be much nicer, from a carnal perspective, to skip Bethlehem and go right to Zion. But the journey to our highest destiny starts with little responsibilities. It may mean being neglected, pushed aside, and ignored. But this significant season lays the foundation for success later on. It's an essential, inescapable part of the journey from which nobody is exempt, not even the Messiah. Both David and Jesus had their small beginnings in Bethlehem, yet both were destined to rule with God's authority. If the eternal King started in Bethlehem, so will anyone who follows Him.

PRAYER STARTER

Father, so often my life seems filled with "small days." When I am consumed with insignificant details, filled with little thoughts, and paralyzed with inadequacy within myself, cause me to recognize that You are in the little things and that You have destined me to experience Your power and authority.

**THIS IS THE PLACE WHERE WE LEARN TO FIND
OUR SATISFACTION NOT IN THE PROPHECY OR
PROMISE BUT IN GOD.**

DAY 255

Therefore Saul sent messengers to Jesse, and said, "Send me
your son David, who is with the sheep."...So David came to Saul
and stood before him. And he loved him greatly, and he became his
armorbearer. Then Saul sent to Jesse, saying, "Please let David stand
before me, for he has found favor in my sight."
—1 Samuel 16:19–22, NKJV

After Samuel anointed David, the Spirit of the Lord departed from
Saul, and a distressing spirit troubled him. As a cure for his ugly mood,
Saul's servants recommended David to play music to comfort him. So
David moved to the city of Gibeah, the capital of Saul's government.
He lived there from approximately the time he was seventeen to when
he was twenty-three. Saul was greatly pleased with him, and David
found favor in Saul's eyes. David also found favor with the entire
nation of Israel, which had been in full-scale military crisis because of
Goliath the Philistine. David was used by God to pull the nation out
of a disaster. He became a national hero and brought the nation into
a significant victory. God snatched him out of the hills of Bethlehem,
significantly increased his salary, and gave him favor before man. What
David probably didn't know is that in all this early success, God was
testing the character of his love and servanthood. Would he continue
to draw on his spiritual identity in God, or would he begin to find
value and importance from his new position of honor?

PRAYER STARTER

*Father, when You have placed me in my Gibeah where You are testing
my love and servanthood for You, help me to recognize that any promotion
that comes to me comes from You. It is not because of me; it is because of You
and Your love for me.*

**THIS WAS THE TEST OF PROMOTION GOD SET BEFORE
DAVID IN GIBEAH.**

DAY 256

Young men, in the same way be submissive to those who are older. All of you, clothe yourselves with humility toward one another, because, "God opposes the proud but gives grace to the humble." Humble yourselves, therefore, under God's mighty hand, that he may lift you up in due time. Cast all your anxiety on him because he cares for you.
—1 Peter 5:5–7

When David was promoted to Gibeah, he continued to live from his heart as he did in Bethlehem, faithful to his small responsibilities. Though he was beginning to taste the favor and esteem of men, he continued to be faithful in insignificant tasks. God knew this season of favor would only be temporary. He wanted David to learn to respond with humility and love whether in Bethlehem or Gibeah, isolation or the national spotlight. Often, the Lord will give us a certain amount of success to equip us for the wilderness years that are yet ahead. We will suddenly find ourselves in a position of prominence or leadership where people value our time and opinions. But that's never the end of the story. Life alternates between times of promotion and times of struggle, times of favor and times of difficulty. When we learn how to lean on Him alone in times of success, we will know how to find Him in times of difficulty.

PRAYER STARTER

Father, never let me lose sight of the fact that all I am and all I have come from You. Give me a heart of humility and love for You, and help me to be faithful in the little things. My source is in You, alone.

MOST PEOPLE NEVER IMAGINE THAT THE SEASON OF SUCCESS WILL CHANGE, BUT IT ALMOST ALWAYS DOES.

DAY 257

No one from the east or the west or from the desert can exalt a man. But it is God who judges: He brings one down, he exalts another.
—*Psalm 75:6–7*

Joseph experienced early promotion and demotion. He received favor from his father, but that got him in trouble with his ten older brothers. He was sold as a slave to the Egyptians, then found himself over the whole guard in Potiphar's house. He may have thought all the promises were coming to pass and he was on the permanent high road, but there was another dungeon ahead. He was sent to prison for a number of years. Finally he was entrusted with all the wealth of Egypt. Saul of Tarsus, who would become the apostle Paul, had a supernatural encounter with Jesus on the way to Damascus (Acts 9). The whole Christian world was talking about this new convert. But after his immediate international success, he spent at least fourteen years in the desert without anything happening in his ministry. Then, for a while, he had a successful healing and evangelism ministry, but then it was off to prison and beatings and death. These men learned to find their identities in God in the character-testing time of early success. Have you tasted success? Did you realize your character was being tested? God wants you to establish your identity fully in Him and learn to handle the favor of men in the same way you handled the obscurity. If you pass the test, you "graduate" to the next season—though you may wish you hadn't.

PRAYER STARTER

Father, let me learn from Joseph and Paul the lesson of establishing my identity firmly in You alone. Let my heart be pure before You, and let me honor You, for You alone are the lifter of my head.

PROMOTION COMES NOT FROM THE EAST, WEST, OR SOUTH BUT FROM THE NORTH—FROM THE LORD.

DAY 258

David left Gath and escaped to the cave of Adullam....All those who were in distress or in debt or discontented gathered around him, and he became their leader. About four hundred men were with him.

—1 Samuel 22:1–2

After the praises and promotion in Gibeah, David's career took a sharp turn. He lost all favor in Saul's court. Saul rose up to kill him and enlisted three thousand men to chase, capture, and murder him. Seldom has there been such a dramatic reversal. David, probably confused and exasperated, at least initially, fled and made his headquarters in the dark, damp wilderness cave of Adullam. There he gathered four hundred men together, and for about seven years they and their families wandered the wilderness. Gibeah had tested him with praise and success. Now Adullam was testing him with hardship. God put David in Adullam for seven long years to firmly root his identity in God. The lessons of this season, though extremely difficult to learn, would prove to be his protection when he became king of Israel. In the same way, God doesn't want us to get our identity even a little bit from our anointing or earthly success but from being loved by God and being a lover of God. Our ministry can fall apart. The people who admired us can leave. The blessing of the Spirit can lift off our labors for a season. We can lose our building, our home, and our financial base, but if we love God and He loves us, we are still successful. This is the sure inheritance the Father has promised us.

PRAYER STARTER

Father, I've spent time in Adullam. I have lived on the backside of the desert in my spiritual life. Help me never to forget that even in the wilderness You love me, protect me, and bring me to a mature, intimate relationship with You.

WE MUST REMEMBER WHEN WE SUDDENLY ARE SHOVED INTO AN ADULLAM SEASON THAT GOD HAS A DIVINE PATTERN FOR MATURING US.

DAY 259

Now he who supplies seed to the sower and bread for food
will also supply and increase your store of seed and will enlarge the
harvest of your righteousness. You will be made rich in every way
so that you can be generous on every occasion, and through us your
generosity will result in thanksgiving to God.
—*2 Corinthians 9:10–11*

Adullam was tough for another reason as well. The people who gathered to David were not exactly Israel's best and brightest. Their spiritual roots were not deeply anchored in God. They were in distress, in debt, and discontented with Saul and the government. They came to David and said, "Take care of us. It's time somebody else thinks for me!" Idealism and naïveté about relationships are removed from us in Adullam. This is the place where we discover that God is real and He alone is our supply even in greatest distress, not the people He sends our way. The good news of Adullam is that it gives you hints and foreshadowing of what you can expect in the time of God's full release of your destiny. So the struggles you are visited with in Adullam turn out to be training for the way God wants to bless you in Zion. In your time of deepest struggle you will see hints of what's to come in your life.

PRAYER STARTER

*You alone supply the things I need—whether in Gibeah or Adullam.
Teach me to look only to You for my supply. Help me to show others that You
are all I need, all they need.*

GOD DOESN'T WANT US TO GET OUR IDENTITY EVEN A LITTLE
BIT FROM OUR ANOINTING OR EARTHLY SUCCESS BUT FROM
BEING LOVED BY GOD AND BEING A LOVER OF GOD.

DAY 260

In the course of time, David inquired of the LORD. "Shall I go up to one of the towns of Judah?" he asked. The LORD said, "Go up." David asked, "Where shall I go?" "To Hebron," the LORD answered.
—2 Samuel 2:1

After approximately seven difficult years in the wilderness, the season finally changed with the death of King Saul. David came out of the desert at about thirty years of age. Upon hearing of Saul's death, his first response might have been, "At last, I can be king over all Israel!" His men jumped to this assumption. They cried with a sense of relief, "David! You're finally king. Let's move in." But David did the unexpected thing. He sought God's heart. He demonstrated what people who are intimate with God do before making big decisions. An open door in the natural stood before him, but he refused to enter it without the direct leading of the Lord. Beloved, this is how we must behave! Just because things seem to be falling together doesn't mean the right time has come. We must sense in our spirits and discern if an open door is of God or if it leads down a false path. The Holy Spirit will give us wisdom about this at the time of decision.

PRAYER STARTER

Father, as You lead me from place to place, from season to season, give me clear vision and focused thinking so that I can only move through doors that You have opened for my life.

WE MUST NEVER THINK WE CAN ADVANCE WILLY-NILLY WITHOUT SEEKING THE LORD'S HEART FOR A SITUATION.

DAY 261

Be completely humble and gentle; be patient, bearing with one
another in love. Make every effort to keep the unity of the Spirit
through the bond of peace. There is one body and one Spirit—just as
you were called to one hope when you were called—one Lord,
one faith, one baptism; one God and Father of all, who is over all
and through all and in all.

—*Ephesians 4:2–6*

The Lord told David to go to Hebron and only take a little bit of
the kingdom. There were twelve tribes of Israel, and Hebron represented only one. God was testing and training David once again. He
wanted David to find his identity in God, not in being king of Israel.
Therefore, God only released a partial fulfillment of the full destiny
promised to him. God will do this to us, too. It's an agonizing experience, but it builds incredible patience in us. David spent seven more
years limited to the city of Hebron. Still, he didn't become angry with
God for making him wait through another season of testing. He knew
the Lord would give him all of Israel when it was time. He was after
the perfect will of God and would not settle for less. The only reason
David could act this way lay in his identity: being king of Israel was
not the key to his sense of importance. And we too will triumph in the
lesson of Hebron when we see we are already successful before God and
don't strive for success before men by going after position and honor.

PRAYER STARTER

*Teach me, Father, that the accumulation of blessings that You have
brought into my life pale in importance to the intimate relationship You long
to share with me. Let me dwell in Hebron, the place of partial fulfillment of
Your destiny for me, content to find my identity in You and You alone.*

**GOD WANTS YOU TO FIND YOUR IDENTITY IN GOD,
NOT IN EARTHLY SUCCESS.**

DAY 262

"You will seek me and find me when you seek me with all your heart. I will be found by you," declares the LORD, "and will bring you back from captivity. I will gather you from all the nations and places where I have banished you," declares the LORD, "and will bring you back to the place from which I carried you into exile."
—*Jeremiah 29:13–14*

One reason God gave David only one-twelfth of the kingdom in Hebron was because He wanted David's core of fighting men—the future army of Israel—to become mature and seasoned. God wanted a core of submitted, committed leaders free of ambition. To their credit, these men became righteous warriors, using their strength for the greater glory of God and Israel instead of doing their own thing. They found the secret that working together produces far greater results than going it alone. Hebron speaks to us of finding God in times of partial fulfillment of His promises. This can be a painful season in our lives. The blessing seems to come so slow. You may pass the test of isolation and obscurity in Bethlehem, the test of early promotion in Gibeah, and the test of adversity in Adullam. But many of God's servants stumble in this place represented by Hebron. We must keep our identities in Him even when the promises are at our very fingertips. Even in that place of tantalizing closeness, God demands a righteous response.

PRAYER STARTER

Father, when my Hebron seems empty and lonely, and only a few others seem willing to fellowship with You, teach me that a few is mighty in Your power. Raise us up a mighty army You can use to make Your name great among our nation. Make us righteous in our Hebron.

OUR GREATEST PRIVATE AGENDA MUST REMAIN TO BE LOVED BY GOD AND TO BE A LOVER OF GOD.

DAY 263

When all the elders of Israel had come to King David at Hebron, the king made a compact with them at Hebron before the LORD, and they anointed David king over Israel.
—*2 Samuel 5:3*

David waited for the season of God's promotion. It arrived one day when Ishbosheth was murdered by wicked men. David had arrived. This season of Zion speaks to us of the full release of what God promised David during his earthly lifetime. This is when the full prophetic destiny for our lives begins to be manifest. David would soon capture Jerusalem, referred to as "Zion" in Scripture, and set up his capital there instead of Gibeah. There is no substitute for the confidence we feel upon arriving at our destiny in God's time and in His way. Many people work hard to get their ministry moving and happening. They strive at work to attain a certain position. But sometimes they feel God hasn't moved fast enough on their behalf, so they hurry it along with unholy manipulation. They may get the position or prominence they want, but they lack any confidence in it. They are consumed with fear that somebody will take over their territory or steal their position. They live with anxiety because they can't be sure God gave the ministry or position to them in the first place. They have built on a faulty foundation. Beloved, I exhort you for the sake of your purpose and destiny in this life, allow God to take you to your Zion! You either arrive legitimately with the confidence of heaven behind you, or you arrive illegitimately and riddled with anxiety.

PRAYER STARTER

Father, stay my hands from hindering Your plan for me with unholy manipulation. Keep the fear and anxiety of human position from destroying me. Raise me up and set my feet on the path to Zion.

DON'T STEP OUT OF LINE; DON'T RUSH. THERE IS NO SECOND BEST IN THIS.

DAY 264

When the LORD brought back the captives to Zion,
we were like men who dreamed.
Our mouths were filled with laughter,
our tongues with songs of joy.
Then it was said among the nations,
"The LORD has done great things for them."
The LORD has done great things for us,
and we are filled with joy.
—*Psalm 126:1–3*

God doesn't bring us to Zion for our personal enrichment. Often the Lord's blessing will rest on a person, congregation, nation, or city, and they start thinking the blessing was given mostly to add to their personal prestige or lifestyle. This is a danger we must avoid once we arrive at our destiny. Some people imagine that when they finally reach the fullness of their promise and place of destiny, they will have only joy. They picture complete contentment in their anointing and prominence. But it doesn't work that way, even in the grace of God. In our place of destiny, we will still experience pressures, persecutions, and pain. As you prepare to enter your destiny, set your expectations correctly.

PRAYER STARTER

Father, when I am tempted to believe that pressure, persecution, and pain are keeping me from reaching my potential in You, cause me to remember that You bring me to Zion for Your pleasure and Your plan, not for my own personal enrichment.

> ARRIVING AT ZION IS ABOUT SERVING THE KINGDOM IN
> GREATER MEASURE—A PRIVILEGE FAR GREATER THAN
> MONEY OR FAME.

DAY 265

Blessed are those whose strength is in you,
who have set their hearts on pilgrimage.
As they pass through the Valley of Baca,
they make it a place of springs;
the autumn rains also cover it with pools.
They go from strength to strength,
till each appears before God in Zion.
—*Psalm 84:5–7*

Zion is a prophetic picture of Jesus being made King over all the earth just as David was king over all Israel. It would be a shame to miss this beautiful portrait of what's coming. The Father has promised His Son an inheritance, a bride who will be His eternal partner. She will love Him in this age and the age to come. She will find her fulfillment in Him just as David found fulfillment of his earthly purpose in Zion. I want to assure you that there's a divine pattern in your life. In the pain and the maze of things, it seems as if there isn't a plan and you are wandering aimlessly from cave to cave, pursued by armies much stronger than you, and surrounded by losers. Yet God has a strategic plan and is bringing you to a specific purpose. Each one of us will, God willing, stand before Him one day in Zion. When we submit to His divine leadership in every season of our lives, we will ascend out of the wilderness entirely dependent on Him. He alone will be the reward of our hearts through every season of life.

PRAYER STARTER

Father, I rest in the knowledge that You have a perfectly designed pattern of destiny for my life. Help me to understand that You are in each season of my life, are directing each step I take, and will never leave me or forsake me.

GOD HAS A PROPHETIC PILGRIMAGE FOR EVERY ONE OF US.

DAY 266

It was now about the sixth hour, and darkness came over the whole land until the ninth hour, for the sun stopped shining. And the curtain of the temple was torn in two. Jesus called out with a loud voice, "Father, into your hands I commit my spirit." When he had said this, he breathed his last.

—*Luke 23:44–46*

The truth that empowered David through the obstacle course of opposition on the way to Zion and his destiny is so powerful that it was among the last words of Jesus. When Jesus's broken body hung on the cross, moments before His final breath, darkness loomed over the soul of the God-man as He who knew no sin became sin. Jesus felt the agony of separation from the Father. He knew that on the other side of the agony was the awesome promise that God would raise Him from the dead and enthrone Him over all created order. But before the fullness of the promise came to pass, He experienced the greatest pressure and opposition any man has faced. In that dark delay, He lifted His voice and cried out, "Into Your hands I commit My Spirit" (Luke 23:46, NKJV). Jesus decided this was the most appropriate heart response He could have while waiting for the light and promise to break forth. When God gives a promise, we usually experience a time of darkness before He brings it to pass. We have a hard time seeing what season we're in or where it's all leading. In the hour of the impossible situation, what should you do? Grab hold of those seven words, and commit your spirit into the Father's hands.

PRAYER STARTER

Father, when I face pain and opposition and death, remind me of the example Your Son gave as He felt the silence of His Father and the cruelty of man. Teach me to say, "Father, into Your hands I commit my spirit."

"INTO YOUR HANDS I COMMIT MY SPIRIT."

DAY 267

Free me from the trap that is set for me,
for you are my refuge.
Into your hands I commit my spirit;
redeem me, O Lord, the God of truth.
—*Psalm 31:4–5*

The "trap" in this verse can represent many things to us, like spiritual, physical, financial, or relational quagmires. In Jesus's experience, the trap was His bearing the sin of the world before His exaltation. He cried, "Father, pull Me out of the impossible situation, for You are My strength." He knew He could not deliver Himself as He hung in the dark place between promise and fulfillment. His confidence rested in His Father alone. In our own times of trouble and personal injustice, the Lord is looking for that same cry to come forth from our hearts. God is calling us to this place of dependence. He is beckoning us to depend on Him with every hope for breakthrough, every need for provision, every dream of success. We must surrender our deepest desires to God's keeping. We are utterly unable to bring our prophetic promises to pass. Only He can change the times and seasons and bring the breakthrough we long for.

PRAYER STARTER

Father, Your Son's confidence as He faced death did not lie in circumstances or people—His confidence rested in You alone. Call me to this place of total dependence upon You; teach me to surrender myself completely to You.

BELOVED, IN OUR DIFFICULT SEASONS OF LIFE, WE MUST COMMIT OUR DEEPEST PASSIONS AND PROPHETIC PROMISES TO GOD.

DAY 268

Free me from the trap that is set for me,
for you are my refuge.
Into your hands I commit my spirit;
redeem me, O Lord, the God of truth.
—*Psalm 31:4–5*

What does it mean to commit our spirits to the Lord? Our spirit is the part of us that touches our deepest desires and dreams. It is the repository for our greatest passions and hopes for our lives. As He hung on the cross, Jesus was saying, "Father, I commit to You the things I treasure the most. I surrender to Your hand what I have lived for and believed in." I believe Jesus was declaring the secret of how He lived His entire earthly life. At the end of His life He knew this spiritual principle would again prove reliable and true. God was His source, and God is our source. Committing our spirits to Him means asking the Father to take care of those things that matter most to our hearts. It is recognizing that we can't make God's promises come to pass in our own strength. When you commit something into God's hands, the devil cannot steal it. The only person who could stop the will of God in David's life was David. And only you can stop God's will from happening in your life by disconnecting from communion with God.

PRAYER STARTER

Teach me, Lord, that only as I surrender myself completely to You will I discover the secret to fulfilling Your will for my life. Keep me from stopping Your will from happening in my life. I will never disconnect myself from constant communion with You.

WHEN OUR SPIRITS ARE HIDDEN IN HIM, THE ENEMY CAN'T LAY A FINGER ON THEM.

DAY 269

I will extol the LORD at all times;
his praise will always be on my lips.
My soul will boast in the LORD;
let the afflicted hear and rejoice.
Glorify the LORD with me;
let us exalt his name together.
—*Psalm 34:1–3*

Committing our spirits into God's hands is an act of aggressive spiritual warfare, not passive indifference. David did it to bring God into his conflicts. He wasn't kicking back and saying, "Whatever happens, happens; I really don't care, Lord." No, he was using a spiritual tactic to bring God into the situation of his personal injustice. He engaged in this kind of spiritual warfare from his youth to the end of his life. When he entrusted a specific situation to God, there was a reaction and a release in the spirit realm. God moved on David's behalf. David became a model of how God settles the score when we war according to His way. One key characteristic in David's life was the way he processed pain, mistreatment, disappointment, and injustice, a process recorded so richly in the Book of Psalms. He learned to war in the spirit by giving up his right to revenge. Other men and women of God such as Daniel, Joseph, and the patriarchs of old operated in this principle as well.

PRAYER STARTER

Help me to recognize that committing my spirit to You is spiritual warfare. Teach me to be an aggressive spiritual warrior, entrusting You with every moment of my life. You are the defender of my faith, and I place my hope and trust in You alone.

THE LORD BECKONS US TO ENTER HIS HEART AND LEAVE
THE AGENDA OF JUSTICE TO HIM.

DAY 270

But I say to you who hear: Love your enemies, do good to
those who hate you, bless those who curse you, and pray for those
who spitefully use you....But love your enemies, do good, and lend,
hoping for nothing in return; and your reward will be great, and
you will be sons of the Most High. For He is kind to
the unthankful and evil.
—*Luke 6:27–28, 35, NKJV*

When we place the injustice done to us in God's hands, we allow room
for His vengeance. If we act in an angry spirit and try to vindicate
ourselves, God steps back and lets us fight alone. His plan is that He
takes revenge however He sees fit, and we bless our enemy even as He
works vengeance. He is a God who mostly wants to bless and be merciful, and as we bless our enemies, we exhibit His character even as He
doles out justice. That's His idea for showing mercy even when justice
is needed. When we are kind to our enemies, we mirror the Father's
kindness for evil and ungrateful men, and we come into unity with
the ruler of the universe. There is no form of spiritual warfare more
powerful than that.

PRAYER STARTER

*Teach me, Lord, that vengeance belongs to You. Teach me to bless my
enemies, to extend mercy and love instead of seeking to extract justice. You
will fight for me, and I will love for You.*

**VENGEANCE BELONGS IN GOD'S HANDS. HE SETTLES
SCORES PERFECTLY.**

DAY 271

Do you not know that your body is a temple of the Holy
Spirit, who is in you, whom you have received from God? You are
not your own; you were bought at a price. Therefore
honor God with your body.
—*1 Corinthians 6:19–20*

When you want to retaliate, remember that the fundamental reality in
the kingdom of God is found in the words of our Scripture today: "For
you were bought at a price;…in your body and in your spirit, which
are God's" (NKJV). Beloved, when you show kindness to your enemies,
it declares you belong to another. Your resources belong to God, your
reputation belongs to Him, and your time belongs to Him. When your
enemies bring pressure on you, malign your reputation, or steal your
resources or your time, the Lord invites you to make a transfer of ownership and put your complete self into His hands. This makes room for
His vengeance and His agenda. He is your defense and your ally. This
is the path to true liberty and true power. Every time someone harms
you, it's another divine opportunity to shout to the world that the Lord
owns you and will defend you according to His righteousness.

PRAYER STARTER

*Jesus, what an incomprehensible price You paid to redeem my soul from
hell. Let me never forget that I belong to You. Be my defense, be my ally, and
show me the path to true liberty and power.*

> IF HE IS NOT CONCERNED TO PUNISH IMMEDIATELY
> THE INJUSTICE DONE TO YOU, THEN NEITHER SHOULD YOU
> BE WORRIED—YOU BELONG TO HIM.

DAY 272

But I trust in you, O Lord;
I say, "You are my God."
My times are in your hands;
deliver me from my enemies
and from those who pursue me.
—*Psalm 31:14–15*

David said, "My times are in your hands." It's one thing to commit our spirits into God's hands; it's quite another thing to trust God with the timing of His breakthrough. Each "committing" has its own challenges and anxieties. After we commit our spirits into God's hands, the test of time comes. One year turns into two, and two years turn into ten. We begin to question, "What about the breakthrough? What about the promises?" Though we have committed our spirits to Him, the years have multiplied. David saw there were two steps to this. First, he committed his spirit; then he committed the timing of those dreams. He learned to rest in God's sovereignty. We too must give ourselves to this two-part progression. First, we commit our spirits and dreams into God's hands by living lives of prayer and fasting as we seek their fulfillment. Second, we trust Him for the season of release.

PRAYER STARTER

Father, in all my life, You have never been one minute too early or one minute too late. When I am tempted to question Your timing in the future, help me to remember Your track record from the past. I rest in You and wait for Your promises.

WHEN WE STAND BEFORE GOD IN ETERNITY, WE WILL REALIZE HE WAS NEVER ONE MINUTE LATE.

DAY 273

I have chosen the way of truth;
I have set my heart on your laws.
I hold fast to your statutes, O LORD;
   do not let me be put to shame.
I run in the path of your commands,
   for you have set my heart free.
—*Psalm 119:30–32*

David faced many external enemies, but he also triumphed over a much more formidable foe: his own heart. He knew how to commit his spirit into God's hands when confronted by his own weakness. This is one of the hardest things to figure out in the Christian walk, but to be people after God's heart, we must. The glory of the human story is that we can't exhaust God's mercy. Our weakness never disqualifies us if we sincerely repent. David discovered that there is a contingency for human weakness, which comes to us by God's grace. In his times of weakness, he ran toward God instead of away from Him.

PRAYER STARTER

Father, like David, I choose Your truth. My heart desires to know only Your Word. I cling to Your promises and trust Your plans. In the times of my greatest weakness, I will run to You and find Your strength and power.

THE GLORY OF THE HUMAN STORY IS THAT WE CAN'T EXHAUST GOD'S MERCY.

DAY 274

David said to Achish, "If I have now found favor in your eyes, let them give me a place in some town in the country, that I may dwell there."...So Achish gave him Ziklag that day....Now the time that David dwelt in the country of the Philistines was one full year and four months.
—1 Samuel 27:5–7

Even though God had sent a message right to David that He would protect him, fear conquered his heart, and he doubted the promises. In the final lap of the race before God made him king, David stumbled into great compromise in the Philistine city of Ziklag. He chose physical security outside the will of God. And to make things worse, he promised loyalty to Achish, an archenemy of Israel. David lived with terrible tension inside of him. He was a man divided. On the one hand, he still had great zeal for the Lord. On the other hand, he was living in compromise and using the favor and anointing of God in a wrong way. For his entire time in Ziklag, David lived a charade, neglecting his destiny, disobeying the prophet's word, disregarding his other prophetic promises, betraying Achish with lies, and endangering his own men and their families. We have looked at David as the great worshiping warrior king with the heart after God's, but here we see him riddled with the same fear, doubt, and insecurity we see in ourselves.

PRAYER STARTER

Father, may I never forget the lesson David learned in Ziklag—where he sought to protect himself and left the security of Your will. Keep me from trying to use my own human powers instead of trusting You in faith. I don't want to find myself in Ziklag riddled with fear, doubt, and insecurity.

DAVID'S FAITH IN DIVINE PROTECTION WAS WAVERING BIG-TIME. HE HAD REACHED THE END OF HIS COURAGE.

DAY 275

David and his men reached Ziklag on the third day. Now the
Amalekites…attacked Ziklag and burned it, and had taken captive
the women and all who were in it, both young and old…. When
David and his men came to Ziklag, they found it destroyed by fire
and their wives and sons and daughters taken captive. So David and
his men wept aloud until they had no strength left to weep.
—1 Samuel 30:1–4

For sixteen months, David's Ziklag strategy seemed to be working, but God was about to kick the props out from under him. One day, David and his men came home and saw their city burned to the ground. God allowed Ziklag to burn so David would come face-to-face with Him. It was this very trauma that caused David to return to God and depart this period of disobedience. Each of us, I daresay, has a city of compromise, a Ziklag to which we retreat at some point in our lives. Our Ziklag is a place of supposed refuge that empowers us to continue in disobedience. It's the place where we devise little systems that give us sinful pleasure and false comfort when God's will becomes too intense for us. The Lord does not reject us during these times, but He doesn't approve of our sin, either. He looks for ways to restore us, not destroy us. He devises means so that His banished ones are not expelled from Him (2 Sam. 14:14). But He almost always allows our city of compromise to be burned.

PRAYER STARTER

Teach me, Father, to turn to You before my disobedience destroys my hopes and dreams. When I fall to compromise and apathy, find me and restore me to Your presence. Bring me face-to-face again with You.

OUR ZIKLAG IS LIKE A CUBBYHOLE WHERE WE ESCAPE FROM
THE REALM OF GOD'S PROMISES AND RETREAT INTO THE
ENEMY'S TERRITORY WHERE WE FEEL SAFER.

DAY 276

David was greatly distressed because the men were talking of
stoning him....But David found strength in the LORD his God. Then
David...inquired of the LORD, "Shall I pursue this raiding party? Will
I overtake them?" "Pursue them," he answered. "You will certainly
overtake them and succeed in the rescue."
—1 Samuel 30:6–8

Ziklag's destruction was an agonizing tragedy for David and his men.
But David did the right thing. As a result, we know what to do when our
Ziklag is burned and compromise is no longer an option. When everything was falling apart, David returned to his root system and "found
strength in the LORD his God." He went to the Lord and said, "Lord,
I am Yours. I love You, and I know You love me. Help me, Lord." One
of the greatest miracles that can happen in the life of a discouraged
believer is knowing the Lord's mercy and delight so deeply that we run
toward Him in our time of greatest sin. Have you awakened one morning and realized you were living in a place of compromise? David knew
what God was like, so he confidently approached the Lord instead of
slinking away in shame. This led to his complete recovery. If you run
away from God instead of to Him in time of crisis, you can't be restored,
but the complete solution will be found when you run to Him.

PRAYER STARTER

*Father, when everything around me is falling apart, cause me to do as
David did and "strengthen myself in the Lord." Give me Your miraculous
grace and mercy, and help me to run to You instead of away from You.*

HAVE YOU WATCHED GOD BURN YOUR ZIKLAG—YOUR PLACE
OF DISOBEDIENCE?

DAY 277

You number my wanderings; put my tears into Your bottle; are they not in Your book? When I cry out to You, then my enemies will turn back; this I know, because God is for me.
—*Psalm 56:8–9, NKJV*

Psalm 56 develops more of the insight that helped David's confidence in God's mercy. This psalm was written while David was still living in compromise. David said to the Lord, "God, You know I'm wandering. You take notice of my compromises. I'm out of Your will, and my ways are not hidden from You." Neither are we hidden from Jesus when we hide out in Ziklag. We are not deceiving God when we are stuck in compromise. But after this, David reached for the gold ring of God's mercy and said, "[You] put my tears into Your bottle; are they not in Your book?" (v. 8, NKJV). David knew that his tears of despair and broken dreams, his tears of disobedience for lying and resisting the prophetic word, were treasured by God. David had many different kinds of emotions churning within him. His tears were of a man who had lied and not trusted the Lord. He had endangered his friends. Yet he still loved the Lord. He wanted to be wholly God's. He knew that God was scooping his tears up in His hand and storing them in His bottle because our tears of repentance are precious to God.

PRAYER STARTER

Thank You, Father, that none of my ways are hidden from You. See my tears and brokenness, and forgive my disobedient spirit. I love You with my whole heart, and I long to be restored to Your holy presence.

GOD WILL REVEAL HIMSELF AS GENTLE TO US WHEN WE ARE IN ZIKLAG, THE PLACE OF COMPROMISE.

DAY 278

Record my lament; list my tears on your scroll—are they not
in your record? Then my enemies will turn back when I call for help.
By this I will know that God is for me. In God, whose word I praise,
in the LORD, whose word I praise—in God I trust; I will not be
afraid. What can man do to me?

—*Psalm 56:8–11*

I imagine David sitting somewhere by himself, crying, "O God, I hate
disobeying You. I love You—You know that—but I'm so afraid. I
know I'm disobeying the prophetic word. I know that I am telling lies
and deceiving people. But I am so afraid right now." We have all been
there, crying tears of repentance. Maybe one of David's men walked up
to him and said, "Get up and quit crying, you hypocrite! God doesn't
want to hear your blubbering. If you really loved God, you would stop
sinning and go back to Israel like He commanded. Obey God or shut
up." Yet in this moment, the Lord whispered in David's ear, "I have
captured every one of your tears and put them in My bottle in heaven."
David knew his tears were not despised by God; they were precious.
Though the men around him likely thought he was a hypocrite, God
saw genuine love in David's heart. David believed that God was for him
while he was in Ziklag, and this was the secret to his recovery.

PRAYER STARTER

*Father, like David, I hate my disobedient spirit. I long to be Your
obedient child. How precious to me is the thought of You scooping up my tears
and placing them in a bottle. You care so much for me. Revive my cold heart
and help me to burn with love for You.*

**WE NEED TO PUT OUR COLD HEARTS BEFORE THAT SAME
FIRE OF REVELATION THAT WARMED DAVID'S HEART.**

DAY 279

The LORD is compassionate and gracious,
slow to anger, abounding in love.
He will not always accuse,
nor will he harbor his anger forever;
he does not treat us as our sins deserve
or repay us according to our iniquities.
—*Psalm 103:8–10*

David opened his heart again in Psalm 103 to express what he knew about the way God's heart worked. He was saying, "When I deserve to be punished, He forgives me and restores me in love." David knew that God had removed his sins as far as the east is from the west. This was David's revelation of God's heart. He learned to relate to God on the basis of God's passion for him rather than his own performance. Beloved, only a student of God's emotions can recover so quickly after grievous compromise. God forgives us today so we will grow in the fear of God tomorrow. If He wiped us out today, we would never become mature, God-fearing people. This is God's strategy toward us. He wants to deal gently with us even though it requires burning our Ziklags. He does not want to mark our iniquities but to forgive them so we can go on to be great in love. He wants our confidence to be based in the revelation of His desire for us and His work on the cross.

PRAYER STARTER

Lord, if You treated me as I deserve, You would banish me from Your presence. Yet it is my sins that You remove, taking them as far away as the east is from the west. Thank You so much for raising me up to walk with You again in holiness. Complete Your work in me.

DO YOU NEED TO OVERCOME A SPIRIT OF FEAR THAT GETS IN THE WAY OF YOUR INTIMACY WITH GOD?

DAY 280

One thing I have desired of the LORD, that will I seek: that
I may dwell in the house of the LORD all the days of my life....For in
the time of trouble He shall hide me in His pavilion....And now my
head shall be lifted up above my enemies all around me....Hear,
O LORD, when I cry with my voice!...When You said, "Seek My
face," my heart said to You, "Your face, LORD, I will seek."
—*Psalm 27:4–8, NKJV*

What is the path to overcoming great fear in the end times? The
examples of Jesus and David make it clear: they overcame fear by seeking God's face in intimacy. They gazed upon the heart of God, encountering His beauty. The trouble David talked about was manifold, but
mainly it was the trouble of people seeking to harm him. It is awful to
walk around with that sinking feeling in your stomach because somebody at work, church, your neighborhood, or school is out to get you.
You want to repair the situation, but often you can't, so you learn to
live with the reality of having an enemy, as David did. He practically
walked around with a big target on him from the day Saul rejected him.
But he proclaimed that God would hide him in His shelter. His words
shine a big light on the answer of how to carry our hearts in the hour
of persecution and great trouble that comes from evil people.

PRAYER STARTER

*Father, keep me from the fear of what others might say or do to me.
Keep me from feeling the sting of rejection and hatred from others. When
evildoers threaten to destroy me, let me overcome their evil by living in the
security of Your love.*

**THE LORD WILL ANOINT US WITH ANSWERS TO COMFORT
FAINTING OR FAILING HEARTS.**

DAY 281

The LORD is my light and my salvation; whom shall I fear? The LORD is the strength of my life; of whom shall I be afraid? When the wicked came against me to eat up my flesh...they stumbled and fell. Though an army may encamp against me, my heart shall not fear; though war may rise against me, in this I will be confident.
—*Psalm 27:1–3, NKJV*

The first claim David made was, "The LORD is my light." With these words, he declared that the Lord would help him with the spirit of revelation. One of the privileges God has given the church is access to divine information. We receive it in a general sense through His Word, which makes our hearts strong for the days ahead. Many believers don't study enough the powerful information freely offered in the Word. This is God's number-one way of equipping us for the coming pressures. In the Bible, God reveals His plan for the end times and for eternity, everything we can expect to happen to us as believers. But He also gives us divine information in a more personal and specific way through the prophetic anointing, which David referred to here. I along with many others believe that the Lord is now raising up and releasing the prophetic ministry in the church all over the earth on a scale nobody has yet seen.

PRAYER STARTER

Father, I want to receive Your spirit of revelation. Equip me to face an uncertain future by having access to Your divine information. Release Your prophetic ministry to Your people in this day.

GOD WILL SURELY GIVE US INFORMATION ABOUT THINGS JUST AROUND THE CORNER, DIVINE REVELATION THROUGH DREAMS AND VISIONS.

DAY 282

The Lord is my light and my salvation— whom shall I fear?
The Lord is the stronghold of my life—of whom shall I be afraid?
When evil men advance against me to devour my flesh, when my
enemies and my foes attack me, they will stumble and fall. Though
an army besiege me, my heart will not fear; though war break out
against me, even then will I be confident.
—*Psalm 27:1–3*

Each believer has a personal history in God that has been developed
through the years. It may be lengthy or it may be thin, but the Lord
wants to give each of us as individuals a substantial private history so
we can write our own faith book, so to speak. David's history in God
was constantly growing. Each time he stepped out of fear and into the
strength and boldness of God, a new page was added to his personal
faith book. How do we gain history in God? By getting out of the boat
as Peter did to walk on the water. You won't get a fat book of personal
history with Him unless you leave the safe zone. When the dark night
comes and we face the great troubles prophesied in Luke 21, we will
draw upon our private history in God. Why should our hearts faint for
fear like the unbelievers? We will overcome fear through a personal history in His faithfulness. We should agree with David's testimony and
say, "I will not be afraid because I remember that God has continually
been my salvation and deliverer."

PRAYER STARTER

*Like David, my history in You, God, is constantly growing. When
I look back upon my life, I see Your miraculous interventions and blessing.
I have the confidence to step boldly into my future with You, trusting You to
continue to be my constant salvation and deliverer.*

**WHEN WE ARE IN DIFFICULTY, GOD WANTS US TO PRESS IN
AND SEEK HIM FOR A BREAKTHROUGH.**

DAY 283

I pray that out of his glorious riches he may strengthen you
with power through his Spirit in your inner being, so that Christ
may dwell in your hearts through faith.
—*Ephesians 3:16–17*

David also said that God was his emotional strength, the strength of his heart. This is another facet of our intimacy with Him that shields us from fear. Paul prayed that divine might would touch our inner man, that our emotions would be made strong. He was referring to our emotional being. God fills our souls with strength that we might stand in confidence. This is a supernatural gift and an anointing on the inside of us that enables us to keep going though it appears we have every reason to quit. Not quitting is itself an act of God's grace within us. But He will do more than that: He will cause your heart, your emotions, to become buoyant and powerful, to be alive in God. When the Lord delivers us from fear, it doesn't mean we will never feel fear again, but that it's no longer a predominant reality in our life. Fear is no longer our preoccupation. It becomes something the enemy unsuccessfully tempts us with, a sideshow of his failure.

PRAYER STARTER

Father, fill me to overflowing with Your supernatural anointing that allows me to stand undefeated regardless of circumstances. Heal the wound of my spirit and cause me to be alive in You. Deliver me from the fear of my enemy.

**BELOVED, THERE IS AN EMOTIONAL STRENGTH
OFFERED US BY GOD.**

DAY 284

Sing to him, sing praise to him;
tell of all his wonderful acts.
Glory in his holy name;
let the hearts of those who seek the LORD rejoice.
Look to the LORD and his strength;
seek his face always.
—*Psalm 105:2–4*

The breakthrough anointing over fear is found in the secret place of God's beauty. Fear does not dominate the heart there because a superior pleasure upholds the heart. It is a lifestyle of encounter and intimacy with the beauty of God that rescues us from fear. This was a drastically new concept when David put it forth. Moses, who lived five hundred years earlier, popularized the teaching that you cannot see the face of God and live. In Exodus 20:19, the people said, "Do not have God speak to us or we will die." David answered that paradigm of God with his own experience, which created a vastly different paradigm: "God Most High told me that He wanted to show me His face." This is the first time God ever said to the human race that He desired us to seek His face. David was the first person to declare this. His new teaching was that the God of heaven does not want to strike us dead when He shows us His face, but He desires to bring us into the experience of closeness and comfort with Him.

PRAYER STARTER

Father, I seek Your face. I know that You desire to show us Your face, and I long to behold Your beauty. I declare with David, "Lord, show me Your face."

FEAR IS NO LONGER OUR PREOCCUPATION.

DAY 285

These I will bring to my holy mountain
and give them joy in my house of prayer.
Their burnt offerings and sacrifices
will be accepted on my altar;
for my house will be called
a house of prayer for all nations.
—*Isaiah 56:7*

David knew that the fullness of God would not come to pass in his generation without night-and-day prayer, which is why he was consumed with zeal for the house of God. This vision so consumed him that he set up a prophetic worship ministry to the Lord with four thousand musicians and two hundred eighty-eight singers (I Chron. 23–25). One of the central themes of Scripture ever since that time is how God has been building the house of prayer throughout the generations. There is struggle in the process of fulfilling God's purpose. Through the Word we see how He gathers the people, they fall and stumble in the process, then He gathers them again and gives them victory. He allows struggle so that when the victory comes, our hearts are protected by the grace of humility. At the end of natural history, God says, "My house will be called a house of prayer for all nations."

PRAYER STARTER

Father, I recognize with David that there is struggle in the process of fulfilling Your purposes for my life. Teach me to make my life a life of prayer. Let me bow before you night and day, that I might be a house of prayer upon this earth.

WE HAVE A LOT TO LEARN FROM DAVID, WHO WAS A
GLORIOUS PROPHETIC PICTURE OF THE END-TIME HOUSE OF
PRAYER GOD WILL ESTABLISH ACROSS THE EARTH.

DAY 286

When the day of Pentecost came, they were all together in one place. Suddenly a sound like the blowing of a violent wind came from heaven and filled the whole house where they were sitting. They saw what seemed to be tongues of fire that separated and came to rest on each of them. All of them were filled with the Holy Spirit and began to speak in other tongues as the Spirit enabled them.

—*Acts 2:1–4*

Many elements in this passage reveal how God started His church on the Day of Pentecost. I want to highlight three of these elements. First, God sent the "wind" of the Spirit, then the "fire" of the Spirit, and then the "wine" of the Spirit. When God sends the wind of the Spirit, we can expect to see great signs and wonders. The fire of God will enlarge our hearts in the love of God. The wine of God is linked in the Book of Joel to the outpouring of the Holy Spirit, God's ministry of bringing joy inexpressible and refreshment to weary, burdened souls. As God restores the church before the Second Coming, I believe the order will be reversed. First, He is sending the wine of the Spirit to refresh and heal the weary church. Then He will send the fire of the Spirit to enlarge our hearts in God's love. Last, He will send the wind of the Spirit, which includes a manifestation of the ministry of angels. This demonstration of the Holy Spirit's power will bring countless numbers of new people to saving faith in Jesus Christ.

PRAYER STARTER

Spirit, send Your "wind" and "fire" and "wine." I long to see Your mighty signs and wonders and to have my heart enlarged by Your love. Give me a fiery passion for Jesus and a heart of compassion for others.

I BELIEVE THAT ACTS 2 IS A DIVINE PATTERN OF HOW GOD VISITS HIS CHURCH IN POWER.

DAY 287

These are not drunk, as you suppose, since it is only the third
hour of the day. But this is what was spoken by the prophet Joel.
—*Acts 2:15–16, NKJV*

The Joel 2 prophecies concerning the outpouring of the Holy Spirit
are partially fulfilled in Jerusalem on the Day of Pentecost. But just
because the outpouring at Pentecost was "what was spoken by the
prophet Joel" doesn't mean that was *all* of the outpouring. The Spirit
fell on one hundred twenty people in a small room in Jerusalem. That's
not big enough for the complete fulfillment—even if you include the
three thousand who were converted and baptized that day. I am convinced that the fullness of Joel 2 is yet to be seen. The greatest and
fullest manifestation of the kingdom of God—the Day of the Lord,
the restoration of all things, and the outpouring of the Holy Spirit—is
reserved for the consummation of all things at the end of the age.
I believe there will be an unprecedented revival in which all believers
will experience dreams, visions, and everything Joel prophesied just
before the Second Coming of Christ.

PRAYER STARTER

*Father, I long for the fulfillment of Your prophetic word to pour Your
Spirit out upon this world. I wait eagerly for revival to fill our land and for
Your people to experience dreams and visions from You.*

THE PROPHECY WILL HAVE A WORLDWIDE SCOPE TO IT
WHERE ALL FLESH—THAT IS, ALL BELIEVERS, NOT JUST
PROPHETS—WILL HAVE DREAMS AND SEE VISIONS.

DAY 288

But when he, the Spirit of truth, comes, he will guide you into all truth. He will not speak on his own; he will speak only what he hears, and he will tell you what is yet to come. He will bring glory to me by taking from what is mine and making it known to you.
—*John 16:13–14*

A lot of things will begin to happen as a result of this outpouring of the Spirit. It will have so many multidimensional expressions that it cannot be called simply an evangelism movement, a healing movement, a prayer movement, a unity movement, or a prophetic movement. Above all things, it will impart and renew deep, affectionate passion for Jesus through the Holy Spirit. The increase of prophetic ministry in the local church involves more than verbal, inspirational prophecy. In my understanding, it includes angelic visitations, dreams, visions, and signs and wonders in the sky, as well as an increase in prophetic revelation, even the kind given through the subtle impressions of the Holy Spirit.

PRAYER STARTER

Lord, bring a revival that fills Your people with deep, affectionate passion for You. Fill Your people with angelic visitations, dreams, visions, and signs and wonders. Increase Your prophetic revelation to Your children.

THE HOLY SPIRIT LONGS ABOVE ALL THINGS TO GLORIFY JESUS IN THE HUMAN HEART.

DAY 289

Your sons and daughters will prophesy, your young men will
see visions, your old men will dream dreams. Even on my servants…
I will pour out my Spirit in those days, and they will prophesy.
I will show wonders in the heaven above and signs on the earth below,
blood and fire and billows of smoke….And everyone who calls
on the name of the Lord will be saved.
—*Acts 2:17–21*

Confirmation of prophetic words by the acts of God in nature is not
a common topic in the church. But signs in the heavens as well as the
very forces of nature on Earth will serve as a dramatic testimony to the
church and to unbelievers. The greatest fulfillment of Joel's promise
will be just prior to Christ's Second Coming. Acts 2:17–18 speaks of
the outpouring of the Spirit and the increase of prophetic revelation
on the entire body of Christ. Verses 19–21 are dedicated to the great
increase of the acts of God in nature. The last days will be accompanied by a multiplication of all four elements of the Joel 2 prophecy:
the outpouring of the Spirit, prophetic dreams and visions, signs and
wonders on Earth and in the heavens, and a wholehearted turning to
Jesus—first for salvation, and then with extravagant love for Him. This
wholehearted calling on the name of the Lord is not only for unbelievers, but it includes the church growing in holy passion for Jesus.

PRAYER STARTER

*Father, help me to be a part of the outpouring of Your Spirit. Give me
prophetic dreams and visions. Help me to pray for mighty signs and wonders. Let
me be a part of causing a wholehearted return to You. Bring revival to me.*

WHEN A BALANCED PROPHETIC MINISTRY FLOURISHES, IT IS
OFTEN FOLLOWED BY SOME FORM OF SIGNS AND WONDERS.

DAY 290

In the last days, God says...I will show wonders in the heaven above and signs on the earth below, blood and fire and billows of smoke....And everyone who calls on the name of the Lord will be saved.
—*Acts 2:17, 19–21*

Signs and wonders in nature are not to be taken lightly, because they are not given for trivial reasons. Don't expect God to show a sign in the heavens concerning which car you are supposed to buy. Fire fell from heaven and consumed Elijah's sacrifice, the Red Sea parted, and a star led the wise men to Bethlehem. These were not insignificant events in the progress of God's plan and purpose. God's power displayed by signs and wonders in nature in the last days will be unprecedented because it will serve to confirm and signify one of the greatest events of all time—the last ingathering of souls and the Second Coming of Jesus Christ. The purpose of the outpouring of the Spirit, the increase of the prophetic ministry, and the signs and wonders in nature is to awaken the church to passionate Christianity and to bring people to salvation.

PRAYER STARTER

Help me to understand Your work in these end days, dear God. Let me always remember that Your Spirit is being poured out upon man to awaken Your church and to bring people to salvation.

THE MAGNITUDE OF GOD'S MANIFEST POWER IS USUALLY PROPORTIONAL TO THE SIGNIFICANCE OF HIS PURPOSE.

DAY 291

We did not follow cleverly invented stories when we told you
about the power and coming of our Lord Jesus Christ, but we were
eyewitnesses of his majesty. For he received honor and glory from
God the Father when the voice came to him from the Majestic Glory,
saying, "This is my Son, whom I love; with him I am well pleased."
We ourselves heard this voice that came from heaven when we were
with him on the sacred mountain.
—2 Peter 1:16–18

Convincing power and irrefutable truth marked the spread of the gospel in the first century. The presence and power of the Spirit provided undeniable evidence of the truth the apostles proclaimed. An important element of the gospel message in those days was that the apostles were eyewitnesses to the fact that Jesus was risen from the dead. Firsthand eyewitness verification of this essential truth was of highest importance in the initial preaching of the gospel. When the apostles assembled to choose a man to replace Judas, the stipulation was that he needed to have been with them from the beginning so, as Peter said, he could "become a witness with us of his resurrection" (Acts 1:22). One fundamental job of the twelve apostles was to provide eyewitness verification to all that Jesus said and did. The church's message in the end times will not only be that Christ is risen from the dead, but that His return is imminent.

PRAYER STARTER

Father, I thank You for those who were eyewitnesses of Your power and glory in the days when Your church began on Earth. I recognize that the great harvest of souls that will soon take place will be a witness to the fact that Your return in imminent. Thank You for this outpouring of mercy and power.

**THE LAST GREAT HARVESTING OF SOULS WILL BE AN
EXTRAVAGANT OUTPOURING OF GOD'S MERCY AND POWER.**

DAY 292

To keep me from becoming conceited because of these
surpassingly great revelations, there was given me a thorn in my
flesh, a messenger of Satan, to torment me. Three times I pleaded
with the Lord to take it away from me. But he said to me, "My grace
is sufficient for you, for my power is made perfect in weakness."
Therefore I will boast all the more gladly about my weaknesses,
so that Christ's power may rest on me.
—*2 Corinthians 12:7–9*

One principle to note is the connection between the abundance of revelation and a higher degree of suffering or testing. According to Paul,
his thorn in the flesh was given to keep him from exalting himself in
light of the abundance of revelation that he had received (2 Cor. 12:7).
The thorn was given *because of* revelation. On the other hand, it seems
that God gives powerful revelation *because of* the testings that some are
about to encounter. Paul received a prophetic vision instructing him to
take his missionary efforts into Macedonia rather than Bithynia. That
decision resulted in Paul and Silas being arrested, dragged before the
magistrate, severely beaten with rods, thrown into the inner prison, and
secured in stocks. Though the thorn can come because of revelation, so
also revelation can come to prepare us for future testings. How greatly
will the saints who are awaiting the physical and visible return of Jesus
Christ be encouraged by the undeniable confirmations of His coming!

PRAYER STARTER

*Father, may I recognize the thorns that come into my own life as evi-
dence that You are testing me and preparing me to be ready for Your coming.
With the thorn comes powerful revelation of Your plan to come again.*

**A POWERFUL PROPHETIC REVELATION WITH
UNDENIABLE CONFIRMATIONS STABILIZES PEOPLE IN A TIME
OF SEVERE TESTING.**

DAY 293

However, as it is written: "No eye has seen, no ear has heard,
no mind has conceived what God has prepared for those who love
him"—but God has revealed it to us by his Spirit.
—*1 Corinthians 2:9–10*

Occasionally, the Lord may give directions to a church that would be difficult to act on without a strong prophetic confirmation. One such event is recorded by Eusebius, the third-century church historian. According to Eusebius, the entire body of believers in the city of Jerusalem picked up and left the city because of a prophetic revelation, and, consequently, their lives were spared. Immediately after their departure, Jerusalem was put under siege by Titus, the Roman general, and was destroyed in A.D. 70. Surely God established the credibility of these prophetic messengers in the eyes of the church before the coming crisis. It must have been a strong enough confirmation to be believed. I believe that there is a quality of prophetic ministry emerging in the body of Christ in our day that will achieve a similar kind of credibility in the eyes of both the church and, to a degree, even secular leaders and society. Many may scoff at this idea, but someday God might use prophetic ministry to actually save them from disaster!

PRAYER STARTER

Father, I thank You that You will raise up a credible prophetic ministry in these last days that will help the world to know Your specific plans and purpose. Father, may we look to Your revelation to guide our lives and protect us from disaster.

**WHAT EXCITING TIMES LIE AHEAD FOR THE BODY
OF CHRIST!**

DAY 294

Watch your life and doctrine closely. Persevere in them, because
if you do, you will save both yourself and your hearers.
—1 Timothy 4:16

One of the most surprising and enlightening things I share with conservative evangelical pastors is that there are people with valid gifts of the Spirit who are themselves still carnal. This challenges a commonly held idea that it is greater truth, wisdom, and character that produce greater power. Many think that only godly, mature people are used by God in demonstrations of power, but there are many exceptions. What is often surprising to both charismatic and noncharismatic pastors is that people can express valid gifts of the Spirit, yet have some pretty significant hang-ups and unresolved issues in their lives. Many leaders have assumed that if there is a definite flaw in a person's doctrine, wisdom, or character, then that is proof positive that the gifts and power in their ministries must not really be from God after all.

PRAYER STARTER

Father, You have determined to give Your spiritual gifts to imperfect, human individuals. Help me to understand that Your words and messages may be given through vessels of clay, imperfect people who may not always have the ability to speak with clarity.

> PROPHETIC PEOPLE MUST BE CLEAR ABOUT MAJOR
> DOCTRINES, BUT ON LESSER POINTS OF DOCTRINE, THEY
> MIGHT BE MISINFORMED.

DAY 295

But one and the same Spirit works all these things, distributing
to each one individually as He wills.
—*1 Corinthians 12:11, NKJV*

The word used in the New Testament for spiritual gifts is *charisma*
or, literally, "gifts of grace." In other words, these gifts are given
freely and are not earned. It was Simon the sorcerer who misunderstood the gifts and power of the Holy Spirit, thinking they could
be purchased (Acts 8:18–24). What a terrible thing, we think. No
doubt Simon had a wrong equation, and Peter severely rebuked him
because of the wickedness in his heart that would allow him even to
consider buying the power of God. But there's not much difference
between earning gifts and buying them. Money is only a function
of effort and labor. Contrary to some commonly held equations,
the gifts and power of God are distributed at the will of the Holy
Spirit. They are not given as a token or a badge of God's approval of
a person's level of spiritual maturity. Neither are they earned by our
consecration. They are grace gifts.

PRAYER STARTER

*Father, teach me that spiritual gifts are gifts freely given because of
Your great grace. I cannot earn these gifts, and nothing I can offer to You will
purchase them. You bestow these gifts freely as the gift of grace.*

SPIRITUAL GIFTS ARE GIVEN FREELY AND ARE NOT EARNED.

DAY 296

O foolish Galatians! Who has bewitched you...? This only
I want to learn from you: Did you receive the Spirit by the works of
the law, or by the hearing of faith? Are you so foolish? Having begun
in the Spirit, are you now being made perfect by the flesh?
—Galatians 3:1–3, NKJV

Paul wrote these words to the Galatians, who had difficulty understanding grace and who kept putting law and works back into their
equation. Apparently, the Galatians had experienced a filling of the
Holy Spirit and, with it, certain manifestations of spiritual gifts. Paul
reminded them that just as being spiritually gifted is by grace, so justification is by grace. You can turn that idea around as well. Just as we
are saved by grace, not by works of merit, we receive the gifts of the
Spirit by grace, not works.

PRAYER STARTER

Thank You, Father, that Your gift of grace has provided justification from my sins and has enabled me to be the receiver of Your gifts of the
Spirit. May I never assume that my works enabled me to receive either of
these blessings.

JUST AS WE ARE SAVED BY GRACE, NOT BY WORKS OF MERIT,
WE RECEIVE THE GIFTS OF THE SPIRIT BY GRACE,
NOT WORKS.

DAY 297

When Peter saw this, he said to them: "Men of Israel, why does this surprise you? Why do you stare at us as if by our own power or godliness we had made this man walk? The God of Abraham, Isaac and Jacob, the God of our fathers, has glorified his servant Jesus.... You killed the author of life, but God raised him from the dead. We are witnesses of this. By faith in the name of Jesus, this man whom you see and know was made strong. It is Jesus' name and the faith that comes through him that has given this complete healing to him, as you can all see."

—*Acts 3:12–16*

The lame man who begged for alms was commanded by Peter and John to walk in the name of Jesus. Peter wanted to make that point clearly and quickly before there were any false assumptions. The manifestation of God's power was not a sign of his personal godliness. The healing was the result of God's purpose in His timing by means of faith in Jesus's name, a faith that comes through Him. That passage contains many implications. But if it says anything, it is that the miracle was not about Peter or about promoting his spirituality. It had to do with God and His purposes.

PRAYER STARTER

Thank You for reminding me, Spirit, that even though I am incapable of possessing any form of godliness except that which comes from You, still You make it possible for me to work miracles in Your name.

THE MIRACLE WAS NOT ABOUT PETER—IT HAD TO DO WITH GOD'S PURPOSES.

DAY 298

But to each one of us grace has been given as Christ
apportioned it....It was he who gave some to be apostles, some to be
prophets, some to be evangelists, and some to be pastors and teachers,
to prepare God's people for works of service, so that the body of
Christ may be built up until we all reach unity in the faith and in the
knowledge of the Son of God and become mature, attaining to the
whole measure of the fullness of Christ.
—*Ephesians 4:7, 11–13*

Paul writes to the Ephesians that "grace was given according to the
measure of Christ's gift" (Eph. 4:7, NKJV). Verse 11 makes it clear that
the *gift* he was referring to is a *ministry gift*. We can't help but notice
the misconception about the anointed people referred to in this passage. We commonly assume that people are given the gift of being a
prophet, pastor, or evangelist. Paul saw it differently. "He...gave some
to be apostles...prophets...evangelists...pastors...teachers" (v. 11,
emphasis added). Clearly, the minister *was the gift* to the church. It was
not an issue of the anointed gift being for the benefit of the minister.
That really changes the way we look at it. God's gifts are distributed to
people who become vessels and conduits of His mercy for the benefit
of others.

PRAYER STARTER

*Father, help me to discern the giftings that You have given to me. And
help me to remember always that the purpose of the gifts You placed in my
spirit are that Your church may come to know You better.*

**GOD'S GIFTINGS ARE NOT ABOUT OUR PROMOTIONS
AND ESTEEM.**

DAY 299

But to each one of us grace has been given as Christ
apportioned it. This is why it says: "When he ascended on high,
he led captives in his train and gave gifts to men."
—*Ephesians 4:7–8*

The gifts of God in a person's life are not merit badges signifying that person's consecration, wisdom, or 100 percent doctrinal truth. You might interpret the meaning of Ephesians 4:7 like this: out of unmerited grace, each person is given gifts for the purpose of being used to bless others. Gifts of the Holy Spirit, whether they are in the form of manifestations of power and revelation or in the form of people given as ministers, are for the purpose of blessing the church. Yet, most of us can hardly avoid the temptation of seeing supernatural power gifts working through an individual as a symbol of God's approval of that person's life, spiritual maturity, and doctrine. The more significant the giftings and power, the more approval from God—or so it would seem. If we understood that the manifestations of the Spirit are for the common good and not for the good of the individual whom God uses, we would be less likely to stumble over the idea that God uses imperfect, often immature people to bless the church.

PRAYER STARTER

Father, use me to bless others. Display Your spirit and Your giftings in my life in such a way that no one sees anything of me, but sees only You.

OUT OF UNMERITED GRACE, EACH PERSON IS GIVEN GIFTS
FOR THE PURPOSE OF BEING USED TO BLESS OTHERS.

DAY 300

You foolish Galatians! Who has bewitched you? Before your very
eyes Jesus Christ was clearly portrayed as crucified. I would like to learn
just one thing from you: Did you receive the Spirit by observing the law,
or by believing what you heard? Are you so foolish? After beginning
with the Spirit, are you now trying to attain your goal by human effort?
Have you suffered so much for nothing—if it really was for nothing?
Does God give you his Spirit and work miracles among you because you
observe the law, or because you believe what you heard?
—*Galatians 3:1–5*

In his rebuke to the Galatians, Paul used the idea of receiving the gifts of
the Spirit by faith and not works as analogous to receiving justification
by faith and not works. This whole idea of grace is completely contrary
to our natural way of thinking—the idea that the gifts, even the gift
of salvation, can be given on the basis of grace through faith alone and
not with reference or regard to meritorious efforts. Every other religion
besides Christianity has at its core a prescription for some kind of
salvation or union with God based on works. In this most commonly
held false equation, man must earn his forgiveness, striving diligently
to bridge the separation between God and man. Indeed, it is hard to
understand it being any other way.

PRAYER STARTER

*Father, how hard it is for man to understand the grace of God. It is
freely given, totally without merit, and based only on faith in You.*

**THIS WHOLE IDEA OF GRACE IS COMPLETELY CONTRARY TO
OUR NATURAL WAY OF THINKING.**

DAY 301

Therefore, since we have been justified through faith, we have peace with God through our Lord Jesus Christ, through whom we have gained access by faith into this grace in which we now stand.

—*Romans 5:1–2*

There is no way anyone will understand justification by grace appropriated only through faith without looking at it from God's perspective. When we see the holiness of God on one hand and the depth of mankind's sin on the other, a lot of things come into a new light. Justification by faith alone makes sense only when you realize that no amount of human effort could bridge that immeasurable gap. No amount of consecration or sanctification could earn the right to the gifts of the Spirit any more than indulgences could gain forgiveness or Simon's money could purchase God's power. Gifts of the Spirit are given based on the grace of God, not on the maturity, wisdom, and character of the vessel.

PRAYER STARTER

Father, there is a great gulf that stands between Your perfect holiness and the sinful, hopeless condition of mankind. Nothing but a simple faith in You can bridge that gulf and cause Your forgiveness and mercy to flood over my soul.

GOD'S SOLUTION ON THE CROSS MAKES SENSE WHEN YOU REALIZE THAT THE HUMAN EFFORT EQUATION IS HOPELESSLY FLAWED.

DAY 302

But the LORD said to Samuel, "Do not consider his appearance
or his height, for I have rejected him. The LORD does not look at the
things man looks at. Man looks at the outward appearance,
but the LORD looks at the heart."
—1 Samuel 16:7

Throughout Bible times, God forgave and extended great mercy to people who, by our standards, did some pretty despicable things. Without diminishing the gravity of some of the more serious sins on our list, Jesus showed everyone that things like pride, hypocrisy, treatment of the poor, unforgiveness, and self-righteousness were more serious to God than we could have ever imagined. It seems He is rather patient and merciful with people who do bad things due to the fact that they are unwise, immature, or just weak. But to those who continue to deliberately disobey God, attempting to misuse God's grace and turn it into an excuse for sin, He often exercises His judgment, exposing such deliberate rebellion. We need to be careful about judging spiritual gifts as invalid because of people's weaknesses and immaturity. God may be more concerned about what He has set out to accomplish in the life of the prophetic vessel than about passing full judgment on that person.

PRAYER STARTER

Holy Spirit, give me the grace to understand that Your purposes are far above what I can see with my human eyes. When I am tempted to discredit a prophetic message from You because of unwise, immature, or weak actions in that prophet's life, remind me that You often speak through weak vessels.

WHEN COMPARED TO THE PURITY AND HOLINESS OF GOD,
THE DIFFERENCES BETWEEN THE BEST OF US AND THE
WORST OF US ARE NOT AS GREAT AS SOME OF US
MIGHT LIKE TO IMAGINE.

DAY 303

> If I have the gift of prophecy and can fathom all mysteries and all knowledge, and if I have a faith that can move mountains, but have not love, I am nothing.
> —1 Corinthians 13:2

Most prophetic people don't have the gift of leadership that is essential for a church to be healthy, balanced, and safe. A church led only by prophets is not a safe environment for God's people. One of the most important things to do in a church that wants to nurture and administrate prophetic ministry is to dial down the mysticism and the carnal desire to look superspiritual. We need to keep our eyes off people and remain focused on Jesus and His purpose for us. This is not a spiritual beauty contest, but it can turn into one very quickly if people see gifts as merit badges rather than something to bless the church. The fact that power and revelation flow through prophetic ministers is not necessarily a sign that God is pleased with the other areas of their lives. Sometimes the prophetic gifts will continue to operate even when there is an inner crumbling taking place in their private lives.

PRAYER STARTER

> Father, keep my eyes focused on the true revelations You want to give to Your people. Cause me to desire nothing more than growing in my love and intimacy with You. Build Your church in whatever manner and with whomever You choose to use.

IT IS NOT ABOUT THE VESSEL. IT'S ABOUT LOVING THE LORD AND BUILDING UP HIS CHURCH.

DAY 304

But the one who does not know and does things deserving
punishment will be beaten with few blows. From everyone who has
been given much, much will be demanded; and from the one who has
been entrusted with much, much more will be asked.
—*Luke 12:48*

People with prominent spiritual giftings, as well as those with callings
to leadership, must constantly guard against high-mindedness. High-
mindedness is simply considering that you, your position, or your purpose is so important that you are judged more leniently. High-minded
people are those who consider that, because they are doing such an
important work for God and because His power is manifest through
them, they are not accountable for things like integrity, honesty, and
kindness—especially in the small and unseen matters of life. It is this
temptation to self-deception that plagues many people in positions of
power and influence. It is a great deception because, in actuality, the
opposite is true. Every person through whom spiritual gifts operate, as
well as every person in a position of privilege or leadership, needs to
be acutely aware that a day of reckoning is coming. We will all stand
before God one day for a final evaluation of our lives and ministries
(I Cor. 3:II–I5).

PRAYER STARTER

*Holy Spirit, convict me of any high-mindedness that is present in my
life. Fill my life and my mouth with integrity, honesty, and kindness. Help
me never to forget that I shall give an account to You for every word I speak
or think.*

**WE WILL ALL STAND BEFORE GOD ONE DAY FOR A FINAL
EVALUATION OF OUR LIVES AND MINISTRIES.**

DAY 305

Those who sin are to be rebuked publicly, so that the others may take warning. I charge you, in the sight of God and Christ Jesus and the elect angels, to keep these instructions without partiality, and to do nothing out of favoritism. Do not be hasty in the laying on of hands, and do not share in the sins of others. Keep yourself pure.
—1 Timothy 5:20–22

God has mercy on weak vessels and will manifest His gifts through them even when things are not totally right inside. But don't be deceived. This will not go on forever. It's like a dog on a long leash. He can chase after a cat to a limit, but eventually and suddenly, he'll come to the end of the leash. Some of God's people have been displayed as examples that He is patient with their sin and that His gifts are without repentance. Others are examples of another fact—that God eventually calls His servants to give account of their stewardship. God's disciplines are manifest more openly to this group, and it causes us to fear God. The message for prophets, leaders, and church people is this: God's gifts are freely given as a sign of His mercy, not His approval. Don't disdain valid spiritual gifts manifested through spiritually immature people. But also, do not be fooled by God's grace and patience with prophetic vessels who remain anointed for a season as they continue in their carnality. Eventually He will call us all to account as stewards of the gifts He has entrusted to us.

PRAYER STARTER

Father, teach me to focus on You, the giver of gifts, rather than on the gifts themselves. Make me a good steward of Your revelation, and help me to leave the judging of others to You.

GOD'S GIFTS ARE FREELY GIVEN AS A SIGN OF HIS MERCY, NOT HIS APPROVAL.

DAY 306

Above all, you must understand that no prophecy of Scripture came about by the prophet's own interpretation. For prophecy never had its origin in the will of man, but men spoke from God as they were carried along by the Holy Spirit.
—*2 Peter 1:20–21*

Methodology or ministry style does not produce power or anointing. Because you were standing in a certain place doing a certain thing when God spoke, moved, or healed doesn't mean that the circumstances had anything to do with it. Nevertheless, people find themselves trying to re-create the setting so they can see God's power again. I've seen all kinds of people from all over the body of Christ imitating styles and methods because they think that the method is the key. But the person of the Holy Spirit is the key to operating in the power of God. We have to beware constantly of thinking that if we get the early morning prayer meeting going just the way it was before and the same worship leader back up there with those same anointed songs, then maybe God will do the comet thing again. That's spiritual superstition.

PRAYER STARTER

Spirit, speak through me in any way You choose. Keep me from creating methods or mannerisms or styles for rating acceptable prophecy. Give me the clear vision to hear Your voice through others without attempting to judge their delivery style.

PROPHETIC PEOPLE ARE OFTEN TEMPTED TO THINK THAT THEIR PARTICULAR METHOD AND STYLE IS ESSENTIAL TO THE ANOINTING WORKING THROUGH THEIR LIVES.

DAY 307

Follow the way of love and eagerly desire spiritual gifts,
especially the gift of prophecy. For anyone who speaks in a tongue
does not speak to men but to God. Indeed, no one understands him;
he utters mysteries with his spirit. But everyone who prophesies
speaks to men for their strengthening, encouragement and comfort.

—1 Corinthians 14:1–3

There is the natural tendency in some of us to try to systematize spontaneous experiences. We sometimes think that if we discover the method-key, then we can control it. If people are successful in their ministry (or only appear to be), then they might start using the methods to manipulate people as well. People who are perceived as anointed men or women of God possess a potential for the power of suggestion. Whether it is being suggested that people will fall down, get a prophetic word, or speak in tongues, this is manipulative power of suggestion. Ministers with power and prophetic giftings who are not in relationship with a balanced local church team often allow their method-as-power tendencies to dominate their ministry. It is simply much more difficult to get away with manipulation and pretense when you relate closely to a balanced team of people who live in the real world.

PRAYER STARTER

Holy Spirit, I love the spontaneity of Your revelations to man. Keep me from manipulation or predictability in the use of the spiritual gifts You have given to me. And cause me to allow others the liberty to express Your words whenever and however You choose to use them.

THE GIFTS AND MANIFESTATIONS ARE GIVEN AS THE HOLY SPIRIT DESIRES.

DAY 308

> But he said to me, "My grace is sufficient for you, for my power
> is made perfect in weakness." Therefore I will boast all the more
> gladly about my weaknesses, so that Christ's power may rest on me.
> That is why, for Christ's sake, I delight in weaknesses, in insults,
> in hardships, in persecutions, in difficulties.
> For when I am weak, then I am strong.
> —*2 Corinthians 12:9–10*

We want to undermine the false equation that says if you follow a formula, God will manifest His power every time. I believe that on certain occasions He strategically does not manifest His power in order to win people's hearts away from the minister and his methods. Sometimes He will withdraw His Spirit in order to keep from perpetuating our confidence in methodology. Our desire is never to look weak, but Paul's testimony was that he delighted in weakness, that the true power of Christ might work through him. A spiritual mystique is intrinsically woven into prophetic ministry. When open and hungry people get around a prophetically anointed person, they are both hopeful and fearful that this person will reveal secrets and divine perspectives to them. They often cling to every word such a person may utter. This dynamic makes both parties vulnerable to unique temptations.

PRAYER STARTER

> *Father, You are not a God of formulas and methods. Continue to manifest Your presence and power in whatever form You choose. Rid my mind of any desire for spiritual mystique in prophetic ministry. Do what You want—in me and in others.*

**AFTER ALL, HEARING DIRECTLY FROM THE LIVING GOD
ABOUT ANYTHING IS A RATHER AWESOME THING.**

DAY 309

At the time of sacrifice, the prophet Elijah stepped forward and prayed: "O LORD, God of Abraham, Isaac and Israel, let it be known today that you are God in Israel and that I am your servant and have done all these things at your command. Answer me, O LORD, answer me, so these people will know that you, O LORD, are God, and that you are turning their hearts back again." Then the fire of the LORD fell and burned up the sacrifice, the wood, the stones and the soil, and also licked up the water in the trench.
—1 Kings 18:36–38

I have observed that it is easier to get one's identity wrapped around the prophetic ministry more than any other role one may have in the body of Christ. Prophetic people often submit to others' expectations that they constantly hear from God—whether God is saying anything to them or not! I believe there is a sense in which we should make things a little "harder on God" when it comes to showing His power. Let me explain. I have pondered how Elijah poured water on the sacrifices on Mt. Carmel (1 Kings 18). He didn't add lighter fluid and strike a match behind his back! He was confident that if the genuine fire of God fell, then it could consume even a wet sacrifice. I would challenge prophetic ministers to put some "water on the sacrifices" they prepare and really trust God to prove His power without their feeling the pressure of trying to help God out so much. Then when His power is demonstrated, the people will not glorify the prophet of God, but the God of the prophet.

PRAYER STARTER

Father, remove from me the desire to "set up" the scene or circumstance for You to reveal Your power. Let the power and revelation come from You, not from any "help" that I attempt to give You.

I ENCOURAGE YOU TO STAY IMPRESSED WITH GOD AND HIS POWER WITHOUT BECOMING IMPRESSED WITH YOURSELF.

DAY 310

Many will say to me on that day, "Lord, Lord, did we not prophesy in your name, and in your name drive out demons and perform many miracles?" Then I will tell them plainly, "I never knew you. Away from me, you evildoers!"
—*Matthew 7:22–23*

One of the tough parts of effective prophetic ministry is keeping personal opinions out of the way. On the other hand, teachers have a platform on which to declare many of their own thoughts. Prophetic people often chafe against this restraint on them that is not upon teachers. It is so important that prophetic ministers are part of a local church team that includes gifted teachers. If they are not in a team, then they are often tempted to assume too much responsibility and thereby venture outside their calling. When prophetic people and evangelists become separate from the local church, they are often tempted to establish doctrine, just as a gifted teacher with a large following sometimes does. Some of the unbalanced doctrine so widespread in the body of Christ has come from such people who have a large following through television and radio. They teach the multitudes who have gathered because of the supernatural gifts of the Spirit that operate through them. However, if they don't have a teaching gift that has been cultivated through proper training in the Scriptures, they are sure to teach unbalanced doctrine to their followers.

PRAYER STARTER

Father, keep me from a public ministry of any kind until I have allowed Your Spirit to give me the training I need in Your Word through a local community of believers and teachers whom You have placed in authority over me. Provide a covering of authority for me so that I may never wander into error.

PROPHETIC MINISTERS NEED TO BE WARY OF MANY POSSIBLE PITFALLS.

DAY 311

So also you, since you are zealous of spiritual gifts, seek to
abound for the edification of the church.
—*1 Corinthians 14:12, NAS*

False assumptions about spiritual gifts and what they signify can
eventually cause us to throw out something good or accept something
bad. Power gifts do not necessarily endorse character or methodology.
Nor do a prophet's great miracles validate all his doctrine. The most
important thing to remember is that "the manifestation of the Spirit
is given to each one for the profit of all" (1 Cor. 12:7, NKJV). Spiritual
gifts are for the purpose of blessing the body of Christ, not exalting
the person through whom they come. God delights in using weak and
imperfect vessels in order that He might receive the glory.

PRAYER STARTER

*I thank You, Spirit, for the blessing of the spiritual gifts You have
placed in our midst within Your body. May I never forget that the purpose of
Your gifts is to bless Your people. Thank You for using weak and imperfect
vessels to proclaim Your glory.*

DON'T LET BEING USED BY GOD IN PROPHECY AND HEALING
MIRACLES BECOME "COMMON" TO YOU.

DAY 312

> Therefore, my brothers, be eager to prophesy, and do not
> forbid speaking in tongues. But everything should be
> done in a fitting and orderly way.
> —1 Corinthians 14:39–40

We Christians have created a lot of religious assumptions about how God deals with us. He is a gentleman, we say, who will never barge in, but who politely stands at the door, quietly knocking and patiently waiting. The Holy Spirit is often thought of as being extremely shy or skittish. If we want the Holy Spirit to move, we get very quiet and still. If a baby cries, some think the Spirit might be quenched or perhaps scared off. This sounds ridiculous, but some Pentecostals and conservative evangelicals alike operate under notions such as these. Paul instructed the Corinthians not to forbid tongues or prophecy but to "let all things be done decently and in order" (I Cor. 14:40, kjv).

PRAYER STARTER

> Holy Spirit, how grateful I am that You are indeed a gentleman. Thank You for patiently waiting for me to open my heart to the revelation You want me to have. Help me to always move as You prompt and only as You determine.

THE HOLY SPIRIT IS A GENTLEMAN WHO NEVER BARGES IN.
HE STANDS AT THE DOOR, QUIETLY KNOCKING
AND PATIENTLY WAITING.

DAY 313

Then Peter stood up with the Eleven, raised his voice and addressed the crowd: "Fellow Jews and all of you who live in Jerusalem, let me explain this to you; listen carefully to what I say. These men are not drunk, as you suppose. It's only nine in the morning! No, this is what was spoken by the prophet Joel."

—Acts 2:14–16

Biblical examples of the move of the Holy Spirit teach us this: *the Holy Spirit does not appear to be overly concerned about our reputations.* The outpouring of the Spirit didn't do much for the respectability of those in the upper room. "These men are not drunk, as you suppose," said Peter. Some people seem to be drunk as a result of the filling of the Holy Spirit. I can imagine Peter preaching his Acts 2 sermon while still feeling the effects of some of the holy hilarity of heaven himself. Peter directed his first sermon to the out-of-town visitors who were in Jerusalem for the feast of Pentecost. Many of those were the people who were amazed and perplexed at hearing praises to God in their own language (Acts 2:8–12). But Peter also preached to those who were the most religious of all, the Hebraic Pharisees of Judea who, being offended in their minds, scoffed, "They are full of new wine" (v. 13, NKJV). The disciples' behavior might have seemed out of order to these religious leaders, but it was, nevertheless, the work of the Holy Spirit.

PRAYER STARTER

Forgive me, Holy Spirit, for being concerned about the appearance of my response to Your anointing. Forgive me for judging others for their responses to You. I will allow You to work in any way You choose.

THE HOLY SPIRIT DOES NOT APPEAR TO BE OVERLY CONCERNED ABOUT OUR REPUTATIONS.

DAY 314

For since in the wisdom of God the world through its wisdom did not know him, God was pleased through the foolishness of what was preached to save those who believe. Jews demand miraculous signs and Greeks look for wisdom, but we preach Christ crucified: a stumbling block to Jews and foolishness to Gentiles, but to those whom God has called, both Jews and Greeks, Christ the power of God and the wisdom of God.

—*1 Corinthians 1:21–24*

In contrast to the polite, shy, gentlemanly image we have of the Holy Spirit, *He intentionally offends people.* It pleased God that the Gentiles were offended by the foolishness of the gospel message and that the Jews were tripped up by the stumbling block of the cross. Paul warned the Galatians that if they required circumcision as demanded by the Jews, then "the offense of the cross has ceased" (Gal. 5:11, NKJV). The implication is that the gospel is sometimes offensive by God's design. By offending people with His methods, God reveals the pride, self-sufficiency, and feigned obedience that lie hidden in people's hearts.

PRAYER STARTER

Father, prepare me for the times when Your Spirit offends me or others. Remind me that You may choose offense to reveal my pride, self-sufficiency, or feigned obedience.

THE HOLY SPIRIT INTENTIONALLY OFFENDS PEOPLE.

DAY 315

*I am the living bread which came down from heaven.... Most
assuredly, I say to you, unless you eat the flesh of the Son of Man
and drink His blood, you have no life in you. Whoever eats
My flesh and drinks My blood has eternal life,
and I will raise him up at the last day.*
—*John 6:51, 53–54, NKJV*

A good example of God intentionally offending people is in John 6.
Jesus fed five thousand people with the multiplied fish and loaves. Now
they expected that the Messiah would prove Himself with some great
sign, something more than multiplying bread or healing people. They
were asking Jesus to do something like the manna-from-heaven thing
again. Jesus offended them in their minds theologically by saying that
He was the bread that came down from heaven. He offended their
expectations by refusing to give them the expected sign. He offended
their sensibility and their dignity by suggesting that they eat His flesh
and drink His blood. Jesus knew their hearts—that most of them
loved their tradition more than God. He also knew that those who followed Him as told in John 6 did so with mixed motives. He revealed
their hearts by intentionally offending their minds.

PRAYER STARTER

*When I feel offended by Your Spirit, cause me to immediately repent
and to remember that You offend to redeem. Reveal my heart through Your
offense, and bring me to repentance and restoration.*

**GOD'S OFFENSE IS REDEMPTIVE. HE OFFENDS PEOPLE'S
MINDS IN ORDER TO REVEAL THEIR HEARTS.**

DAY 316

Now to each one the manifestation of the Spirit is given for the common good. To one there is given through the Spirit the message of wisdom, to another the message of knowledge by means of the same Spirit, to another faith by the same Spirit, to another gifts of healing by that one Spirit, to another miraculous powers, to another prophecy, to another distinguishing between spirits, to another speaking in different kinds of tongues, and to still another the interpretation of tongues. All these are the work of one and the same Spirit, and he gives them to each one, just as he determines.
—1 Corinthians 12:7–11

Prophetic ministry cannot be an end in itself. Its purpose is always to strengthen and promote something greater and more valuable than itself. People get off track when they allow themselves to become more focused on the unusual means of the message rather than God's purpose in that message. It is not so important whether the message comes from a five-star prophet with mountain-moving confirmations, or if it is something that simply seems good to everyone involved. The message is always more important than the method. The subjective side of our faith is always to be scrutinized in the light of the objective side, but both are essential. God is always working to bring the Word and the Spirit together. If we have the Word and the Spirit, we grow up.

PRAYER STARTER

Holy Spirit, may I never seek to merely know about You. Give me a passionate desire to know You, Your personality and being.

OUR DESIRE IS FOR GOD, NOT JUST KNOWLEDGE ABOUT HIM.

DAY 317

The LORD Almighty is the one you are to regard as holy, he is
the one you are to fear, he is the one you are to dread, and he will be a
sanctuary; but for both houses of Israel he will be a stone that causes
men to stumble and a rock that makes them fall. And for the people
of Jerusalem he will be a trap and a snare.
—*Isaiah 8:13–14*

The Pharisees and the disciples both misunderstood Jesus, and consequently, they were both offended. Those who were offended and who turned away from Jesus when He said, "I am the living bread which came down from heaven" (John 6:51, NKJV), were not Pharisees but His disciples (followers other than the Twelve). Though He taught with great wisdom and did a few mighty works in His hometown, His friends "were offended at Him" (Matt. 13:57, NKJV). The most commonly used Greek word in the New Testament for *offend* is also translated "to stumble." The Greek word is *skandalizo*, from which our English word *scandal* is derived. By offending people's minds, God reveals the things in their hearts that cause them to stumble. Jesus is revealed in the Bible as the way, the truth, the Bread of Life, and the door. He is also "a stone of stumbling and a rock of offense" (Isa. 8:14, NKJV). What is most revealed in the offended heart is a lack of hunger for God and a lack of humility. In God's eyes, these are two important characteristics of the heart.

PRAYER STARTER

Father, if there are hidden things within my heart that could cause me to stumble, then reveal them to me by Your spirit that I may lay them at the altar and find Your perfect will.

**GOD EVEN SCANDALIZES OR OFFENDS HIS OWN
PEOPLE'S MINDS.**

DAY 318

I keep asking that the God of our Lord Jesus Christ, the glorious Father, may give you the Spirit of wisdom and revelation, so that you may know him better. I pray also that the eyes of your heart may be enlightened in order that you may know the hope to which he has called you, the riches of his glorious inheritance in the saints, and his incomparably great power for us who believe.

—Ephesians 1:17–19

Neither functioning in New Testament prophetic ministry nor moving in the supernatural ministry of the Holy Spirit is an exact science. These things challenge our improper control issues and our religious codes. They've been designed by God for this very purpose! We are called to embrace the mystery of God and not to lust after neatly tying up every doctrinal or philosophical loose end that we encounter. Our hunger for a personal relationship with God Himself should overpower this drive within us to perfectly comprehend every fact. Our humility before God should instruct us that we will never have all the answers, at least not in this age. We are hard enough to live with as it is. As long as we're in this flesh, I don't think possessing omniscience would help us be any easier to live with.

PRAYER STARTER

Father, as much as I want to know more about *You*, my heart's desire is to have a dynamic intimate relationship with *You*.

> TRUE CHRISTIANITY IS A DYNAMIC RELATIONSHIP WITH A LIVING GOD, AND IT CANNOT BE REDUCED TO FORMULAS AND DRY ORTHODOXY.

DAY 319

You search the Scriptures, for in them you think you have
eternal life; and these are they which testify of Me. But you are not
willing to come to Me that you may have life. I do not receive honor
from men. But I know you, that you do not have the love of God in
you....How can you believe, who receive honor from one another,
and do not seek the honor that comes from the only God?
—*John 5:39–42, 44, NKJV*

Jesus directly addresses the root problems of self-satisfaction and
religious pride. The religious Jews were deceived by equating their
knowledge of Scripture and their association with the religious community with the knowledge of God. Yet, truthfully, they were stub-
bornly refusing to enter into a personal relationship with God through
His personal representative, Jesus. They boasted in their knowledge
of Scripture while rejecting the author of Scripture. God puts before
us strategic stumbling blocks in the gospel and in our walks with
the Holy Spirit to test our hearts. If we become hungry for God and
humble in heart, these stumbling blocks actually become the stepping
stones that lead us forward in His purposes for our lives.

PRAYER STARTER

*Father, rid my life of self-satisfaction and religious pride. Test my
heart, and strengthen me in humility to be prepared to fulfill Your purposes.*

ANY OF US SHOULD WELCOME WHATEVER IT TAKES TO
ENTER INTO AND ENJOY A MORE INTIMATE RELATIONSHIP
WITH THE FATHER, SON, AND HOLY SPIRIT.

The LORD said to me, "Go, show your love to your wife again, though she is loved by another and is an adulteress. Love her as the LORD loves the Israelites, though they turn to other gods and love the sacred raisin cakes." So I bought her for fifteen shekels of silver and about a homer and a lethek of barley. Then I told her, "You are to live with me many days; you must not be a prostitute or be intimate with any man, and I will live with you." For the Israelites will live many days without king or prince, without sacrifice or sacred stones, without ephod or idol. Afterward the Israelites will return and seek the LORD their God and David their king. They will come trembling to the LORD and to his blessings in the last days.

—Hosea 3:1–5

God will often make the lives of His prophetic vessels prophetic illustrations of the messages they are called to proclaim. Sometimes God deals with His servants in a way that is hard for us to understand. That is one of the burdens of the prophetic calling. When people's lives are used to illustrate God's point, these message bearers feel God's heart in the matter. The prophet Hosea is one of the best examples of this. God instructed him to embrace and marry a harlot. In doing so, Hosea demonstrated God's love and forbearance toward the harlot nation of Israel. This was undoubtedly a painful thing for Hosea, but it enabled him to feel the heart of God. God wants His servants not only to *say* what He is like, but to *be* like Him; not only to *say* what He wants, but to *do* and *demonstrate* His will; not only to *declare* His heart, but to *feel* His heart.

PRAYER STARTER

Holy Spirit, deal with my spirit in whatever way You need to deal with me. I want only to be like You and to do Your will.

SOMETIMES GOD DEALS WITH HIS SERVANTS IN A WAY THAT IS HARD FOR US TO UNDERSTAND.

DAY 321

To keep me from becoming conceited because of these
surpassingly great revelations, there was given me a thorn in my
flesh, a messenger of Satan, to torment me. Three times I pleaded
with the Lord to take it away from me. But he said to me, "My grace
is sufficient for you, for my power is made perfect in weakness."
Therefore I will boast all the more gladly about my weaknesses,
so that Christ's power may rest on me.
—*2 Corinthians 12:7–9*

God often sends a thorn in the flesh to those to whom He gives abundant revelation, in order to protect their hearts from destructive pride. The apostle Paul said that he had been given a "thorn in the flesh" in order that he would not exalt himself. This was due to the fact that his ministry was surrounded by "surpassingly great revelations" (2 Cor. 12:7). For some, the beauty of God's work in them is never put on a public stage and is seldom noticed, except by a few. In such cases, those peoples' lives are perfected for God's pleasure and the impact on individuals around them. Sometimes the Holy Spirit works inwardly for almost a lifetime before that person is given the full platform to release the message. Still others are called to be proclaimers of the message. Some have been given an early platform and are allowed to preach beyond the maturing work of the Holy Spirit in their lives.

PRAYER STARTER

Father, reveal my life message to me. Show me the work You want me to do. Make me a vessel fit for Your service—whatever that service may be.

**GOD HAS PURPOSED TO WORK A LIFE MESSAGE
THROUGH EACH OF US.**

DAY 322

The Lord is not slack concerning His promise, as some count slackness, but is longsuffering toward us, not willing that any should perish but that all should come to repentance.
—*2 Peter 3:9, NKJV*

The Scriptures suggest that God extends His grace to people and patiently waits for them to change. God desires that all of us examine ourselves carefully in the light of His Word and become sensitive to the Holy Spirit's conviction in areas that need to change. But eventually, if we don't recognize the problems and deal with them, all kinds of external circumstances can be used to bring to light the unresolved or carnal issues in our lives. If we really love God, He gives us the chance to respond voluntarily to the Spirit. But if we don't respond, He will often extract submission from us.

PRAYER STARTER

Father, when I feel a thorn pricking at my spirit, help me to remember that the purpose is to allow me a chance to deal with Your conviction and to respond in submission to Your will.

THE THORN IN THE FLESH PRODUCES HUMILITY OVER TIME IN THE LIVES OF SINCERE YET IMMATURE FOLLOWERS OF CHRIST JESUS.

DAY 323

Our fathers disciplined us for a little while as they thought best; but God disciplines us for our good, that we may share in his holiness. No discipline seems pleasant at the time, but painful. Later on, however, it produces a harvest of righteousness and peace for those who have been trained by it.
—*Hebrews 12:10–11*

Remember that the purpose of God's discipline is to equip our hearts in Christlikeness. The prophetic message that He gives us is in essence to embrace the various dimensions of Christlikeness. His overall prophetic goal for all Christians is "to be conformed to the image of His Son" (Rom. 8:29, NKJV). God wants us to embody the prophetic message that He entrusts to us. It is never enough to proclaim a message. In one sense, God wants His Word to become flesh in our lives. Therefore, He sends various forms of redemptive discipline to help us see the unperceived weaknesses in our lives, those hidden fault lines beneath the surface. We can despise His discipline and decide to quit pursuing the Lord as fervently as we once did. We can become bitter at God for administering it. Or we can respond in the only right way, which is to endure His redemptive discipline, knowing that it is for our good that we might share in His holiness.

PRAYER STARTER

Lord, I welcome Your disciplining Spirit, for it equips me to live in Christlikeness. Keep me from becoming bitter or from rejecting Your purposes for the discipline.

WE MUST SEEK TO LIVE THE MESSAGE WE PROCLAIM BEFORE WE CAN GENUINELY CLAIM TO HAVE A PROPHETIC MESSAGE AND A PROPHETIC MINISTRY.

DAY 324

The LORD said to him, "Who gave man his mouth? Who
makes him deaf or mute? Who gives him sight or makes him blind?
Is it not I, the LORD? Now go; I will help you speak and
will teach you what to say."
—*Exodus 4:11–12*

In Old Testament times there were usually only a few prophets on the
whole earth at any one time. Sometimes prophets were contemporaries
(Haggai and Zechariah, Isaiah and Jeremiah), but for the most part
they operated in isolation as the lone mouthpiece of God. They often
were not incorporated into the daily religious life and traditions but
stood apart, separated unto God. No prophet exemplified this more
than Elijah, who stood alone against King Ahab, the prophets of Baal,
and the sins of a rebellious people. John the Baptist fits that mold
as well—the man of God coming out of the wilderness to proclaim
repentance because the Day of the Lord was imminent. These prophets
spoke with a clear and unmistakable, "Thus saith the Lord!" The
authority of God's prophets was not limited to the general content or
the main ideas of their message. Rather, they claimed repeatedly that
their very words were the words that God had given them to deliver.

PRAYER STARTER

*Lord, if You call me to the ministry of prophecy, I recognize that
I must only speak the words You place within my spirit. Give me the courage
to deliver Your words—and just Your words, none of my own.*

> **THERE WAS NEVER A QUESTION ABOUT ACCURATELY
> DISCERNING THE GENUINE WORD FROM GOD. FOR THE
> PROPHET, IT WAS ONLY A MATTER OF WHETHER HE HAD
> THE COURAGE TO DELIVER IT.**

DAY 325

Instead, speaking the truth in love, we will in all things grow
up into him who is the Head, that is, Christ. From him the whole
body, joined and held together by every supporting ligament, grows
and builds itself up in love, as each part does its work.
—*Ephesians 4:15–16*

Under the new covenant we don't usually see prophets who live by themselves in the wilderness. The prophetic ministry is a vital part of the greater body of Christ. Prophetic ministers are validated by their involvement in and with the local church, not by their separateness. The church becomes evangelistic through its evangelists, caring through its pastors, serving through its deacons, and prophetic through its prophets. Prophetic ministers serve within the church to help it fulfill its function, enabling it to be the prophetic voice in the earth. But just because we have called and ordained evangelists, pastors, and deacons, that doesn't mean every believer cannot share the gospel, care for others, and serve the church and the world. In the same way, the prophetic word can be manifested through any believer, not just those called by God as prophets.

PRAYER STARTER

Lord, I thank You for permitting me to be a part of Your body and to fellowship with the local church where You have placed me. Show me Your will for me in that place.

**PROPHETIC MINISTERS ARE VALIDATED BY THEIR
INVOLVEMENT IN AND WITH THE LOCAL CHURCH,
NOT BY THEIR SEPARATENESS.**

DAY 326

Answer me, O LORD, out of the goodness of your love;
in your great mercy turn to me.
Do not hide your face from your servant;
answer me quickly, for I am in trouble.
Come near and rescue me;
redeem me because of my foes.
—*Psalm 69:16–18*

One of the more difficult things to deal with as a prophetic minister is coming face-to-face with people in great need only to find God completely silent on the matter. This awkward situation, which will inevitably arise, presents a real test of character and maturity for the prophetic person. The pressures of people's expectations and assumptions push many prophetic ministers into dangerous waters that can eventually shipwreck their integrity as well as their ministry. Notwithstanding the pressure of people's expectations or his own desire to help a person in need, a prophetic minister must discipline himself to remain silent when God is silent. Manufacturing a word in his own mind, whether it is out of compassion or the pressure of our ministry credibility, can work directly against the purpose of God in the life of a church or an individual. A lack of integrity never builds people's faith over the long haul, even though the people may be excited for the moment over a man-made prophetic word.

PRAYER STARTER

Father, may I never speak a word until You have filled my mouth and disciplined my spirit to be Your servant. Teach me the integrity of keeping my mouth shut when it is filled with my words only.

THE GREAT TEMPTATION IS TO GIVE A WORD YOU DON'T
HAVE IN ORDER TO RELEASE THE PRESSURE OF
THE MOMENT.

DAY 327

My God, my God, why have you forsaken me?
Why are you so far from saving me,
so far from the words of my groaning?
O my God, I cry out by day, but you do not answer,
by night, and am not silent.
—*Psalm 22:1–2*

God's silence or inactivity at a time when *we* desperately want God to act or speak serves to reveal the spiritual maturity of both the people and the prophet. Each believer must go through the struggle of learning to walk with God when He is silent. It's an inescapable part of spiritual growth, and a prophetic minister must understand God's strategy of silence. As one who supposedly speaks for God, a prophetic minister must understand that God does not always speak, even in the most desperate of situations. If he cannot grasp this, he will inevitably manufacture words for people when God's specific purpose is for him to say nothing. Regardless of his well-intentioned efforts to make God *look good*, he becomes a stumbling block for those whom he seeks to help.

PRAYER STARTER

Teach me to understand the silence when I cannot hear Your voice. May I never manufacture words to speak for You. I would rather say nothing than to become a stumbling block to others.

EACH BELIEVER MUST GO THROUGH THE STRUGGLE OF LEARNING TO WALK WITH GOD WHEN HE IS SILENT.

DAY 328

Who among you fears the LORD?
Who obeys the voice of His Servant?
Who walks in darkness and has no light?
Let him trust in the name of the LORD
And rely upon his God.
—*Isaiah 50:10, NKJV*

Isaiah 50 describes the person who walks in the fear of the Lord. Part of the process of spiritual maturity is coming to the edge of our understanding, then walking on ahead without knowing what will happen next. God sometimes calls us, as He called Peter, to walk on water—to proceed in faith, but with uncertainty. Walking in darkness as it is used here doesn't refer to moral darkness that comes from sin or demonic oppression. It simply means walking in unknown territory without clear light and reassuring direction. God's silence forces us to grow in our confidence in Him as a person while we walk through the darkness, lacking a sense of direction. We eventually realize He was nearby all along. In this way, we develop our own personal history with God.

PRAYER STARTER

Give me the courage, Father, to walk with You in blind faith, even when I do not understand Your plan and purpose. As long as I can sense Your presence in the darkness, I will confidently place my trust in You.

DO NOT MANUFACTURE AN ARTIFICIAL LIGHT OUT OF YOUR FRUSTRATION WITH THE DARKNESS.

DAY 329

I am still confident of this:
I will see the goodness of the LORD
in the land of the living.
Wait for the LORD;
be strong and take heart
and wait for the LORD.
—*Psalm 27:13–14*

God's personality is infinite in its complexity and creativity. We think of God as being *perfect* in every way. God has a divine personality, perfect in His wisdom, love, and goodness. His dealing with each of us is in terms of building a relationship of love. But more often than not, our monolithic misunderstanding of how God *should* act in a given circumstance sometimes causes His action to seem contrary to our way of thinking. One of the things we should learn from the Gospels is that Jesus often did not answer people in the way we think our Lord should have. Then, when we think He should have answered, He was silent. At times when we suppose He should have intervened, He was inactive. If for no other reason than this, prophetic ministers should be careful not to presume what God should say or do in any given situation.

PRAYER STARTER

Keep me, Spirit, from drawing conclusions about Your ways. You are infinitely more wise and knowing than I could ever understand. I will patiently wait to see what You have planned for me and for Your people.

WE SOMETIMES DRAW WRONG CONCLUSIONS FROM
GOD'S SILENCE OR HIS PRESUMABLE LACK OF INTERVENTION
ON OUR BEHALF.

DAY 330

Now Jesus loved Martha and her sister and Lazarus. So,
when He heard that he was sick, He stayed two more days
in the place where He was.
—*John 11:5–6, NKJV*

Because of our preconceived notions, we sometimes draw wrong conclusions from God's silence or His presumable lack of intervention on our behalf. We often conclude that God's love for us has waned or that we are unworthy of His attention or perhaps that we are being punished for something. But that was certainly not the case with Lazarus. The Scriptures say several times that Jesus loved Lazarus along with his two sisters, Mary and Martha, but His delay in coming to help Lazarus in his greatest need was precisely calculated. We know that Jesus's seeming lack of response had nothing to do with lack of love, but had everything to do with fulfilling the redemptive purpose of God. The ensuing miracle was a prophetic sign to many of His own resurrection. But for Lazarus, Martha, and Mary it was something more—a lesson to trust God always, even when they must walk in darkness beyond the edge of their understanding.

PRAYER STARTER

Father, like Martha I often cry out, "Why didn't You come when I called?" Teach me the lesson of placing my ultimate trust in You even when I cannot understand Your plan and purpose.

WE OFTEN CONCLUDE THAT GOD'S LOVE FOR US HAS WANED
OR THAT WE ARE UNWORTHY OF HIS ATTENTION OR PERHAPS
THAT WE ARE BEING PUNISHED FOR SOMETHING.

DAY 331

I wait for your salvation, O LORD,
and I follow your commands.
I obey your statutes,
for I love them greatly.
I obey your precepts and your statutes,
for all my ways are known to you.
—Psalm 119:166–168

We stumble over the fact that God doesn't speak or act the way we think He should. But from Isaiah we learn not to manufacture our own light when we walk in darkness. From Saul we learn not to run ahead of God when the answer is delayed. From the Gospels we learn that God's silence does not mean we are rejected or unloved; it must be understood in the light of God's redemptive purposes. For those who have allowed the Holy Spirit to perform His work in their lives, the "Why, God?" questions are accompanied by a growing peace and trust rather than disillusionment and unbelief. God wants us to learn to be at peace in our souls by virtue of our relationship with Him, not by virtue of the information about our circumstances that we sometimes receive from Him. People searching for God's peace and comfort often look for it by asking God for information about their future. But He wants our peace to come first by fixing any problems in our personal relationship with Him.

PRAYER STARTER

Father, how often I run ahead of You and question, "Why?" Teach me to be at peace with Your purposes because of the trusting relationship I have with You.

OUR "WHY, GOD?" QUESTIONS ARE A NORMAL PART OF THE WALK OF FAITH FOR ALL OF US UNTIL THE VERY END.

DAY 332

Woe to the wicked! Disaster is upon them! They will be
paid back for what their hands have done.
—*Isaiah 3:11*

A vital test of a prophet is in his willingness to speak a hard word from
God, then his willingness to accept the resulting reproach and persecution that is the normal burden of prophetic ministry. This is a test
of surrender and consecration to God. Another vital test is being able
to remain silent when God has not spoken, regardless of the apparent
need of the moment. This is a test of honesty and integrity before God.
A third vital test is the willingness to remain silent about something
God has clearly revealed to you yet requires your silence on. This is a
test of maturity and security in God. Some prophets want to ensure
that they are always credited with having received revelation from God.
Sometimes they're like children who know a secret and just can't stand
it; they have to tell it to someone.

PRAYER STARTER

*Test my surrender and consecration to You, O God. Build me in
honesty and integrity before You. Cause me to grow in maturity and security
in You. Then I will be prepared to be Your spokesman.*

JUST BECAUSE GOD DIVINELY OPENS YOUR EYES TO A
CERTAIN REVELATION DOESN'T NECESSARILY MEAN YOU ARE
SUPPOSED TO SHARE IT.

DAY 333

But one and the same Spirit works all these things, distributing
to each one individually *as He wills.*
—*1 Corinthians 12:11, NKJV, emphasis added*

Being called into some kind of prophetic ministry is not necessarily the
reward for how diligent you have been to seek to mature in prophecy.
It's not even determined by how eager you are to grow in wisdom and
character. It is a matter of God's sovereign call. The same thing is true
with regard to each individual manifestation of the Spirit. We serve a
personal God who has His own purposes for each individual. God is
not an impersonal force. A Tibetan monk may go through exercises
and disciplines, thinking these will help him become an ascended
master. But the gifts and callings of God are not primarily based on
our striving, seeking, or searching, but they are based on His sovereign choice and His grace. It is not a matter of our efforts to attain
or develop spiritual skills. It is all about God's sovereign calling and
God's gracious giftings.

PRAYER STARTER

*Father, help me to understand the purpose for the giftings You have
given to me. Show me why You have called me to these gifts, and enable me to
respond as Your grace gives me strength.*

THERE IS A PLACE FOR DILIGENTLY SEEKING TO GROW
IN GIFTING, CHARACTER, AND MATURITY. BUT WHILE
DILIGENCE CAUSES YOU TO GROW WITHIN YOUR CALLING, IT
DOES NOT DETERMINE YOUR CALLING.

DAY 334

The voice of the LORD is over the waters;
the God of glory thunders,
the LORD thunders over the mighty waters.
The voice of the LORD is powerful;
the voice of the LORD is majestic.
The voice of the LORD breaks the cedars;
the LORD breaks in pieces the cedars of Lebanon....
The voice of the LORD twists the oaks
and strips the forests bare.
And in his temple all cry, "Glory!"
—*Psalm 29:3–5, 9*

Music is a heavenly thing in its essence, a part of creation that reflects and proceeds from the very heart and personality of God Himself. This makes music prophetic in nature. Our Father loves music. He is a singing God (Zeph. 3:17). He has a powerful and majestic voice (Ps. 29). Jesus the Son composed the song of all songs that will be eternally fresh—the "song of the Lamb" (Rev. 15:3–4). The Holy Spirit inspires songs and melodies. There is a whole book of them in the Bible—the Book of Psalms. Music has always provided a means of communion and connection between God and His creatures above and below. Spirit-filled Christians are to occupy themselves with singing psalms, hymns, and spiritual songs, singing and making melodies in their hearts to the Lord (Eph. 5:19). Music has intrinsic power to move the inner affections and the outer actions of people.

PRAYER STARTER

Inspire me, Holy Spirit, to sing psalms, hymns, and spiritual songs to You, allowing my life to be a melodious symphony of praise for Your goodness to me.

THE HOLY SPIRIT INSPIRES SONGS AND MELODIES.

DAY 335

I will declare Your name to My brethren; in the midst of
the assembly I will sing praise to You.
—*Hebrews 2:12, NKJV*

This scripture implies that one of the deepest longings within the heart
of Jesus is to sing the praises of His Father in the midst of and through
the instrumentality of the congregation of the believing. In light of the
nature and importance of music, it should not surprise us that God has
used minstrels to inspire and activate the prophetic (2 Kings 3:15). Nor
should it be surprising that prophetically inspired people will be led to
sing in the Spirit, communicating the heart of God to His people and
the heart of His people back to God. This is the essence of what some
have termed the "song of the Lord." This phrase, popularized by the
charismatic renewal of recent decades, refers to the scriptural references
to the Lord's song (Ps. 137:4), spiritual songs (Eph. 5:19), and singing a
new song to the Lord (Ps. 33:3; 96:1; 98:1; 149:1; Isa. 42:10).

PRAYER STARTER

*Free my spirit to express the songs of Your Spirit. Help me to com-
municate the heart of God to Your people through my unfettered expressions
in the Spirit.*

THE RISEN CHRIST LOVES TO IMPART SOME OF THE
PASSION HE HAS FOR HIS FATHER INTO THE HEARTS OF HIS
YOUNGER BROTHERS AND SISTERS THROUGH GIVING THEM
HIS SONGS BY THE SPIRIT.

DAY 336

For the Spirit searches all things, yes, the deep things of God.
For what man knows the thing of a man except the spirit of the
man which is in him? Even so no one knows the things
of God except the Spirit of God.
—*1 Corinthians 2:10–11, NKJV*

Jesus promises to proclaim the Father's name as He sings in the midst
of the congregation (Heb. 2:12). This implies that the Holy Spirit gives
the church a deeper revelation of the nature and personality of God
in prophetic messages through song. It also encourages extolling and
declaring the majesty and beauty of God and His ways through prophetic prayers that are sung. Romans 8:26 states that the Holy Spirit,
who resides within believers, helps them communicate the depths of
their being to God in prayer that is in harmony with His will. Still, I
think there will be an intensification of the Spirit's work in releasing
His songs before the Second Coming of Jesus. Perhaps one aspect of
the depths of God is the treasury of heavenly music that the Holy Spirit
will impart to prophetic musicians within the body of Christ for the
blessing of all mankind and the furthering of God's kingdom. This
music will reflect a full range of the attributes of our awesome God,
from His tender mercy to His terrible judgments.

PRAYER STARTER

*Teach me, Spirit, to recognize the beautiful bridge that music builds to
link the revelations of our awesome God to us, His people. Let me show Your
beauty through my expressions.*

**THE HOLY SPIRIT IS THE COMMUNICATION LINK BETWEEN
GOD AND HIS PEOPLE.**

DAY 337

And Hezekiah commanded to offer the burnt offering upon the altar. And when the burnt offering began, the song of the Lord began also with the trumpets, and with the instruments ordained by David king of Israel.
—*2 Chronicles 29:27, KJV*

God has been releasing His songs throughout the centuries. The Book of Revelation indicates that God's work and Satan's work both take on new levels of manifestation and power just before the end of the age. I view this as a cosmic and earthly clash of holy and unholy passions. Attending the increase of prophetic ministry will undoubtedly be an increase of inspired prophetic music to impart passion for Jesus and His Father in the hearts of believers. Undoubtedly, the enemy will increase his counterfeit anointing to musicians and songs that will draw people's allegiances after him and his unholy spirits. The Scriptures exhort us to sing a new song unto the Lord. The Holy Spirit stands ready to anoint and inspire many prophetic musicians and singers who will risk getting so intimate with the Godhead that they will discern the fresh music of heaven and release it to us for our enjoyment, refreshment, instruction, and admonition.

PRAYER STARTER

Holy Spirit, cause my spirit to burst forth with the fresh music of heaven. Raise up a symphony of prophetic musicians and singers to spread the songs of heaven into a world saturated with the music of the enemy.

THE SCRIPTURES EXHORT US TO SING A NEW SONG UNTO THE LORD.

DAY 338

He who prophesies speaks edification and exhortation
and comfort to men.
—1 Corinthians 14:3, NKJV

Practically everyone who is filled with God's Spirit is able to prophesy on an inspirational level (what I have referred to as Level I prophecy), especially in a worship service where the Holy Spirit's presence is more easily recognized. The result of what we call *inspirational prophecy* was described by Paul in our verse for today. The purpose of this type of prophecy is to inspire and refresh our hearts without giving any correction or new direction. This kind of prophecy is usually a reminder from the heart of God about His care and purposes for us, and it often emphasizes some truth we already know from the Bible. Inspirational prophecy can be a very profound revelation, or it can be (as it usually is) something very simple, such as, "I feel the Lord is saying that He really loves us." That message, if it is given at a divinely prescribed time, can be powerful and effective.

PRAYER STARTER

Holy Spirit, fill my spirit with the inspiration of Your marvelous love and care for Your children. Help me to be willing to inspire others with the overflow of revelation that You give to me.

IF INSPIRATIONAL PROPHECY OCCURS TOO FREQUENTLY, IT
WILL BECOME TOO COMMON, AND PEOPLE WILL NO LONGER
PAY ATTENTION TO WHAT IS BEING SAID.

DAY 339

I want you to know, brothers, that the gospel I preached is not something that man made up. I did not receive it from any man, nor was I taught it; rather, I received it by revelation from Jesus Christ.
—*Galatians 1:11–12*

One of the characteristics of prophetic revelation is that it is sometimes allegorical or symbolic, and it is fully understood only after future events have taken place. From the Old Testament perspective, it was not altogether clear what the Messiah would look like. The prophets foretold the coming of both a kingly Messiah and a suffering servant, but no one even remotely considered that both were the same person. Obviously, kingly messiahs aren't servants, and they don't suffer. Even the disciples had a hard time with it. The Gospels, especially the synoptic Gospels (Matthew, Mark, and Luke), show how baffled the disciples were. The messianic secret is a theme that runs throughout all the synoptic Gospels. They had a very difficult time figuring out who Jesus was and the nature of His eternal kingdom. We have to be careful about locking in on our interpretation of prophetic revelation lest we miss what God is trying to say to us and do with us.

PRAYER STARTER

Father, I love when You speak through Your Spirit to me with revelation that helps me to understand the allegorical and symbolic examples You have placed in Your Word to reveal Yourself to Your people. Help me to clearly understand Your revelation through these methods.

CARELESSLY INTERPRETED PROPHETIC REVELATION CAN CAUSE CHAOS IN SOMEONE'S LIFE.

DAY 340

Then the disciples went out and preached everywhere, and
the Lord worked with them and confirmed his word
by the signs that accompanied it.
—*Mark 16:20*

When you receive a prophetic word from someone, you must hold it at
arm's length until God *Himself* confirms it in your heart. If a prophetic
minister receives accurate and authentic revelation from God that, for
example, you are going to have a street ministry, all they are doing is
giving you an advance warning that *you* personally are going to hear a
new direction from God about a street ministry. This prophetic noti-
fication is sometimes God's way of confirming ahead of time what you
will hear for yourself later on. On other occasions, prophetic words can
confirm something you have already heard very clearly. But you should
not step out and act on the prophetic word alone if you haven't received
the confirmation.

PRAYER STARTER

*Father, keep me from allowing false or misdirected prophetic messages
and interpretations from entering my spirit. Confirm Your words through
others to me and help me to hear only authentic divine revelations from You.*

IT IS IMPORTANT THAT YOU KNOW THE DIFFERENCE
BETWEEN WHAT IS PUT FORTH AS DIVINE REVELATION,
WHAT IS CONFIRMED, AND WHAT IS ASSUMED TO
BE THE INTERPRETATION.

DAY 341

> So Paul and Barnabas spent considerable time there, speaking boldly for the Lord, who confirmed the message of his grace by enabling them to do miraculous signs and wonders.
> —*Acts 14:3*

Revelation itself is not going to help the body unless it goes through the process of interpretation and application. The interpretation may be accurate, but if a person jumps the gun and gets ahead of God in the application, a considerable amount of hurt and confusion may result. Consequently, there is as much need for divine wisdom in the interpretation and application as there is in the revelation. God never works as fast as people think He should. Don't get involved with prophetic people and words if you are not willing to wait on God to bring them to pass. God will declare His intention through the prophetic gift, but if the application is not in His timing, you'll find yourself trying to step through a door that is not open. The way is not yet prepared, and the grace is not yet sufficient.

PRAYER STARTER

> *Father, help me to understand that when Your Spirit speaks through Your prophets to Your people, we must clearly know how You desire Your people to apply those words to our lives. Don't let me get ahead of You or fail to respond when You speak to me.*

GOD NEVER WORKS AS FAST AS PEOPLE THINK HE SHOULD.

DAY 342

The testimony of Jesus is the spirit of prophecy.
—*Revelation 19:10, NKJV*

This means that the fresh revelation of Jesus's heart is the essence of His testimony. This includes the revealing of who He is along with what He does and how He feels. The spirit (purpose) of prophecy is to reveal these aspects of Jesus's testimony. Passion for Jesus is the result of this prophetic revelation. Such holy passion is the highlight of the prophetic church. It is a ministry that passionately *feels* and *reveals* the divine heart to the church and the world. Prophetic ministry has to do not only with information but also with the ability to experience in some measure the compassion, grief, and joy of God, and then to gain a passion for God. Out of experiencing God will come the revelation of some of His future plans and purposes. If you "desire earnestly to prophesy" (1 Cor. 14:39) by merely seeking information from the *mind* of God, you have bypassed the cornerstone and the essence of prophetic ministry—the revelation of His heart.

PRAYER STARTER

Father, may I never forget that the revelations You place within my spirit for others must be given out of a heart that passionately loves You and desires to reveal Your heart of compassion and love for Your people.

THE PROPHETIC MINISTRY IS TO BE STAMPED AND SEALED
WITH AN AFFECTION FOR AND SENSITIVITY TO
THE HEART OF GOD.

DAY 343

It is like a mustard seed which, when it is sown on the ground, is smaller than all the seeds on earth; but when it is sown, it grows up and becomes greater than all herbs, and shoots out large branches, so that the birds of the air may nest under its shade.

—*Mark 4:31–32, NKJV*

Throughout the last two millennia, all the powers of hell have been unable to eliminate the gospel or the church. It has only continued to grow. The church in its survival and growth is living out the prophetic word. Its very presence is a continuing witness to prophecies fulfilled. The church is also a prophetic witness in its mission. Just as the apostles were in the early days, the church today is *the* witness to the death and resurrection of Jesus Christ. As the bride of Christ, all that the church does in order to make herself ready—gathering together, worshiping, celebrating Communion, witnessing, preaching the gospel, casting out demons, healing the sick, being peacemakers—is a prophetic trumpet to the world of the relationship of Christ to His church and of the fact that Christ is coming again. The next time you are sitting in a church service, remember that even though we are almost two thousand years removed from the first-century church, the very fact that you are gathering with others in His name is both a prophetic fulfillment and a prophetic statement to the world.

PRAYER STARTER

Jesus, what an incredible privilege it is to gather with Your people and prepare together to become Your bride. May our worship, preaching, witnessing, and works of spiritual service show an unsaved world Your love and draw them into a relationship with You.

THE CHURCH'S PRIMARY TASK HAS ALWAYS BEEN TO PRESERVE AND PROCLAIM THE GOOD NEWS OF HIS DEATH, RESURRECTION, AND HIS COMING AGAIN TO JUDGE THE WORLD.

DAY 344

Preach the Word; be prepared in season and out of season;
correct, rebuke and encourage—with great patience and
careful instruction.
—*2 Timothy 4:2*

The New Testament epistles were not written like lessons for a Sunday school curriculum. They were written as letters to people like us who were at times going through very difficult situations. When we as a church hear about the conflicts that caused the writing of 2 Corinthians or discover the drama that is the background of the letter to the Hebrews, we begin to identify with the *people* of the New Testament, not just with the exhortations to them. Not only does this make the New Testament come alive, but it also gives the church a sense of connection with those who began the race. The church as a prophetic community must realize that we are a continuation of what they began. We must feel that connection. The torch has been passed so many times that it is easy to lose sight of the fact that we are running the same race they started. Their leg of the race has been completed, and they have now gathered at the finish line to cheer us on. The church is the living testimony of the prophetic purpose of God in history.

PRAYER STARTER

Holy Spirit, help me to understand the heart and emotions of those early Christians who became Your servants. Let me feel connected to them, and give me a heart that desires to separate myself to You just as they did.

**THE CHURCH IS A PROPHETIC COMMUNITY THAT IS TO
PRESERVE AND PROCLAIM ACCURATELY THE WORD OF GOD.**

DAY 345

> You did not trust in the LORD your God, who went ahead of
> you on your journey, in fire by night and in a cloud by day, to search
> out places for you to camp and to show you the way you should go.
> —*Deuteronomy 1:32–33*

The church must discern the current move of the Spirit. Just as the
children of Israel followed the cloud through the wilderness, the
church needs to move when the Holy Spirit says to move. The relationship that exists between the church and the Holy Spirit is not static.
The Spirit is forever doing a new thing with the church as a whole and,
separately, with each congregation. The Ten Commandments given on
Sinai are forever true and unchangeable, but the people of Israel were
changing locations constantly as they moved around in the wilderness.
The kind of moving I am referring to is the changing emphasis placed
on elements of truth, structure, and strategy. The greatest expression
of the church as a prophetic community is in those congregations or
denominations that move on with the cloud but carry with them all the
wisdom, experience, and maturity of their history.

PRAYER STARTER

> *Spirit, may I never be so content with my spiritual life that I fail
> to see the moment-by-moment, day-by-day ways that You are moving and
> revealing Yourself to Your people. Do a new thing in my heart, in my church,
> and in Your world.*

> WE ARE MOVING AROUND WITHIN THE BOUNDARIES OF THE
> UNCHANGEABLE TRUTH OF GOD'S WORD.

DAY 346

This salvation, which was first announced by the Lord, was
confirmed to us by those who heard him. God also testified to it
by signs, wonders and various miracles, and gifts of the Holy Spirit
distributed according to his will.
—*Hebrews 2:3–4*

The demonstration of the supernatural power of God in and through
the church is a dimension of the prophetic ministry. As in the days
of Elijah, miracles attest to the truth of God's Word. The written
Word includes the witness of the apostles, and if attesting miracles
were needed when they personally testified within a few years of the
Resurrection, how much more are attesting miracles needed today to
confirm the veracity of their written accounts? Attesting miracles are
also valuable as a dimension of the prophetic community because, more
than anything else, they make people aware that God is actually present
with them. The working of miracles jolts our sensibilities and makes
us joyfully (or frightfully) aware of the fact that He is in our midst by
the presence of the Holy Spirit and that He is very close to each of us.
Through the miraculous, the church prophesies and proclaims that
He is alive!

PRAYER STARTER

*Lord, I long to see miracles and signs and wonders of Your mighty
power. Come to Your people in Your power, and give us mighty miracles that
reveal Your presence in our midst.*

IN THE MIRACULOUS, THE LIVING GOD OF THE WRITTEN
WORD SHOWS UP IN A POWERFULLY PERSONAL, INTIMATE,
AND TANGIBLE WAY.

DAY 347

Therefore go and make disciples of all nations, baptizing them in the name of the Father and of the Son and of the Holy Spirit, and teaching them to obey everything I have commanded you. And surely I am with you always, to the very end of the age.
—*Matthew 28:19–20*

The church has the responsibility to be a "prophet to the nation" concerning injustice, repression, and the unrighteousness that eventually causes a nation to provoke the judgment of God. Many times prophets to the nation speak from a secular platform, not necessarily as those who represent the church. Joseph and Daniel were two biblical examples of people who represented God in a position of secular power. Abraham Lincoln and Martin Luther King Jr. prophetically stood for justice and righteousness in our social order. Yet they were not seen as prophetic from the traditional position of being on a church staff. It is my conviction that the church as an institution should be as a prophet standing for the advancement of righteousness without indebtedness to political party affiliations.

PRAYER STARTER

Dear Father, may Your people, Your church, stand strong and tall as a prophetic voice to this world pronouncing Your righteousness to all. Keep us from division, and keep our motives and purposes pure.

THE CHURCH AND THOSE WHO SPEAK FOR THE CHURCH MUST UNDERSTAND WHERE TO DRAW THE LINE.

DAY 348

And we have the word of the prophets made more certain, and you will do well to pay attention to it, as to a light shining in a dark place, until the day dawns and the morning star rises in your hearts.
—*2 Peter 1:19*

God has raised up leaders in the church throughout the generations who have functioned as prophets of God crying out against the sins of the people. John Wesley, for instance, turned England back to God when the people's personal unrighteousness and apathy had brought them to the edge of societal chaos. This outcry is similar to the prophetic cry against social injustice, but different in that it is specifically directed to the people in the church. It is less like Jonah prophesying against Nineveh and more like Isaiah and Jeremiah prophesying to Israel and Judah. People such as Billy Graham, Charles Colson, John Piper, David Wilkerson, and A. W. Tozer stand out in my mind as prophetic ministers raised up to cry out against unrighteousness in the church as they revealed the deep things about the knowledge of God. Their words have been anointed by the Spirit to awaken hearts to holiness and passion for Jesus.

PRAYER STARTER

Father, give us a clear understanding of the men and women of God whom You are using as prophetic ministers to our world today. Anoint their spirits and awaken their hearts to holiness and passion for Your Son. Cause us to be attendant to their words, that we do not miss the revelations of Your Spirit that they bring.

GOD USES SUCH PROPHETIC VOICES, JUST AS HE USED JOHN THE BAPTIST, TO PRICK THE CONSCIENCE OF BELIEVERS UNTO FULL REVIVAL.

DAY 349

With that same spirit of faith we also believe and therefore
speak, because we know that the one who raised the Lord Jesus
from the dead will also raise us with Jesus and present us
with you in his presence.
—*2 Corinthians 4:13–14*

Someone once asked the intriguing question, "Where does God live?"
Another with a sharp wit answered, "Anywhere He wants to!" A good
answer indeed. When Solomon dedicated the first temple, he said,
"The heavens, even the highest heaven, cannot contain you. How
much less this house I have built!" (1 Kings 8:27). So where does
God really live? Where is His presence? First, He lives in heaven itself
where He dwells in unapproachable light. Second, He is omnipresent,
and there is no place where He is not. Third, He has condescended
to live within His "temples." In the Old Testament, it was first the
tabernacle and then the temple in Jerusalem. In the New Testament,
it is the church—the corporate body of Christ as well as each believer
in Christ. Fourth, He and His Word are one, and thus He is present
in the Holy Scriptures. Fifth, He is present in the sacraments of the
church. And finally, He also periodically "visits" specific people and
places by His "manifest presence." In other words, God "comes down"
and interfaces with the natural realm.

PRAYER STARTER

*Father, You have manifested Yourself to us in many ways. You choose
to dwell in our midst and to reveal Yourself through Your Word and church.
I long to have Your presence in my life and for You to "come down" in special
visitation to my life.*

**WE ARE CALLED TO VALUE AND ESTEEM EVERY DIMENSION
OF THE PRESENCE OF GOD.**

DAY 350

For we commend not ourselves again unto you, but give
you occasion to glory on our behalf, that ye may have somewhat
to answer them which glory in appearance, and not in heart. For
whether we be beside ourselves, it is to God:
or whether we be sober, it is for your cause.

—*2 Corinthians 5:12–13, KJV*

Paul was challenging the mentality of some who were looking on outward things and not properly discerning the heart of a certain matter at
hand. What could this matter have been? The next verse tells us. Paul
reveals that this controversy centered around two different general states
of being that he and other believers were experiencing periodically. This
first *mode* he called being "beside ourselves." The only other time that
this Greek word is used in the New Testament is when the people of
Nazareth accused Jesus of being mad. We get our English word *ecstatic*
from a Latin word that means "being outside oneself." Paul seems to be
referring to what are classically understood as ecstatic spiritual experiences and phenomena. He was exhorting the Corinthian believers to
not stumble over this genuine holy activity that didn't appear *dignified*
or even always *rational*. Instead he challenged them to *glory*—that is,
to rejoice greatly—that such visitations were occurring among them
and releasing greater passion in their hearts for God. Visible joy upon
believers is possibly the best advertisement for the gospel.

PRAYER STARTER

*Spirit, reveal Yourself to me through whatever method You choose.
Make me willing to be "beside myself" with the joy of Your presence. Release
greater power and passion in my heart for Christ, and let others see Your
love in my life.*

WE ARE TO SERVE THE LORD WITH GLADNESS.

DAY 351

Jesus did many other things as well. If every one of them were
written down, I suppose that even the whole world would not have
room for the books that would be written.

—John 21:25

The Bible does not record all possible divine or legitimate supernatural
activities and experiences that have occurred or may yet occur among
men and nations. Rather, it records examples of divine activity and
legitimate supernatural experiences that fall into broader categories
that are typical of how the Holy Spirit works. This concept is taught
in John 21:25, in which John states that if all the wonderful works
that Jesus did had been recorded, all the books in the world could not
contain them. The Bible nowhere teaches that God is bound to do
only what He has done before. In fact, there are many prophecies of
Scripture that speak of God doing things He has never done before.
One friend of ours has said, "God has this *problem*, you see—He thinks
He's God!" Truly, He is God, and He can do anything He wants to.

PRAYER STARTER

*Remove the hindrances of my finite human mind to comprehend the
many ways that You reveal Yourself to Your people. Help me to understand
that You can do whatever You want—and do whatever You want in me.*

GOD IS ALWAYS AND FOREVER FREE TO DO UNPRECEDENTED
THINGS THAT ARE CONSISTENT WITH HIS CHARACTER AS
REVEALED IN SCRIPTURE.

DAY 352

So I say to you: Ask and it will be given to you; seek and you
will find; knock and the door will be opened to you. For everyone
who asks receives; he who seeks finds; and to him who knocks, the
door will be opened. Which of you fathers, if your son asks for a
fish, will give him a snake instead? Or if he asks for an egg, will give
him a scorpion? If you then, though you are evil, know how to give
good gifts to your children, how much more will your Father in
heaven give the Holy Spirit to those who ask him!
—*Luke 11:9–13*

In this passage, Jesus is both inviting and challenging His disciples to
pray in a specific way and for a specific thing. The verbs translated
"ask," "seek," and "knock" are in a continuous tense in the original
manuscripts. This gives the phrases the sense that the desired blessings must be pursued with repeated action and with perseverance. God
wants us to really want what we desire and not be passive or nonchalant
about it. Any temporary denial serves only to deepen the hunger for
the thing denied. He also reveals that the requests for the good things
of His kingdom can be summarized by asking for the release of the
ministry of the Holy Spirit. God is a generous and wealthy Father who
truly wants to give the Holy Spirit's ministry to us, but He also wants
us to earnestly desire the Holy Spirit to come upon us with His gifts,
fruit, and wisdom.

PRAYER STARTER

*Thank You, Father, that I can come boldly and confidently into Your
presence. Teach me to approach You with specificity, expressing my deepest
longings before You. Minister to me through Your Spirit.*

WE SHOULD ASK CONFIDENTLY AND BOLDLY FOR HIS
PRESENCE AND PURPOSES, KNOWING THAT IN TIME IT SHALL
BE DONE—IF WE DON'T FAINT OR DOUBT.

DAY 353

You have made known to me the path of life;
you will fill me with joy in your presence,
with eternal pleasures at your right hand.
—*Psalm 16:11*

Some people seem to be more susceptible to the occurrence of outward manifestations. Other people seem less susceptible. Still other people have various kinds of barriers that hinder the flow of the Spirit into and through their lives. Bring the burden of possible barriers honestly to the Lord in prayer and trust Him to reveal if there are any. This is an easy prayer for God to answer! Once you have done this, don't become too introspective about the issue—it may be that you will not experience much of the outward manifestations or phenomena. This does not mean that you haven't received from the Holy Spirit. Many people have reported having much fruit and power of the Spirit being released through their lives after "soaking" in the presence of God in renewal settings without having any outward awareness that they were being filled up. It is not the outward effects of spiritual renewal that we must focus upon or draw attention to, but rather the inner transformation of our souls into the likeness of Jesus.

PRAYER STARTER

Remove the barriers, dear Spirit, that hinder the flow of Your presence into my life. Allow me to "soak in Your presence" and to be transformed by Your ministry that I become more like Christ in all my ways.

BRING THE BURDEN OF POSSIBLE BARRIERS HONESTLY TO THE LORD IN PRAYER AND TRUST HIM TO REVEAL IF THERE ARE ANY.

DAY 354

But the fruit of the Spirit is love, joy, peace, patience, kindness, goodness, faithfulness, gentleness and self-control. Against such things there is no law.
—*Galatians 5:22–23*

The various aspects of the fruit of the Spirit are important to consider as we allow the Holy Spirit to move us out to personally minister to others. Today's devotional and the following eight daily devotional lessons will consider how each fruit of the Spirit applies to the prayer ministry of Spirit-filled individuals.

Love. Love can be viewed as the overarching characteristic from which the other aspects of the fruit of the Spirit flow. Really, the fruit of the Spirit is nothing less than the character of Jesus Christ being manifested in and through believers. As we pray for others, we must view ourselves as servants and not heroes. As we pray for others, we should be conscious that it's much more their moment than ours. A spirit of love will help keep this in view.

PRAYER STARTER

Father, I know that love must begin, flow through, and permeate my entire life. Give me a spirit of love like Yours.

THE SPIRIT OF SERVANTHOOD IS THE MOST OUTSTANDING SIGN OF TRUE LOVE.

DAY 355

Nehemiah said, "Go and enjoy choice food and sweet drinks,
and send some to those who have nothing prepared.
This day is sacred to our Lord. Do not grieve, for the
joy of the Lord is your strength."
—*Nehemiah 8:10*

Joy. We need to approach praying for others with the joyful awareness
of the privilege we have been given. Even if you aren't emotionally *up*,
you need to draw on the waters of joy that reside within you. You
might do this by meditating and focusing upon the fact that you are a
Christian, a temple of the Holy Spirit, forgiven of your sins, destined
for heaven, useful to God, the recipient of many blessings, and so on.
In other words, try to back up and get the big picture of who you are in
Christ and who He is in Himself. Then we are able to put our personal
pressures temporarily behind us and focus on the needs of the one
before us. If you are still unable to draw such joy forth, then confess
your weakness to the Lord and ask Him to graciously compensate for
it on that occasion and pray about it later.

PRAYER STARTER

*I want Your joy, dear Spirit. Flood over my soul with inexplicable joy
that radiates from my life to others.*

> **SEEK TO LET HIS JOY SHOW THROUGH YOUR EYES AND ON
> YOUR COUNTENANCE.**

DAY 356

Peace I leave with you; my peace I give you. I do not give to
you as the world gives. Do not let your hearts be troubled
and do not be afraid.
—*John 14:27*

Peace. We have been given the authority to impart the blessing of peace
to others in the name of Jesus. We should seek to lead others into the
experience of being at peace with God, themselves, and others. We
should seek to approach them with a peaceable spirit—a heart that is
at rest in God's ability to work through us, weak though we are.

PRAYER STARTER

*Your peace, dear Spirit, causes me to rest in You and trust You with my
life. Allow my life to bring Your peace into this lost and chaotic world.*

**WE SHOULD SEEK TO LEAD OTHERS INTO THE EXPERIENCE
OF BEING AT PEACE WITH GOD, THEMSELVES, AND OTHERS.**

DAY 357

The fruit of righteousness will be peace; the effect of righteousness will be quietness and confidence forever.
—*Isaiah 32:17*

Patience. We need to slow down and take our time in praying for others. The Holy Spirit doesn't like to be pushed—He wants to do the leading. Usually, He takes His time in showing His power. In quietness of soul we are able to better receive the impressions of the Spirit upon our spirits, minds, emotions, and bodies. "Soaking" prayer is often very necessary to remove stubborn strongholds of the evil one.

PRAYER STARTER

Spirit, how much I need Your patience. Cause me to understand that as I confidently and quietly wait for You to work in my life, You will transform me and give me the strength of Your presence.

> IN QUIETNESS OF SOUL WE ARE ABLE TO BETTER RECEIVE THE IMPRESSIONS OF THE SPIRIT UPON OUR SPIRITS, MINDS, EMOTIONS, AND BODIES.

DAY 358

And God raised us up with Christ and seated us with him in the heavenly realms in Christ Jesus, in order that in the coming ages he might show the incomparable riches of his grace, expressed in his kindness to us in Christ Jesus.
—*Ephesians 2:6–7*

Kindness. We will often be praying for people whose lives have been wrecked by sin. Many haven't been taught social skills, and they have unlovely characteristics about them. Many have embraced wrong teachings and even are oppressed by demons. We must be braced to gracefully absorb some of their immaturity and deal kindly with their deception. We must overcome evil with good and be kind to those who are unkind to us. This honors the Lord and gives them the best chance to get His help.

PRAYER STARTER

Make me a kind person, Spirit. Let me express the kindness of our loving heavenly Father. Help me to overcome the evil around and in me with the response of spiritual kindness.

WE MUST OVERCOME EVIL WITH GOOD AND BE KIND TO THOSE WHO ARE UNKIND TO US.

DAY 359

For this very reason, make every effort to add to your faith
goodness; and to goodness, knowledge; and to knowledge, self-
control; and to self-control, perseverance; and to perseverance,
godliness; and to godliness, brotherly kindness; and
to brotherly kindness, love.
—*2 Peter 1:5–7*

Goodness. We need to genuinely care for the needs of others and, therefore, we should seek to be willing to show that care to them in practical
ways on the heels of praying for them. We may not have the resources
ourselves, but maybe we know others who might, to whom we can
direct them. We must seek to break the cycles of injustice in people's
lives rather than perpetuate them, especially in the name of serving
the Lord. Also, we must never take advantage of the sacred trust that
others are giving us when they make themselves vulnerable by allowing
us to pray for them. Evil things, behind the guise of *ministry*, have been
perpetrated on vulnerable people before in the history of Christianity.
Let us make sure that we don't add to the list.

PRAYER STARTER

*Father, there is so much injustice in our world today. Help me to show
Your goodness and to handle carefully the sacred trust You have placed in me
to lead others by Your goodness to Your loving Son's salvation.*

**WE MUST SEEK TO BREAK THE CYCLES OF INJUSTICE
IN PEOPLE'S LIVES RATHER THAN PERPETUATE THEM,
ESPECIALLY IN THE NAME OF SERVING THE LORD.**

DAY 360

Never be lacking in zeal, but keep your spiritual fervor, serving the Lord. Be joyful in hope, patient in affliction, faithful in prayer. Share with God's people who are in need. Practice hospitality.
—*Romans 12:11–13*

Faithfulness. We must become involved in personal prayer ministry knowing that it will call for perseverance on our part. We will often have to pray more than one time for the same people with the same needs. We mustn't become intimidated by apparent failure. We also need to remember the truth that if we are faithful in little, then God will give us more with which to work. The anointing of the Spirit grows stronger upon us as we put into practice what we have learned. Commit yourself to praying for hundreds of people for the rest of your life and see what God will do.

PRAYER STARTER

Above all things, dear Father, I want to be counted faithful to You. Cause me to be faithful in my intercession before You for the souls of others.

COMMIT YOURSELF TO PRAYING FOR HUNDREDS OF PEOPLE FOR THE REST OF YOUR LIFE AND SEE WHAT GOD WILL DO.

DAY 361

Your beauty should not come from outward adornment, such
as braided hair and the wearing of gold jewelry and fine clothes.
Instead, it should be that of your inner self, the unfading beauty of a
gentle and quiet spirit, which is of great worth in God's sight.
—*1 Peter 3:3–5*

Gentleness (meekness). We need to approach praying for others with a fresh
awareness that we don't have the answers for them but that we know
the One who does. This keeps us from presumption and platitudes.
Our movements, both physical and verbal, need to be gentle rather than
abrupt or harsh. If we can help set them at ease by knowing that they
are safe in our presence, then they will be able to receive more easily
from the Lord.

PRAYER STARTER

*Give me a spirit of gentleness, dear Father. Pour Your oil of gentleness
over my spirit, and cause it to flow carefully and consistently into the lives of
others through a gentle spirit.*

OUR MOVEMENTS, BOTH PHYSICAL AND VERBAL, NEED TO BE
GENTLE RATHER THAN ABRUPT OR HARSH.

DAY 362

But mark this: There will be terrible times in the last days.
People will be lovers of themselves, lovers of money, boastful, proud,
abusive, disobedient to their parents, ungrateful, unholy, without
love, unforgiving, slanderous, without self-control, brutal, not lovers
of the good, treacherous, rash, conceited, lovers of pleasure rather
than lovers of God—having a form of godliness but denying its
power. Have nothing to do with them.
—2 Timothy 3:1–5

Self-control. We encourage people to "dial down," both emotionally and physically, as they go to pray for others. If you are being outwardly and manifestly influenced at the moment and involved in an uncontrollable experience with the Spirit, then seek to stay in a receiving mode and wait until you can calm down to get into a giving mode. We must recognize that the danger exists of unwittingly manipulating others by putting a wrong pressure on them to respond to us if we violate this principle. There are exceptions to this general rule. One is if a person specifically asks you to pray for them while you are in such a state. Another could be if the other person is a friend and you know that they would welcome such an experience. And there may be others.

PRAYER STARTER

Father, in my intercession for others, help me to "dial down" as I enter Your presence and to have a calm, receiving spirit that allows Your Spirit to direct my prayers for others.

**WE ENCOURAGE PEOPLE TO "DIAL DOWN," BOTH
EMOTIONALLY AND PHYSICALLY, AS THEY GO TO
PRAY FOR OTHERS.**

DAY 363

He called a little child and had him stand among them. And he
said: "I tell you the truth, unless you change and become like little
children, you will never enter the kingdom of heaven. Therefore,
whoever humbles himself like this child is the greatest
in the kingdom of heaven."
—*Matthew 18:2–4*

Take the posture of being *learners* rather than *experts* in the ministry of
the Spirit. There really aren't that many of our generation who have
gone before us in some of these things. We must continue to become
like little children before our heavenly Father, the Lord Jesus, and the
Holy Spirit. We must be more confident in their ability to teach and
lead than in our ability to learn and follow. Fortunately, their commitment to us is stronger than ours is to them. And this reality is truly the
source of our strength. Be gracious, kind, and patient with differences
in perspectives within the community of believers and various streams
of the body of Christ. If God is the true source of a move of the Holy
Spirit, then He is well able to act independently of our judgments and
criticisms to defend His honor. He will raise up creditable witnesses
and advocates.

PRAYER STARTER

*Father, I have so much to learn about You. If I spend each waking
day of my life in Your presence, I will still have so much more to learn about
Your work, Your love, and Your purposes for my life. Make me a learner,
dear Father.*

**WE DON'T HAVE TO PROVE TO ANYONE THAT SOMETHING IS
OF GOD IF IT REALLY IS!**

DAY 364

Don't be deceived, my dear brothers. Every good and perfect gift is from above, coming down from the Father of the heavenly lights, who does not change like shifting shadows. He chose to give us birth through the word of truth, that we might be a kind of firstfruits of all he created.
—*James 1:16–18*

Give proper liberty and create sufficient opportunities for the Spirit to manifest Himself in the settings that are specifically intended to welcome renewal ministry and its attending activity. Of course, God may Himself break into any gathering with His manifest presence without human mediation. Model and teach proper restraints, and seek to be sensitive to the specific situation and context. What does love *look like* or require in this particular setting? Seek to submit to those in authority for the sake of peace and unity. Mistakes in discernment are bound to happen in the midst of renewal when the heightened fear of both *missing God* and *being deceived* are present. Encourage people to appeal to leaders in private if they disagree with the direction the leaders have given or are giving to the body.

PRAYER STARTER

Father, in all my work and service, in every part of my life, cause me to discern accurately and fully what You are doing and what You want me to reveal to others. Don't allow me to "miss" Your revelation or to cause another to be deceived.

MISTAKES IN DISCERNMENT ARE BOUND TO HAPPEN IN THE MIDST OF RENEWAL WHEN THE HEIGHTENED FEAR OF BOTH MISSING GOD AND BEING DECEIVED ARE PRESENT.

DAY 365

My son, if you accept my words and store up my commands within you, turning your ear to wisdom and applying your heart to understanding, and if you call out for insight and cry aloud for understanding, and if you look for it as for silver and search for it as for hidden treasure, then you will understand the fear of the LORD and find the knowledge of God.

—Proverbs 2:1–5

Search the Scriptures and look for new insights into the ways of God with His people. Study the history of revivals. Wisdom and errors are easier to perceive with the luxury that hindsight affords. Encourage people to rejoice in that, whether or not they have personally been manifestly touched by the Spirit, God is visiting the body in general. Let us not be so individualistic in our thinking. May we all trust the Lord to give us our personal portion in any visitation and be glad for what He is doing in others. This attitude puts us in the best possible condition to be able to receive what God does have for us as individuals.

PRAYER STARTER

Thank You, Father, for all that You are doing in my life. I commit my life to searching Your Word and Your presence for new revelation from You. I want to be fully engaged in Your destiny for my life. I want to be counted worthy of manifesting Your marvelous love to others. I am Yours, Lord. Use me in any way You choose—now and forever.

ENCOURAGE PEOPLE TO REJOICE IN THAT, WHETHER OR NOT THEY HAVE PERSONALLY BEEN MANIFESTLY TOUCHED BY THE SPIRIT, GOD IS VISITING THE BODY IN GENERAL.

WHAT IS THE IHOP-KC MISSIONS BASE?

It is an international missions organization committed to *prayer* (intercession, worship, healing, prophesying, etc.), *fasting* (covering 365 days a year), and the *Great Commission* (proclaiming Jesus to all nations with power as the way to establish His *justice* in the earth). Our work includes equipping and sending missionaries as dedicated intercessors and anointed messengers working to see revival in the church and a great harvest among the lost.

IHOP-KC MISSIONS VISION STATEMENT

To call forth, train, and mobilize *worshiping intercessors* who operate in the forerunner spirit as End-Time prophetic messengers. To establish a 24-hour-a-day prayer room in Kansas City as a perpetual solemn assembly that *"keeps the sanctuary"* by gathering corporately to fast and pray in the spirit of the Tabernacle of David as God's *primary method* of establishing justice (full revival unto the great harvest). To send out teams to plant Houses of Prayer in the nations *after* God grants a breakthrough of His power in Kansas City. The forerunner spirit operates in God's grace in context to the fasted lifestyle (Matt. 6) and prepares others to live in wholehearted love by proclaiming the beauty of Jesus as Bridegroom, King, and Judge.

VISITING IHOP ON WEEKENDS

Encounter God Services: Weekends at IHOP-KC—renewal, conviction, refreshing, impartation, and equipping are what we pray to be released in these weekend meetings at IHOP-KC. On *Friday nights*, Mike Bickle teaches on themes related to intimacy with God. On *Saturday nights*, he teaches on themes related to the End-Times. On Sundays, join the IHOP-KC staff for worship and teaching. Childcare is available. *One-day seminars* are taught on Saturdays.

See www.IHOP.org for details, visitor's accommodations, and more information on joining our staff or attending our internships or Bible school.

Visit IHOP-KC at www.IHOP.org

The International House of Prayer Missions Base Web site has been designed for ease of browsing. We have incorporated the following branches of our community into one cohesive site:

- *IHOP*
- *Onething*
- *Children's Equipping Center*
- *Forerunner School of Ministry*
- *Forerunner Music Academy*
- *Joseph Company*
- *Events & Conferences*
- *Internships & Training Programs*
- *Omega Course*

It's all located at our easy-to-remember address: *www.IHOP.org*. Whether you are interested in visiting IHOP, receiving the Missions Base podcast, browsing the bookstore, watching live Webcasts, or enrolling in FSM's online eSchool, the Web site delivers the information you need and offers many opportunities to feed your heart. With login capabilities that expose you to even more comprehensive IHOP materials, we hope our site will become an ongoing resource for many years to come. Some of the Web site features include:

- *Podcasting*
- *MP3 Downloads*
- *Forums*
- *Free & Subscription-based Webcasts*
- *Sermon & Teaching Notes*
- *eSchool Distance Learning*
- *Internship Applications*
- *Prayer Room Blogs*
- *Online Bookstore*
- *And More!*

Visit us soon at www.IHOP.org!

IHOP INTERNSHIP PROGRAMS

IHOP offers a variety of three-month and six-month internships for all ages. Each internship has the same basic components, including prayer meeting attendance, classroom instruction, practical ministry experience, community fellowship and team building, conference participation, practical service, and Bible study. Internship attendees regularly participate in prayer meetings—between fifteen and twenty-five hours a week—in the prayer room, which can include worship team involvement, intercession for revival, personal devotional time, and study of the Word. Education and instruction cover a wide range of topics, including Christian foundations, prayer, worship, intimacy with God, the Bridal Paradigm of the Kingdom of God, the prophetic and healing ministries, serving the poor, and many others.

Intro to IHOP is a three-month internship for people of all ages, married or single, who want to learn and experience all that IHOP represents— prayer, worship, intimacy, etc.

Simeon Company is a three-month training program for people ages fifty and older who refuse to retire in their desire to radically serve Jesus through prayer, fasting, and worship.

Onething Internship is a six-month daytime internship for young adults between the ages of eighteen and twenty-five who are singers, musicians, intercessors, or evangelists. This program includes housing and eighteen meals a week.

Fire in the Night is a three-month nighttime internship for those between the ages of eighteen and thirty who want to worship and minister to the Lord through the night, midnight to 6:00 a.m. This program includes housing and eighteen meals a week.

Summer Teen Internship is a three-week summer program to equip teens in prophetic worship, intercession, and intimacy with Jesus. Housing is provided with IHOP-KC families.

Please visit *www.IHOP.org* for more information.

FORERUNNER SCHOOL OF MINISTRY

*Redefining Theological Education
Through Night and Day Prayer*

FOUR PROGRAMS:
- Apostolic Preaching Program
  Four-Year Program
- Worship and Prayer Program
  Four-Year Program
- Healing and Prophecy Program
  Two-Year Program
- Biblical Studies Program
  Four-Year Program

ONE ACADEMY:
- Forerunner Music Academy (see below)
  Three-Year Program

THREE INSTITUTES:
- Joseph Company
- Apostolic Missions Institute
- Evangelist Institute

CTEE:
- eSchool – offering access to
  Video/Audio/Class Notes

FORERUNNER MUSIC ACADEMY (FMA)

FMA is a full-time music school that trains musicians and singers to play skillfully and to operate in the prophetic anointing. FMA offers a comprehensive course of high-quality musical training in the context of IHOP's night-and-day prayer and worship. King David understood that prophetic music and songs would release the power of God. He paid 4,000 full-time musicians and hundreds of prophetic singers to gaze night and day upon God as they sang the prayers of Zion. This was their primary occupation in life. They were employed in the Tabernacle of David, which combined worship with intercession that never ceased as it continued 24/7.

CONTACT US:
12444 Grandview Road
Grandview, Missouri 64030
Phone: 816.763.0243
Fax: 816.763.0439
E-mail: FSM@ihop.org
www.IHOP.org

OTHER RESOURCES BY MIKE BICKLE

AFTER GOD'S OWN HEART

This book gives in-depth insight with many practical examples of how to sustain a life of intimacy with God. King David's relationship with God is used as a model of how we can live a radical lifestyle filled with confidence before God while acknowledging our profound weakness.

THE SEVEN LONGINGS OF THE HUMAN HEART

God has placed deep longings in the heart of every human being. We all long for beauty, for greatness, for fascination, for intimacy. We all long to be enjoyed, to be whole-hearted, to make a lasting impact. Only God can fulfill the longings He has given us. When we realize our longings are godly and God wants to fulfill them, we find freedom and joy.

THE REWARDS OF FASTING

Fasting is a gift from God that goes way beyond not eating. Jesus promised we would be rewarded for fasting. Done in the right spirit, fasting increases our receptivity to God's voice and His Word and allows us to encounter God more deeply than we otherwise would. This book explores all the rewards and delights that come to those who fast.

THE PLEASURES OF LOVING GOD

This book invites you on a most unique treasure hunt, a journey of discovery into intimacy with a Bridegroom God that loves, even likes, you and wants your friendship. Dimensions of the forerunner ministry and the House of Prayer are also examined.

GROWING IN THE PROPHETIC

As churches across the country struggle to determine the proper place for the prophetic in their congregations as well as guidelines for the operation of prophecy, the lessons learned by Mike Bickle provide a starting point.

ENCOUNTERING JESUS AUDIO SERIES

"A Prophetic History & Perspectives About the End Times." Over the last twenty years, Mike Bickle has taken time to share bits and pieces of this prophetic history but never as comprehensively as he did in these twelve one-hour sessions! These experiences explain the prophetic history of this ministry in Kansas City as well as establish convictions about the generation that the Lord returns. Although Scripture is our highest standard and guardian of truth, on occasion, the Lord also releases prophetic experiences to encourage our understanding and perseverance.

SONG OF SOLOMON AUDIO SERIES

Mike's completely revised and updated course on Song of Songs, this is his most comprehensive and powerful presentation on this glorious book to date. The CD version includes the Study Guide in PDF format.

STUDIES IN JOEL AUDIO SERIES

As we approach the great and terrible day of the Lord, we will be facing a flood of horrors far greater than in the days of Noah. In his brilliant verse-by-verse teachings from the book of Joel, Mike blows the trumpet and sounds the alarm, offering us a road map of the End-Times.

RESOURCES FROM FORERUNNER MUSIC

ALWAYS ON HIS MIND — Misty Edwards

"Diving deep into intercession, into the Word, into the passionate heart of God." From IHOP-KC, *Always on His Mind* is a live recording that captures Misty Edwards and her team leading worship, intercession, and songs born out of prayer.

CONSTANT — IHOP-KC

Constant is an album that is steady and lyrically inspiring! This collection of songs is thematic of the faithfulness of God. His greatness and our great need for Him are sustained throughout. All the music on this album was written and performed by the International House of Prayer worship leaders.

MERCHANT BAND — Merchant Band

With sounds of Brit pop meets American rock, Merchant Band's self-titled debut album has woven a modern sound with the IHOP messages of intimacy and urgency. Packed with original material that is both fresh and powerful.

ETERNITY — Misty Edwards

This best-selling CD captures the heart of the extravagant worshiper. Misty Edwards is one of the International House of Prayer's most beloved worship leaders. Her unique gifting draws your heart before the Lord, our Majesty, into a deep realm of intimacy with Him.

LIMITED EDITION — IHOP-KC

Connect to the Prayer Room Through Limited Edition

Through IHOP's *Limited Edition* CD subscription club, Forerunner Music now offers you an ongoing glimpse into the International House of Prayer's prayer meetings. We record the worship and intercession that goes on night and day at IHOP. Then we take the best recordings from a two-month period, compile them, and make them available to you. Join IHOP's worship leaders and prayer leaders as they keep the prayer fire burning 24/7.

As the name suggests, these CDs are "limited editions," meaning once we've sold out, no more are available. And the CDs are only available to subscribers. Join the *Limited Edition* CD club, and every other month you will receive the latest CD, as well as other news from the prayer room and regular email updates.

Each *Limited Edition* CD is packed with live worship and prayer. You will find your heart connecting to Scripture and with IHOP's current prayer burdens. We invite you to join us as we seek after the fullness of God. Enter into fiery, passionate intercession with recordings from our corporate intercession sets or sit at the Lord's feet through a Worship With the Word or Devotional set recording. Our desire is that the *Limited Edition* CDs will equip and bless you as you draw nearer to the One you love.

For more information about resources from Mike Bickle and the
International House of Prayer or for a free catalog,
please call 1-800-552-2449 from 8:30 am–5:30 pm Monday–Friday.
Also, visit our Web site and Web store at www.IHOP.org.

WHAT DO YOU SEEK FROM GOD'S HEART?

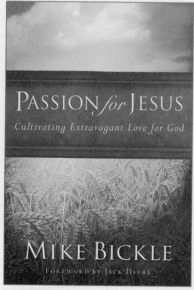

978-1-59979-060-2 /$14.99

Understand why God loves you so much and how you must realize this in order to give Him a surpassing love, like King David.

What does God want from your heart? With an inquisitive heart, you can find out the passion God holds for you and what you can do to strengthen your personal relationship with Him.

"Mike Bickle's book *Passion for Jesus* is filled with wonderful insights into the greatest of all commandments. Mike has spent his adult life attempting, above all else, to acquire a consuming passion for the Son of God."

Jack Deere, ThD

Visit your local bookstore today.